Practical
Punctuation

Praise for *Practical Punctuation*

Practical Punctuation is the thinking child's (and teacher's) guide to punctuation! Gone are endless drills and meaningless exercises that lead to little or no application in children's writing. Dan argues for one focused punctuation study per grade, giving students a year's worth of writing to apply what they've learned. When you consider this approach you'll wonder how you ever taught another way. Dan's think-aloud lesson suggestions make vividly clear how teachers can encourage students to experiment with punctuation to varied effect.

The particular delight of this book comes in the insights of great writers—Frank McCourt, Jimmy Breslin, Natalie Babbitt, Colum McCann—that pepper its pages. These writers afford teachers a real-world view of the power of punctuation in creating meaning. The unrelenting focus throughout this beautifully crafted book is on *meaning*. Dan shows how writers wield punctuation in the way that an artist varies the size and type of her brushes and strokes—all in the service of meaning.

In all the books I've read about written language, Dan is the first to explore the mind's ear. His delicious investigation of how punctuation can "heighten the awareness of rhythm and melody in our own writing," has actually changed the way I read as well as write. How lucky we are to (finally) have an intellectually engaging exploration of what we have too long considered drudgery.

—Ellin Oliver Keene,
coauthor of *Mosaic of Thought*

Practical Punctuation

Lessons on Rule Making and Rule Breaking in Elementary Writing

DAN FEIGELSON
Foreword by Carl Anderson

HEINEMANN • PORTSMOUTH, NH

Heinemann
361 Hanover Street
Portsmouth, NH 03801–3912
www.heinemann.com

Offices and agents throughout the world

Library of Congress Cataloging-in-Publication Data
Feigelson, Dan.
   Practical punctuation : lessons on rule making and rule breaking in elementary writing /
Dan Feigelson ; foreword by Carl Anderson.
      p.   cm.
   Includes bibliographical references.
   ISBN-13: 978-0-325-00906-3
   ISBN-10: 0-325-00906-6
   1. English language—Composition and exercises—Study and teaching (Elementary).
2. English language—Punctuation.   I. Title.
LB1576.F396 2008
372.62′3—dc22   2008031487

Editor: Kate Montgomery
Production: Vicki Kasabian
Cover design: Night & Day Design
Interior photographs: Roy Silverstein
Author photograph: Sue Stember
Typesetter: Publishers' Design and Production Services, Inc.
Manufacturing: Valerie Cooper

Printed in the United States of America on acid-free paper
12   11   10   09   08   ML   1   2   3   4   5

To Sonia, my daughter

and my father Charles

the two who taught me the importance

of listening to children

Contents

Foreword

Several years ago, when Dan Feigelson was principal at PS 6 in Manhattan, I worked as a staff developer in his school. At the end of the last day of my residency, Dan suggested we have a glass of wine at Bemelmans Bar in the Carlyle Hotel, which was a few blocks away on Madison Avenue.

As we walked into Bemelmans, Dan pointed out the murals of whimsical animals that decorate its walls. "Guess who painted them," he said. I looked closely and knew they looked familiar, but I couldn't place the artist. "I'll give you a hint," Dan said, pointing to the group of figures on one wall. I walked over and saw . . . twelve little girls, in two straight lines . . . and the smallest one was Madeline! "Ludwig Bemelmans is the artist," I said—the author and illustrator of the *Madeline* books (and former resident of the Carlyle Hotel).

Spend time with Dan Feigelson, and you find out he knows details about New York City that most people don't. Where you and I might blithely pass by Bemelmans Bar without knowing that the artwork of a beloved children's author adorned its walls, Dan has made it his business to *know* these things.

And if you spend time with Dan Feigelson, you'll also find out he knows and values things about teaching writing that many of us do not—**yet**. Teaching children how to use punctuation wisely and have fun doing so—the subject of Dan's new book—is something many of us don't know much about. Nor do many of us even consider punctuation worthy of extended instructional time in a writing workshop. Dan has made it his business to delve into this topic, and we are all the wiser for the impressive and exciting writing about the subject that he has done in this book.

In *Practical Punctuation*, Dan Feigelson teaches us that punctuation doesn't have to be the dry, boring subject many of us found it to be when we were youngsters. Instead, as Dan writes, punctuation is a tool that writers use to clarify and enhance the meaning they want to get across. Teach punctuation well—and you'll discover how to do exactly that in these pages—and your students become "punctuation zealots," kids who are fascinated by punctuation marks and their many uses, kids who develop new powers as writers because of their newfound knowledge of punctuation.

Practical Punctuation is, above all, a practical book. Inside you'll find units of study for students in different grades, with detailed lessons that specify exactly how to teach students about punctuation. For students in the primary grades, Dan provides a study of end marks (periods, question marks, exclamation marks, and the ellipsis). For students in the middle elementary grades, he unpacks a study of the comma. And for students in the upper elementary grades, he presents a thrilling "cadence study," which involves teaching students how punctuation influences the way writing sounds and shades the meaning of a text. Each unit has been field-tested in real classrooms by experienced teachers, so you can be confident they'll help your students learn to use punctuation not only with purpose, but with joy.

While writing *Practical Punctuation*, Dan Feigelson interviewed award-winning writers—Frank McCourt and Jimmy Breslin among them—about their use of punctuation. These writers have fascinating things to say about punctuation. Clearly, they've given it a lot of thought in the course of crafting their books and articles. Expertly woven throughout, the writers' quotes punctuate Dan's book. As you read along, you begin to anticipate the next writers' insight; they enhance the meaning of the text.

Why teach students to be punctuation zealots? Dan's book gives us many good reasons, and one of the most convincing is this: the writers we revere are punctuation zealots themselves.

Of course, Dan is one, too. He's told me that whenever he revises his work he reads his writing aloud and taps a pencil in order to gauge the cadence of his sentences. He'll show you how to teach kids to do that in Chapter 4.

You should also know that Dan is an experienced and passionate educator. Over more than two decades in education, he's been a teacher, researcher, staff developer, curriculum designer, and principal. Now he leads a network of twenty diverse schools in New York City, a position comparable to that of superintendent in other places. The work that Dan discusses in *Practical Punctuation* rings true because it's written by someone who knows kids, knows classrooms, knows curriculum, and who knows schools.

Today, when I pass Bemelmans Bar, I always think about the paintings inside. Sometimes I stop by to gaze at them for a while. After you read *Practical Punctuation*, you'll notice punctuation more in what you read, and you'll probably stop sometimes to admire the way writers use it. So, too, will your students, as they become writers who are fascinated by punctuation and use it to communicate what they have to say clearly and powerfully.

Carl Anderson

Acknowledgments

For several summers I swam across Queechy Lake each day to stay in shape. The distance was a couple miles, which felt monumental, and as a way to keep going I'd have a conversation with myself from one end of the lake to the other. For the first leg of the swim, all things seemed possible. Once the initial burst of energy faded, the distance to the other side became daunting and I'd think about giving up. To force myself to continue, I set incremental goals—just make it as far as that tree, swim until the halfway point, go to where that rowboat is sitting. This worked for a bit; I felt confident, jazzed, ready to give myself a high five at each passing landmark. When the shoreline didn't get appreciably closer, I'd chide myself for being impatient and alter my stroke to conserve strength. Eventually a more mindless groove would set in and I'd plow ahead with no thoughts at all. Despair, hope and blind determination alternated until at last I'd reach the other side.

Writing a book is a lot like swimming across a lake. After the initial rush of getting started, the distance to the end seems impossible. What makes it different is that the conversations keeping you focused are not just in your head. Voices that have inspired and shaped your thinking emerge to push you on to the next chapter. Those close to you put up with mood swings and endure endless discussions about the smallest details, providing pep talks and reality checks.

I owe many specific lesson ideas in this book to three incredible teachers from PS 6, where I was fortunate to be principal. Ali Marron piloted and helped plan the cadence unit in Chapter 4 with her fifth graders, and was of enormous assistance in simplifying concepts and logistical problems. Barbara Pinto, master first-grade teacher and literacy coach, contributed her ideas about teaching ending punctuation to very young children. Last but not least, Barbara Rosenblum, one of the most inspiring and brilliant teachers on the planet, piloted and co-conceived the comma study in Chapter 3 with her third graders, and spent countless hours discussing punctuation instruction with me over several years. These individuals are truly the co-authors of this book.

In addition to Ali and the Barbs, a few other New York City teachers have contributed to the thinking in this book. At PS 6, fifth-grade teacher Jackie Levenherz helped plan and implement the cadence lessons along with Ali, and Debbie Hartman did amazing second-grade comma work. Fifth-grade teachers Kelly Boland and Pat Faugno also tried out and discussed the internal punctuation and cadence unit. Christian Carter and Alison Rini did some of this work in their fourth-grade classes, and Nathalie Mac, Jenny Fay, Anouk Weiss, and Judy Morehead were intrepid experimenters in their third-grade rooms. When Jane Hsu was my assistant principal she helped design much of the professional development to introduce the ideas to staff.

The fourth-grade teachers at PS 234, Ellen McCrum, Shirley Shum, Lauren Brown, and Cara Gearty, also helped refine the comma study. Joanne Cutitto, Steve Foster, and Kaili Stanley assisted with research and transcriptions.

I am especially indebted to colleague and friend Carl Anderson for his fabulous foreword, reading and critiquing early drafts, and discussing Bob Dylan and the Beatles at length. Lisa Ripperger, Nancy Sing-Bock, and Cheryl Tyler, three freethinking New York City principals, gave valuable feedback on several lessons. Much gratitude is due to the writers who agreed to be interviewed: Natalie Babbitt, Jimmy Breslin, Colum McCann, and Frank McCourt each made wise and irreverent contributions. Our conversations felt like master classes in the art of writing. Last but not least, a deep bow and nod to partner in crime Jon Agee for his spiritual counsel and illuminating outlook on language and life.

The ideas in this book are built on the brilliant work of Mary Ehrenworth, Janet Angellilo, and Edgar Schuster. Their books—*The Power of Grammar* by Mary and Vicki Vinton, Janet's *A Fresh Approach to Teaching Punctuation*, and Schuster's *Breaking the Rules* were major influences. In addition, the conversations I've had with Mary over the years have helped clarify many concepts, concrete and abstract. Of course the foundation for much of this instruction is laid out in the seminal work of Lucy Calkins, who showed so many of us how to look at writing as process and crystallized the way that translates to classroom practice. Finally, my friend, co-conspirator, and fellow renegade Ralph Fletcher's ideas about the craft of writing have informed not just this work but that of teachers around the world—and his uncompromising search for truth on matters professional and personal have helped me past many hurdles.

My career as an educator in New York City has been shaped by a few individuals who have at one time or another pushed me further and deeper: Adele Schroeter, the other half of my educational heartbeat now and for years at PS 321, Livingston Street, and in San Diego; Peter Heaney, principal, mentor, superintendent, and comrade; Bill Casey, a moral compass and the first to hire me as a New York City public school teacher; Judy Chin, Brenda Steele, and Dorita Gibson of the ICILSO, and Gale Reeves of the NYC DOE; Shelley Harwayne, a model for how far you can go when you don't compromise your beliefs; Tanya Kaufman, who taught me to think outside the box as an administrator; Carl Bereiter and Marlene Scardamalia at OISE, who gave me my first job in education, and whose work on writing to learn got me thinking; and Kenneth Bratspies, my fifth-grade teacher, who inspired me to teach in the first place.

Teachers and writers have a lot to learn from jazz musicians. Thanks to Duke Ellington, Charles Mingus, and Carla Bley for showing how planning and improvisation can be balanced to create things of beauty. Many of the ideas in this book have to do with the music of language. Charlie Parker, Dizzy Gillespie, Clifford Brown, Sonny Rollins, Ornette Coleman, Hank Jones, and Max Roach, among many others, have taught timeless lessons about how to shape a line, vary long and short phrases, and create rhythms to get a message across.

During the time it took to complete this book (years!) there were more than a few moments of personal upheaval, and a few folks who made it possible to keep swimming across the lake. I thank Karyn Boyar, Nathan and Andrea Boyar, Naomi Chase, Carolyn Feigelson, Liz Feigelson, Lucia Grauman, Dan Hurley, David Konigsberg, Flavio Pompetti, and John Tintori for their encouragement and understanding at different moments in the process. Kiri Hogue, a girl wise beyond her years, has also taught me a thing or two about moving forward.

Pretty much everything I do is for my daughter Sonia Feigelson, who always questions basic assumptions and has a unique talent for transforming an idea into something new and brilliant. Her restless creativity and searching nature continue to influence her Dad's thinking.

Last but far from least, there are two individuals without whom this book would certainly never have been completed. Kate Montgomery, editor extraordinaire, was patient and demanding at exactly the right times. She is truly the midwife of this project.

Most of all I thank Cara Hogue, my love and partner, for patience, perspective, and perseverance. Her ability to make complicated things simpler and dark moments lighter inspires me at all the most important times, in all the right places.

Teachers, go forth and punctuate.

CHAPTER 1

Purpose Before Particulars

The rules are always true except when they aren't.
—Gary Peacock, jazz bassist and educator

The What and the Why

Like doing push-ups or eating broccoli, punctuation is often perceived as something good for you but not very appealing. Of course a writer must slog through the necessary evil of plugging in commas and periods, but the general consensus is that what makes a text interesting is something else.

Over the last few years when it's come up in conversation that I am working on a book about punctuation, the reactions have been incredulous. With raised eyebrows, people check to be sure I'm not joking before they politely change the subject. "You've got to be kidding," said one well-meaning friend's father, with a look somewhere between contempt and disbelief. It was as though he had thought me an interesting fellow until that moment.

When we think about punctuation (if at all), we think of it as something technical, a set of rules and conventions—in a word, dull.

Like a prim, tightly buttoned spinster in a movie musical who transforms into the beautiful heroine when she lets her hair down, punctuation has another identity beneath its stodgy surface. Though often categorized and dismissed under the heading of conventions, this term is misleading. As with any tool of expression, there are norms and sometimes mandatory guidelines for how to use punctuation marks—but the truth is, most writers think of punctuation as a craft tool more than a set of rules. Quite apart from its organizational role in writing, it can be as useful as poetic language or a well-chosen word to create rhythm, mood, or shades of meaning in a text.

At the very least this idea suggests it is worth taking time to consider the purpose of punctuation, the reasons it is worth learning. Reflecting on purpose is critical not just for teachers, but also for students. A necessary part of any learning process is thinking about why this thing we are spending time on is important to know.

And yet in our rush to show students *how* to do things, we often hurry their reflections. There is pressure to move to the next procedure, no time to linger on the larger purpose. Children are taught rigid formulas for literary essays without understanding why a reader might want to make an argument in the first place. As they learn to subtract, students borrow from the next column without any sense of what amounts the numbers stand for. Information is assimilated and procedures performed efficiently, but the sense behind the steps gets lost. Consequently, some students understand and others don't—but too often the only ones we red-flag are those who get the procedure wrong. How many do we miss that memorize the steps but don't understand what it all means? In an age of accountability and test anxiety, we tend to overdo the *what* at the expense of the *why*.

The teaching of punctuation is a glaring case in point. Ask an elementary school student to explain a period and you'll almost certainly be told that it goes at the end of a sentence. Ask *why* a writer uses a period to end a sentence and you're likely to get a blank stare. Most of us can rattle off certain rules of when to plug in a comma or colon as though reciting a nursery rhyme. We may have a harder time talking about why one works better than another to convey a particular meaning.

Why Learn Punctuation?

Without a sense of why something is important to know, it is hard to care about learning it. It follows that as teachers we need to take time ourselves to consider why punctuation should be taught to young readers and writers. Moreover, we need to be able to convey this purpose to students.

So what is punctuation exactly? What does it do, and why is it worth thinking about? The questions are straightforward enough, but answers are a bit more elusive. When I asked several professional writers to share their thoughts, the answers were more varied than you might expect.

Children's author Amy Hest sighed with what seemed like relief, saying, "I'm so glad you asked me that! Punctuation is such a huge part of what I do, but no one ever asks. I'm constantly trying things new ways, with different punctuation—it's as important as character, setting, and descriptive language in getting my meaning across."

David Konigsberg, a corporate communications writer and editor, said punctuation is "all about rhythm and mood. You can send a message that something is crucial or peripheral just by changing the way it's punctuated."

Novelist Colum McCann expanded on the notion of rhythm, thinking more from the perspective of reader than writer. "It's that little guiding hand, the little hand at the back of the reader's mind that sort of says, OK, halt or, OK, stumble here a little bit or allow yourself a breath or don't allow yourself a breath. . . . It modulates our rhythm. It says this is the music and this is the music sheet. In fact, in a funny way, they do look like musical notations, don't they?"

Newbery Honor winner Natalie Babbitt, author of *Tuck Everlasting*, thought more in terms of speech. "I'm not a theatre person," she commented, "but really the punctuation is like stage directions. It tells you how it's supposed to be said, or heard inside the reader's head."

Poet Naomi Chase added succinctly (and a bit irreverently), "What do I think about punctuation? Good fences make good neighbors."

Pulitzer Prize–winning memoirist Frank McCourt wasn't so sure. "It divides and connects at the same time. . . . You don't go over the fence, but that's a very poor parallel for me. A period is not a fence. A period is a pause—take a breath and then you go on to the next place, but it should go with the last one. And then it is a series of instructions, and maybe the punctuation is the plaster that holds all of them together."

Journalist Jimmy Breslin, another Pulitzer winner, put it simply. "You read with your ear and you write with your ear. . . . [Punctuation] makes it easier to read, purportedly."

As different as these responses are, they suggest a few common threads. According to these writers, punctuation can be used to:

- Place emphasis, i.e., make certain words or passages seem more or less important.
- Separate one idea from another.
- Connect one idea to another.
- Create a rhythm or a *cadence* in the reader's ear.

All of these ideas have to do with *meaning*. Writers use punctuation to get a message across to the reader in a particular way. As wide ranging as their answers may seem at first (e.g., dividing *and* connecting, shading meaning *and* creating rhythm), each author spoke of influencing how a reader experiences and understands text. Interestingly, not one mentioned the importance of following rules.

Of course these writers all have a strong fundamental knowledge of the conventions of punctuation. Elementary school students do not. It is our job to teach these basic norms, but not without conveying the reason we are learning them in the first place. Rules, it is worth reminding ourselves, are created to instill order so something will work more effectively. They exist to *serve* the purpose; they are not the purpose themselves. In the case of writing mechanics, rules are there to help us read with better understanding and write more expressively. A look at punctuation through history shows conventions evolve and change (Schuster 2003), and particular punctuation marks go in and out of fashion. If understanding doesn't come first, rules not only don't help—they can get in the way. Speaking of a particular passage in the newspaper, Jimmy Breslin underscored this point, complaining, "Under the rules, you're supposed to have the commas, but if you look at it with your eye, it's nuts. Too many of them. Who knows what they're talking about after a while?"

As obvious as this point may seem, the way punctuation is traditionally taught puts the cart of conventions before the horse of meaning. We trot out lists of rules to memorize. We pull out worksheets totally unrelated to what students are reading and writing to "practice" using periods or commas or exclamation points. Not surprisingly, the usual reaction is to be turned off. At best young writers learn to plug in rules passively; at worst they can't remember the rules a month after they were taught.

Ironically, punctuation is *always* something writers make choices about; it never has to go just one way. We may need to rewrite a passage so it works as a question rather than a declarative statement, but there are really no ideas that can only be expressed through a single form of punctuation. Our challenge is to impart these norms in such a way that children become *critical thinkers about punctuation*. We want them to make decisions about what works best to convey their meaning, while still "having some consideration for the reader" (Breslin again).

It makes sense then that meaning and choice should be at the forefront in our teaching of punctuation. In order for students to understand its purpose and use it thoughtfully, there are five basic elements we should be sure to include in our planning.

Five Considerations for Studying Punctuation

- Put the *why* before the *what* (purpose before particulars!).
- Allow opportunities for students to experiment with a particular type of punctuation without worrying whether or not it is correct.
- Be sure students watch us model and think aloud as we make punctuation choices in our own writing.

- Teach the conventions explicitly, but not as absolutes.
- Hold students accountable for using punctuation thoughtfully in more formal writing, with opportunities to explain their decisions.

Exactly how these considerations take shape in the classroom will (and should) vary, according to the style of an individual teacher and the strengths and needs of a specific group of students. Nonetheless there are things to consider about each as we plan our individual approach.

Put the *why* before the *what* (purpose before particulars!)

> *I believe in an open mind, but not so open that your brains fall out.*
> —Arthur Hays Sulzberger

Carl Anderson (2000) holds that the most important lens to use in assessing student writing is meaning. Regardless of what we are looking at in a piece of children's work, be it focus, organization, or use of detail, it succeeds or fails according to how well it helps a reader understand. All the discrete elements that go into a piece of writing should serve this objective—and punctuation is no exception. We must establish the mindset that question marks, commas, and all the rest are first and foremost about getting a message across.

But not everything helps a reader understand in the same way, and it is our job to be familiar with the specific things punctuation can do to convey meaning. According to McCourt, Breslin, Hest, and the rest, it has something to do with sound and separation, connecting and cadence. Lofty ideas to be sure, coming from Pulitzer Prize winners. Do they have a place in the elementary classroom?

Interestingly, though abstract when we try to talk about them, these ideas make perfect sense to children who don't know they are supposed to think such things are complicated. "Those curvy lines," comments first grader Jonathan on the purpose of parentheses, "are like big breathy things. You slow down and take a breath, then go back to the sentence." Maddie B., a third grader, arguing with a classmate on the difference between a dash and a comma, was no less thoughtful. "The dash is like a bumpy detour that takes you somewhere else, but the comma is softer. You feel like you're still connected."

Such discussions are convincing evidence that we need not lower the bar or oversimplify our explanations to teach children about the many possibilities for using punctuation thoughtfully. Jonathan and Maddy B.'s high level of thinking is directly related to the fact that they are inventing their own definitions before being taught conventional ones.

Before explicitly teaching conventions, we must allow opportunities for students first to observe the way authors use punctuation in the world and make their own theories *in their own words* about what the particular marks are doing. After putting thought into their own definitions, they have more investment in hearing what others have to say on the subject.

Another important thing to remember is that we need to be as consistent as possible in sending the message that punctuation influences meaning. To do this involves being as specific as possible. How does punctuation influence the way a reader understands? In what ways can writers use it to express more clearly what they have to say? There are several key ideas we want to stress all through our teaching of punctuation, in minilessons, individual conferences, and everything in between.

Six Things We Want Student Writers to
Think About as They Learn to Use Punctuation

- It conveys sound ("what it makes your voice do")—pauses, pitch, speed.

- It connects ideas.

- It separates ideas.

- It emphasizes a particular part of the sentence or passage.

- It "angles" the writing, that is, creates a mood, puts across a point of view.

- It shapes the writing, creating a sense of rhythm, flow, and cadence from one passage to the next.

Allow opportunities for students to experiment with the particular type of punctuation without worrying whether or not it is correct

> *Children are born true scientists. They spontaneously experiment and experience and reexperience again. They select, combine, and test, seeking to find order in their experiences—"which is the mostest? which is the leastest?" They smell, taste, bite, and touch-test for hardness, softness, springiness, roughness, smoothness, coldness, warmness: they heft, shake, punch, squeeze, push, crush, rub, and try to pull things apart.*
> —Buckminster Fuller

There are things you need to know in order to be a good painter. Complementary and tertiary colors are important, as are rules of perspective and composition. A knowledge of what came before is also useful—what Rembrandt brought to the self-portrait, Caravaggio's use of shadow and light, Pollock's tortured textures. Yet no one would assert children should begin learning art by doing exercises in anatomy or engaging in a survey of Italian frescoes. Common sense dictates you start with finger-painting, getting messy, trying out blue next to green and deciding yellow is a better match. Little girls draw endless approximations of ladies in dresses before we worry whether they are getting the proportions right. By first experimenting, learners become curious about conventions and norms and develop a reason and desire to know the technical stuff.

The work of Murray, Graves, Calkins, and Fletcher has made us aware children should be given opportunities to experiment in writer's notebooks and folders before learning to write to a prompt. It is better not to assign "What I Did on My Summer Vacation" essays before allowing students to choose their own subjects, drawing on details and descriptions of what is most important to them. Because of their personal investment, learning how to express themselves more clearly matters.

There exists a curious double standard when it comes to teaching punctuation and mechanics in our reading and writing workshops. Too often, even in strong balanced literacy schools, we see a disconnect in instructional methodology. Our workshops are all about teaching in context, for real purposes, yet when it's time to address paragraphing or commas we resort to minilectures. Often we relegate all mechanics instruction to the editing stage of the writing cycle. The message is that they are an afterthought, something you plug in after most of the work is done. Ironically not a single writer I spoke to thought of punctuation this way; each of them saw it as an essential part of the *drafting* process. "You don't go *back* to put in commas and colons," said Konigsberg, the business writer. "They are part of the plan in the first place."

Our challenge is to teach these critical skills and strategies within a workshop setting, in meaningful contexts—so kids see how they are related to the rest of their literacy learning. As in painting, there are of course rules a writer needs to learn, and it is our job to teach them. But just as we let a child experiment with paints and brushes before teaching her to accurately portray shadow and light, it's important for young writers to make independent judgments about punctuation before we introduce conventions. Primary teachers know invented spelling is the first step in developing theories about *how* to spell, and learning to punctuate effectively is no different. Students need opportunities to mess around with writing conventions. Our job is to choreograph such opportunities so they develop their own theories and strategies. This will lead in the end to a real desire to learn rules, in order to express themselves more clearly and artfully.

When We Begin Teaching Punctuation by Allowing Writers to Experiment . . .

- They develop *strategies* for using punctuation (in the same way they develop strategies for spelling).
- They develop the motivation to learn conventions of punctuation out of a desire to express themselves clearly and artfully.

The need to provide students with opportunities to experiment does not suggest a haphazard approach to planning. On the contrary, to do this well teachers must have content knowledge (i.e., the sorts of choices writers can make about punctuation, as well as at least a fundamental grasp of the conventions) and a good diagnostic sense of children as writers. They must also know how to plan inquiry-style lessons that lead to particular realizations. Good workshop teaching is at times the art of laying bread crumbs to a certain, predetermined result—*choreographing discovery*. The trick is also remaining open to ideas that come up in the moment from students and being willing to forgo our best-laid plans when necessary.

Once students have constructed their own theories and had the chance to mess around without the pressure of producing a finished piece, we switch gears a bit. At this stage students learn the conventions or rules of whatever punctuation they are studying. Indeed they *want* to learn them, if only to see whether their theories were correct. We must be sure that along with this instruction they participate in meaningful writing activities where they can practice what they have learned. Finally, students need to be held accountable for using punctuation more or less conventionally. Just as important, we should insist they use it thoughtfully and, yes, in a way that shows consideration for the reader.

And if this means coming up with a way to break a rule for greater effect, it is something to celebrate.

Be sure students watch us model and think aloud as we make punctuation choices in our own writing

When asked to describe the process of making a painting, Picasso didn't hesitate. "It is a series of choices," he replied. This makes sense; from the moment they put brush to canvas, painters must decide where to put that little dollop of red, at what angle should the shadow fall, whether the figure should lean or stand straight.

We are used to thinking of topic, point of view, even vocabulary, as things a writer makes choices about. Somehow the notion of making decisions about punctuation seems more foreign; after all, isn't it obvious when we need a question mark or a comma? In truth, even the most rule-bound punctuation is in some way a matter of choice. It is mandatory to use ending punctuation when a sentence is finished, but authors decide whether to make it a question or finish with an exclamation point. What type of internal punctuation to use—commas, colons, semicolons, dashes—is almost always a judgment call on the part of the writer. Thinking of punctuation as a matter of opinion is different from saying there are no conventions to learn; once a writer chooses a particular type of punctuation, there are things to know about how to use it. But learning how to make the appropriate choice is what later motivates us to know the rules.

As is the case with learning just about anything, children need to be shown, not told, how to make punctuation decisions. This is best accomplished through demonstration writing, accompanied by think-alouds that model the process of making a choice. In the course of the think-aloud, it is important to articulate the reasons for our decisions, whenever possible ruling out another alternative before arriving at the final choice.

Here's a sample think-aloud:

> "This is a really exciting point in my story, with a lot of things happening very quickly and all at once. The pitcher threw the ball and the batter swung his bat, and all of a sudden the ball was hit right in my direction. To show how fast this all went by, I am going to try writing a long sentence, using commas to separate the different things that happened."

We write on chart paper or overhead:

> The pitcher wound up and threw, the ball whizzed toward home plate, a swing of the bat, a loud crack, and the ball shot sharply in my direction.

And then we go back to thinking:

> "This doesn't quite work though. I want the reader to understand how nervous I was. After all, the ball was hit right in my direction! Also, the comma feels too smooth, like these things happened calmly one after another. The truth is it all felt sudden and jerky, not smooth. It might work better to make it two sentences. I can write a smooth one with commas, to start it off—and then do another with dashes to show when it got scary. Dashes feel much more sudden, so they can show how it all happened before I was ready."

We write again:

> The pitcher wound up and threw, the ball whizzed toward home, and then it all seemed to happen at once. A swing of the bat—a loud crack—I looked up—and the ball was shooting right at me.

We begin by providing opportunities for children to see, hear, and discuss what a writer thinks about when arriving at a punctuation decision. Next, we ask them to try making—and explaining—their own choices.

Teach the conventions explicitly, but not as absolutes

> *I wanted to put semicolons in my camp piece but I wasn't sure how, so Ms. Marron said we should look in one of the punctuation books. We came up with how the first part could be a full sentence, but then you have something after which is too close to go into two different sentences—and it's kind of far to go in a separate sentence by itself. I wrote it down here [reading from her notes]: "The semicolon is entirely a mark of separation or division that is never used to introduce or terminate a statement." So it's not just one sentence, not two sentences—it's kind of like an add-on. And the second part can't introduce a whole new idea; it's got to have something to do with the first part.*
> —Fifth grader Max Zimberg

As students compare how long we pause after a comma with how long we pause after a dash, or think about the differences between an ellipsis and a colon, they are bound to test and discard certain theories. Perhaps a partner will find an example from a book that contradicts their idea; a classmate might pose a convincing argument at a share session that changes their mind. At a certain point they are bound to ask, "What's the *right* way?"

A commonly held misconception is that constructivist teaching means the teacher never gives a direct answer. Students must engage in a sort of Socratic guessing game rather than be privy to world knowledge that adults in the world would look up, google, or ask of a knowledgeable friend. The truth is, children engaged in constructing an understanding are likely to come up with burning, specific questions. In these instances our job is to point them toward places they can find the answers. We needn't worry that we are doing the work for them. When questions come up in context out of a student's genuine desire to know, it is likely the answers will be remembered.

Differences and similarities between the way we use particular types of punctuation are subtle, change over time (Schuster 2003), and vary from one guide to another. Many adults, in or out of the teaching profession, would be hard pressed to say exactly when it would be better to use parentheses or a set of dashes to insert information in the middle of a sentence. Useful guides exist however, which address these issues—and they can be fascinating to look at, especially when the class is having a spirited conversation. For this reason, it is critical to keep a variety of punctuation books available during a study of punctuation. Particularly once they begin to experiment in their own writing, children need to be able to consult reference material. When we are looking at how a book explains a punctuation mark, however, it is important to keep in mind this may not be the final word—several sources should be consulted before coming to a final decision.

These resources should of course be used judiciously, in response to cues from students. It would be a mistake to plan minilessons where we recite the "rules" according to one book or another, or use them to make lists students memorize before they have a chance to research, experiment, and come up with their own theories.

Appropriate Contexts for Using Reference Books

- In individual conferences, when a student comes up with a question about how to use a particular type of punctuation.

- In partner discussions, when students are debating the differences or similarities of one type of punctuation versus another.

- In minilessons or guided shares (see Chapter 4), when the class is discussing how authors use specific types of punctuation to affect meaning or understanding.

Hold students accountable for using punctuation thoughtfully in more formal writing, with opportunities to explain their decisions

Once students have had opportunities to make theories, experiment, and research the punctuation they are studying, it is our job as teachers to assess whether they really understand it. This means they must be held accountable for using the punctuation conventionally and (more important) thoughtfully in a published piece of writing. There are many ways to set up this expectation, depending on the lessons that have come before.

Following a punctuation unit

Sometimes it is a mistake to hold students responsible for producing a finished piece as the final step of a punctuation unit. Doing so may send the unintended message that the experimenting is less important, or secondary, to the final, "correct" writing. But not expecting children to be able to use punctuation conventionally after the study is going too far the other way. After a celebration of experiments and theories (there is an example in the comma study detailed in Chapter 3), we should plan strategically so the next study will provide opportunities for practice. Following a unit on commas, for example, some sort of informational writing might make sense; it often involves lists of facts or steps, and easily lends itself to inserting information in the middle of a sentence. After a study of internal punctuation we could go to a narrative unit, where an author is likely to want different sorts of pauses. Alternatively we could follow up with an open cycle in which children choose their own genre.

None of these ideas are absolutes; pretty much any type of writing can lend itself to practicing any type of punctuation. It may in fact be a good idea to end with a finished piece if this fits with what we have been studying; an example is the cadence unit in Chapter 4, where the point is to use a variety of internal punctuation over several pages of writing. What's important is that children know they will be held responsible at some point for showing what they have learned in their published writing.

Within another writing unit

After students have participated in a unit focusing on punctuation, our hope is that their curiosity will carry over into subsequent writing; once they see these marks as tools for expression, children are likely to want to know more. When such questions come up in conferences or minilessons during other writing cycles, we should go through a similar process of looking at examples, making a theory, experimenting, and researching conventions. After they have gone through this process it is fair to hold them accountable for using the punctuation conventionally.

Regardless of how we hold them accountable, the important thing is not strictly adhering to using conventions correctly but achieving clarity in the writing. A general rule of thumb is that breaking a rule is OK if it serves to get the message across more clearly and if it can be explained by the writer.

Planning a Punctuation Study

I arise in the morning torn between a desire to save the world and
a desire to savor the world. That makes it hard to plan the day.
—E. B. White

It makes sense to do one focused punctuation study (i.e., about a particular sort of punctuation) per grade and to do it early in the year. This quickly establishes the idea that punctuation is a craft tool, not just a set of rules. Doing such a study in October or November allows us to refer back to punctuation in unique ways throughout the school year.

We want students to approach mechanics in the same way they think of vivid language, smooth transitions, or engaging leads. In other words, it should be something a writer makes choices about, to establish a particular voice and make the reader understand in a certain way. Once this lens has been established, teachers can begin to incorporate punctuation decisions into their think-alouds and conferences, whether or not mechanics are the main point of the lesson. They can also include punctuation minilessons within other studies, as one of the things a writer thinks about when drafting, revising, or editing.

Shelley Harwayne wisely points out that the elements of a writing or reading workshop should be thought of as modular furniture, to be moved, adapted, and placed in whatever sequence works best for a given group of children. With this said, there are particular types of activities we want to be sure to include as we plan a punctuation study.

In Planning a Punctuation Study, Provide a Balance Of

- Open inquiry.
- Focused inquiry (with a good measure of teacher manipulation).
- Specific, targeted (i.e., direct) instruction.
- Practice—first informally, then in published writing.

Within That Balance, Provide Opportunities for Children To

- Make reading-writing connections.
- Create, discuss, and argue their own theories of how punctuation works.
- Invent their own names for particular types of punctuation according to their function, before learning correct terminology.
- Observe teacher think-alouds about punctuation decisions.
- Experiment with punctuation in writer's notebooks or folders.
- Rewrite passages using new punctuation, and celebrate these before-and-after experiments.
- Draft, revise, and publish pieces in a variety of genres.

Exactly which of these elements we emphasize will vary first and foremost according to children's needs. Teachers are encouraged to make their own informed decisions about what elements to include, which may need extra time, and whether certain steps should be left out. The important thing to remember is that the curriculum is supposed to serve the students, not the other way around.

What Follows in This Book

The specific focus of a punctuation study will vary according to grade level and the strengths and needs of a particular group of learners. Nevertheless, there are certain things that tend to make sense for particular age groups.

An ending punctuation inquiry usually works well in primary grades (K–2); a comma study is often appropriate for middle elementary students (3–4); and a deeper look at internal punctuation (colons, dashes, semicolons, etc.) and cadence can be the right sort of challenge for older children (grades 5–7).

There are fully fleshed-out lesson plans for each of these studies in the chapters that follow. They are intended as examples of how to balance the activities (open inquiry, focused inquiry, creating theories, experimenting, etc.) suggested in this chapter. The lessons contain:

- Sample minilesson think-alouds about punctuation decisions.

- Ideas for questions that may be appropriate to ask children in individual conferences.

- Suggestions for ways to structure share sessions.

There are at least two types of celebrations a class can work toward at the end of a punctuation study. We might decide that producing a finished product is not the point, and go for a celebration of children's theories, reflections, and writing experiments. The comma unit in Chapter 3 is such a study. Alternatively, it may seem appropriate to have a more traditional culminating event to celebrate a published piece, as in the upper grade cadence unit in Chapter 4. Either type of celebration is equally valid, and a well-rounded school year should have writing celebrations of each type, about punctuation or not.

It is not enough for us to know *how* to teach punctuation if we are not intimately familiar with the accepted conventions and rules ourselves. Therefore, each unit is followed by a selective reference section drawn from a variety of punctuation guides. These may be used by teachers or made available to students when they start asking for the "right" way of doing it.

My longtime colleague Adele Schroeter always stresses that before putting an idea out in the world, we should consider "the worst possible way it can be used." For teachers to take these lesson plans and plug them in more or less as written would not be a terrible thing; some views about punctuation would be stretched, and more than likely some children would discover new vistas to explore in their writing.

My hope however is that educators will use these units as reference points and launching pads for their own thinking. Teachers are encouraged to stretch out lessons over more than one session or skip some entirely if they seem not to fit a particular class. Certainly the suggestions for conferring should vary according to what individual students come up with in the conversation. Best of all would be if some intrepid souls added their own lessons or used these studies as inspiration for new units entirely.

CHAPTER 2

Beginning with Endings
Ending Punctuation Inquiry
(Early Grades)

Let's not have the period be so very somber. It puts an end to a particular thought. But you should have hope then, because you are going into the next sentence, where the previous thought can be expanded. I think it's not to be taken too seriously.
—Frank McCourt

The periods are like little stop signs," Benjamin says when first-grade teacher Barbara Pinto asks why he has put so many in his latest story. Dots are sprinkled throughout, seemingly randomly placed between pairs of words, often three or four to a sentence. "My dog Chija runs around very fast and stops to sniff things or bark or lick people," the young writer explains. "In this part she is running and stopping a lot, and the periods show you." A careful look and Benjamin's logic becomes clear—*Chija likes. to. run. in. the park. and bark. at cats*—not correct, but certainly well thought through. Barbara makes a note of what he has said, intending to use the phrase "stop sign" later with the whole class, crediting Benjamin with the terminology. After complimenting his thinking, she gently shows how the authors of books in the class library just put periods at the ends of sentences. Benjamin agrees this makes the writing easier to understand and goes back to his story to make some punctuation changes.

A hurried assessment might lead us to believe Benjamin's use of conventions indicates a lack of understanding. Certainly he is not making the grade, if the main point is to memorize the rules—and isn't ending punctuation something we want our youngest students to plug in automatically? The answer is yes, eventually. But just as we don't want children to learn even basic mathematical algorithms with no sense of what the numbers stand for, primary grade writers are better able to use interesting punctuation later if they are taught to think critically about even simple periods early on. Benjamin's conceptual awareness of periods and punctuation possibilities is quite sophisticated if the point of our instruction is to think inventively and make informed judgments.

It is not at all obvious how to teach children to be good decision makers when it comes to ending punctuation. Periods, question marks, and exclamation points are on the surface the most rule-bound family of punctuation. It is never an option to end a sentence without one of them, and most of the time it's clear which is the most appropriate in a given situation.

And yet, as straightforward as this seems, there are many ways to end a sentence. How an author chooses to complete a thought depends on the specific information the sentence contains, its intended effect on the reader, and what information came before (to name just a few factors). Though the number of ending punctuation marks to choose from is limited, deciding where and when and how to use them so our writing feels varied and balanced is not so simple.

Even our earliest lessons in punctuation should send a clear message that as with all elements of writing and reading, authors must be purposeful in how they use these marks. There may be strict rules attached to periods and question marks, but rules exist to serve meaning and expression; children remember to follow them when they understand why they matter. The implication for teaching ending punctuation is that it's critical first and foremost to make the purpose clear.

This ending punctuation inquiry, ideal for first grade, asks children to imagine what writing would be like if sentences were *not* separated. Once students see the need to do so, they explore different possibilities of *how* to separate them—the different ending punctuation marks. After they have some knowledge of the purpose and the possibilities, children need opportunities to experiment and articulate their own theories, as Benjamin did with his too frequent stop signs. Finally, after looking at mentor texts, noticing what authors typically do and don't do, and being explicitly taught rules in context, they learn conventions so they remember them and use them consistently.

A typical scenario in many elementary school classrooms is the phenomenon of the student who *knows* when to use periods, can explain when you are *supposed* to use periods, and consistently forgets to do so. Drilling the skill never seems to work, and teachers' frustration levels rise with every new run-on sentence. The undercurrent here is that once we teach students the rules for when and where to use periods, punctuation instruction stops or is put on hold. It's not uncommon for children to go months or even entire school years with no opportunities to make decisions about punctuation. Incorporating revision lessons on how to rewrite passages with new ending punctuation is one way to send a message that it is more than something you repair just before publishing. An added bonus is that making new ending punctuation choices forces normally resistant seven- and eight-year-olds to rewrite entire passages, a battle well known to any teacher of this age group. Such lessons fit well into most second- or third-grade writing units, and a sample is included in this chapter.

The bottom line is that we want to teach these conventions—rules—by giving children opportunities to put meaning and intention first. Like most things, understanding why and being given an element of choice makes ending punctuation not only less dry but pretty interesting to learn.

What Are Those Dots Doing at the End of the Sentences?

Rationale/Purpose   As they learn to read, small children notice all sorts of things about print. From different letters to different fonts to words all in caps to familiar chunks of words, everything seems there for a reason. Before they are explicitly taught about ending punctuation, our youngest readers wonder what those dots are doing at the end of the line.

The purpose of an early grade punctuation inquiry is to harness young children's natural curiosity. This mini-unit, adapted from master first grade teacher and literacy coach Barbara Pinto, begins by asking students to think about how periods help us as readers. From there they investigate the different types of ending punctuation (period, exclamation point, question mark, ellipses) and experiment with them in their writing. Throughout the inquiry children are given opportunities to:

- Form theories about what each type of ending punctuation does.
- Reflect on the ending punctuation *choices* authors make and why.
- Explain their own ending punctuation choices.

Though it is presented in three parts, the study should last a minimum of a week. It may take a couple of days for the class to read through a text and form theories about the author's ending punctuation (Lesson 2). Certainly students will need more than one writing period to experiment with and explain their own ending punctuation choices. For writers who already have a basic knowledge of periods, Lesson 1 may be skipped entirely. Adaptations are encouraged depending on the needs, strengths, struggles, and interests of a particular group of students.

Materials/ Preparation   Teacher:
- A passage (from a familiar picture book, piece of shared writing, morning message, or your own writing) with all periods removed, copied onto chart paper or an overhead transparency.
- The same passage, with periods included.
- Chart paper and markers, to record children's ideas about periods.

Students:
- Book baggies with just-right texts, one for each child.
- Writing folders, paper, pencils.

Summary	The class will examine a familiar text (from a picture book, piece of shared writing, morning message, or your writing) in two different versions. First, students will see and hear it read aloud with no periods at all and notice how difficult it is to read. Then, they will see and hear it in the original version, fully punctuated, and discuss how the periods helped it make sense. Last, children will go off to write, explaining their own decisions of when to use periods.
Sample Language/ Sequence	"Our class has been noticing so many interesting things about how authors write their words," you might begin. "Today we are going to think about some of the other marks, *besides* the letters, that they use to help readers understand." Using an exaggeratedly rushed and breathless voice, read aloud the passage with no periods. The idea is to bring out how the text makes little sense without any pauses or breaths.

> Today is Monday It is a little cold outside We will go to art today and try out some new paints It may get pretty messy There is pizza for lunch This is our favorite We will try not to eat too much and get sick

You might end with a dramatic touch, wiping your brow or falling off your chair in mock exhaustion. "Wow!" you might continue, "I am out of breath after reading that. Turn and talk to your partner about how we could make this writing easier to read."

As students have brief conversations (one or two minutes), listen in and choose comments to share with the group. "Ayana and Susannah said it was confusing to listen to that morning message, since one thing went right into the next. Jorge and Jeanene said it would be better if there were some breaths so we could hear each thing one at a time. Now let's look at the same morning message a different way and see what we notice about how it has changed."

> Today is Monday. It is a little cold outside. We will go to art today and try out some new paints. It may get pretty messy. There is pizza for lunch. This is our favorite. We will try not to eat too much and get sick.

As you read the version with periods included, slow down and emphasize the pauses without overdoing it. Though the first reading was exaggeratedly rushed, this one should be as natural as possible. Once students have had time to hear and look at the text, again ask them briefly to discuss with a partner what they have noticed. Listen in, identifying children who have come up with the particular ideas you want to bring out in the class conversation. By the end of the lesson students should be aware that the dots at the end of the sentence:

- Create pauses and let us breathe.
- Make the writing easier to understand.
- Separate one idea from another.
- Are called periods.

After listening to their observations, open up the conversation to the larger group. Circle the periods at the end of the sentences as students point them out, and record their ideas on a chart that will remain on display. If the above notions don't come out in the conversation, pose questions that will push children's thinking in the right direction.

Also emphasize that writers *make choices* about where to put periods, and give examples of how they make their decisions. "When I was writing about trying out the new paints in art class," you might explain, "I thought it would make people laugh if I talked about how it could get messy. Since I wanted the reader to notice that part, I put a period just before it. That way you read it right after taking a breath, and it feels especially important."

After discussing and charting some of the reasons authors use periods, give students the opportunity to try using them in their own writing. "When you go off to write, think about when you should be using those dots—periods—in your own writing. When is it important to separate one thing from another? Are there any parts where people will be confused if you don't help them by putting in a period? As you work I will be coming around to talk to you about your period decisions."

Independent Work When children begin to try out punctuation in their own writing, don't be too concerned whether they are using it correctly. This will come in time, and in the case of periods it is sure to happen quickly. It is more important to convey the idea that *all* punctuation is something writers make choices about. Though ending punctuation is certainly more rule bound than other sorts, an author chooses when to write a sentence ending in an exclamation point, when to lead with a question, and when to go with the period. Experienced authors know to use exclamation points and question marks in moderation, but young children need to understand that even something as mandatory as ending punctuation involves thinking about how we want the reader to understand our writing.

Questions and suggestions to pose to children as you confer with them during independent writing may include:

- Where is a place you really want your reader to notice something important? How can a period help show that part is special?

- Tell me a list of the things that happen in your story. Is each thing separated with a period? Why or why not?

- How are you deciding when to use periods in your story? Tell me about one place you decided to use one. Tell me about one place you decided not to use one.

Keep records of your conferences, and note suggestions for things children can try in their writing. In order to highlight the notion that periods are something an author makes decisions about, identify two or three students who are particularly articulate about their use of periods, so you can call on them during the class share.

Share Session

Using what students have told you in conferences, choose a particular focus for the share. Points to bring out might include using periods to:

- Separate ideas that would be confusing if they were all together.
- Make a reader pay special attention to a certain part.
- Show where to take a breath after you are done telling about one thing.

Whatever the focus, frame it by clearly repeating back to students what they "can all learn from the writer(s) that shared today."

Possible Follow-Up Activities

Students may speak to their partner about the way authors have used periods in the books they are reading independently. When are they using them to separate different parts of the story? When are they there to bring out something special? You might have a special share session in which children show examples of how periods are used in their favorite books.

Other Sorts of Endings

Rationale/Purpose Once young students have investigated periods, they are likely to be curious about other ways authors end sentences. The remaining types of ending punctuation—question mark, exclamation point, and ellipses—produce very different effects. It is almost always the case that children tend to overuse these marks after first learning them. This is a developmental trait and needn't be of concern. Such experiments ultimately open students to the idea that writers make choices about punctuation.

Materials/ Preparation Teacher:

- Typed-out text copied from a familiar picture book (e.g., *The Little Mouse, the Red Ripe Strawberry, and the Big Hungry Bear*, by Don and Audrey Wood [1984]; *Moo Baa La La La*, by Sandra Boynton [1995]; or *Where's My Teddy?*, by Jez Alborough [1994]) that includes examples of all types of ending punctuation.

- Overhead transparency or SMART Board of pages from the same familiar picture book, as well as markers to write on it.

- *Optional:* A copy of the picture book.

- Transparencies of pages from a second text, preferably familiar, showing all types of ending punctuation.

Students:

- *Optional:* Class sets of the familiar picture books.

- Book baggies with just-right texts, one for each child.

- Writing folders, paper, pencils.

Summary This lesson picks up where Lesson 1 left off, again emphasizing that punctuation at the end of a sentence helps us read writing more easily and is something authors make choices about.

   As a class, students read through the text of a familiar picture book that includes examples of each type of ending punctuation, discussing the differences as they go. You'll display the typed or photocopied text on an overhead transparency or SMART Board, circling the punctuation and writing children's theories in the margin. (It's helpful but not necessary for you and the students to have individual copies of the book as well.) Once students have discussed the different things ending punctuation can do, they test and add to their thinking by looking at a second text individually or with a partner. Finally they experiment with different types of ending punctuation in their own writing. Doing this thoughtfully and allowing for discussion and experimenting will likely take more than one class period.

| **Sample Language/ Sequence** | Once students are gathered in the meeting area, the first step is to make a connection between what you have discussed about periods and the idea that there are different types of ending punctuation. It is important to include language and ideas generated by students in earlier discussions, so they feel invested in the inquiry. "Our class agrees that without periods, writing is pretty hard to read," you might begin. "Benjamin said periods act like stop signs that keep the sentences from crashing into one another, and Paolo thinks they help us remember to breathe. Periods aren't the only punctuation used to end a sentence, though. Today we will look at one of our favorite books, *The Little Mouse, the Red Ripe Strawberry, and the Big, Hungry Bear*, and notice all we can about the *other* marks that end sentences. I'm very excited to find out what you have to say about how they help us read, and what you can do with them in your own writing. Let me know when you see one of these punctuation marks and what you are noticing." |

> Hello, little mouse. What are you doing? Oh, I see. Are you going to pick that red, ripe strawberry? But, little mouse, haven't you heard about the big, hungry bear? Ohh, how that bear loves red, ripe strawberries! The big, hungry bear can smell a red, ripe strawberry a mile away . . . especially, one that has just been picked. BOOM! BOOM! BOOM! The bear will tromp through the forest on his big hungry feet, and SNIFF! SNIFF! SNIFF! find the strawberry. . . .
>
> —Don and Audrey Wood, *The Little Mouse, the Red Ripe Strawberry, and the Big, Hungry Bear*

Read the text aloud, stopping when students raise their hand to share their thoughts. It is important that explanations be in the children's words and not to insist on correct terminology as long as the essential idea is on track. Circle the new punctuation on the transparency as students point it out, write their theories in the margins of the text, and facilitate the conversation. This may involve summarizing similar ideas or occasionally asking a question to push children to go deeper. Ideally students will build on one another's ideas and reach a consensus on what each type of ending punctuation does. Encourage students to respond directly to one another rather than to the teacher.

Although the theories should come from students if at all possible, be sure it's clear that each new type of ending punctuation:

- Changes the way our voice sounds (our inflection rises at the end of a question, we act excited/speed up/get louder when we see an exclamation point, we slow down and drift off when we see ellipses).

- Makes us feel a certain way when we read (we are curious, excited, filled with suspense).

- Is something a writer makes a choice about.

Questions you might ask to bring out these ideas include:

- When would you choose to use this kind of punctuation in your writing?

- How does it make your voice sound? Does it always make it sound the same way? When is it different?
- How do you think the writer wants us to feel when she uses a question mark/exclamation point/ellipsis?

After the conversation, consolidate the group's thinking on a chart, perhaps identifying by name which children came up with which ideas.

Once you have finished, have students, individually or with a partner, do the same sort of work with another familiar text, either a transcription or a published copy. "When you go back to your tables," you might instruct, "I will give you this sheet, which I've copied from another of our favorites, *Where's My Teddy?*, by Jez Alborough. Circle the ending punctuation marks you find and talk to your partner about them. Let's see if you notice the same things or if you change your mind about anything. Once you've finished with the sheet, go to your writing folder and try using these marks in your own stories."

> He tiptoed on and on until . . . something made him stop quite still. Look out! He thought. There's something there! What's THAT?
>
> —Jez Alborough, *Where's My Teddy?*

Independent Work Circulate and confer, emphasizing once again how different ending punctuation marks change the way we read. As students circle and discuss the marks on the sheet, you might ask:

- Why do you think the author used that question mark/exclamation point/ellipsis here?
- How is this question mark/exclamation point/ellipsis different from the one we looked at together as a class?
- When should a writer use a question mark/exclamation point/ellipsis instead of a period?

Once children have begun writing themselves, questions you could ask them about their punctuation decisions might include:

- Why did you use a question mark/exclamation point/ellipses in this place in the story?
- How did you want your reader's voice to sound in this part? Did the ending punctuation help?
- We have noticed that writers sometimes use periods and sometimes use these other ending punctuation marks. Why did you decide to use a period in this part of the story but an exclamation point/question mark/ellipsis over here?

While making your way around the room, note which students do a particularly good job explaining their punctuation decisions, and select two or three to share.

Share Session   Today's share session has two parts. Begin by reviewing the second example with the whole group, comparing its ending punctuation to the examples in the text used earlier in the lesson. You may want to display a transparency of the example and write students' observations in the margins as before, pointing out similarities and differences.

In the second part of the share, have the two or three children you've preidentified show their work and explain their punctuation decisions. It is important that students see the writing and that it is read aloud with appropriate, even exaggerated, vocal inflections (rising of the voice with a question mark, getting excited with an exclamation point). Summarize what students are noticing as readers and trying as writers, and frame their observations in terms of future writing work. "Our class is coming up with such great ideas about how to end a sentence," you might conclude. "For one thing, we have noticed authors use different types of ending punctuation in the same story—not *all* question marks, or just exclamation points. We decide as writers when to use one thing and when to use another. For example, many of us noticed that exclamation points make our voice get louder and a little faster, but ellipses slow us down and stretch the words out. From now on we will be thinking about how we want readers to *say* the words in our writing, and we'll use different ending punctuation to help them."

Thinking About Our Punctuation Decisions

Rationale/Purpose The first two lessons of this inquiry have stressed the idea that punctuation is something writers make choices about. Though it is never an option to leave out ending punctuation entirely, we decide when to use a period versus a question mark or exclamation point depending on the desired effect. Young children are, not surprisingly, quite open to this idea, although their early attempts are often determined more by the novelty of a new punctuation mark (making it sound exciting by using an exclamation point, for example) than truly thinking about what they want to do as writers. This lesson models the process of making an ending punctuation choice that takes into consideration the way we want a reader to think about the story.

Materials/Preparation Teacher:
- Blank overhead or chart paper, to use in your demonstration.
- Markers.
- Sticky notes cut in the shape of arrows.

Students:
- Writing folders, paper, pencils.
- Sticky notes shaped like arrows.

Summary In this lesson you will think aloud about ending punctuation as you write in front of the class, modeling the way authors make such choices. Once your students have seen you do this, they will identify places in their own stories where they made a specific ending punctuation decision. In order to make the idea more concrete, they will label one or more such examples with a sticky-note arrow that explains their thinking.

Sample Language/Sequence "We have been thinking a lot about using different types of ending punctuation in our writing so people read our stories in a certain way," you might begin. "Today I will demonstrate how I make choices about which ending punctuation to use in my own story. As I think out loud, be a spy and listen to the sorts of things I think about. When I am finished, I will ask you to report back on the important things you noticed.

"First of all, I need to decide what will be an interesting subject to write about. I think my cat Fabala would work well, because she does lots of exciting and funny things. That could give me a chance to use exclamation points. Since I want my reader to get interested in hearing about Fabala right away, I can start the story by asking a question." Pause and write the first sentence of your demonstration piece.

> Have you ever met a cat that loves to jump on kitchen tables?

"Now that I have made people curious, they will probably want to keep reading. But if I don't say more about cats jumping on tables, they may get frustrated. I'd better give them some information. Since I started off with a question, my next sentence should end in a period, to keep things calm."

> Have you ever met a cat that loves to jump on kitchen tables? My cat Fabala does it every day when I come home from school.

"One thing I noticed when we studied ending punctuation in books is that periods were used more than anything else. So I think my next sentence should have a period too, before I try something different."

> Have you ever met a cat that loves to jump on kitchen tables? My cat Fabala does it every day when I come home from school. I pet her and push her on to the floor.

"Next I want to show how she jumps down and sometimes crashes into dishes. First I'll write a sentence with another period, and then do one with an exclamation point to show the loud sound she makes."

> Have you ever met a cat that loves to jump on kitchen tables? My cat Fabala does it every day when I come home from school. I pet her and push her on to the floor. Sometimes she jumps right into one of the dishes. Crash!

After leading a brief discussion (one or two minutes) about what students have noticed, turn to the class and ask for their help with the next sentence. "Turn and talk to your partner about what sort of ending punctuation I should use next," you might instruct, "and be sure to say why you have made that choice."

As students have brief conversations, listen in and choose two suggestions to share. Call children back to attention and present both possibilities, reinforcing the idea that there is no one right answer when making a punctuation decision. "Both of these could work well," you might continue. "The important thing is to have a good reason for our decision. When we have our writing celebration, part of what we want to show is how smart we are with our ending punctuation choices. To do this we will choose at least one place where we really thought hard about what punctuation to use. Then we will put a sticky note shaped like an arrow next to that place and write on it what we were thinking. Watch as I do this with my story."

Using a large sticky-note arrow, demonstrate choosing an instance of ending punctuation and explaining your thinking. "I liked the part where the exclamation point makes the crash sound exciting. That could be one place to put my arrow. But the question mark in the beginning gets readers into the story by making them curious about my cat. That might be a better place to show what I have learned about using ending punctuation to make a story interesting." Place your arrow so it points to the first sentence, and write a few words on it to explain your thinking.

> I like how the question mark makes people want to keep reading. ⇨

"When you go off to do your own writing today," you might conclude, "be thinking about what ending punctuation to use, and how it will help the reader. After you have written for a while, I will come around with sticky-note arrows so you can label a place you made a really good punctuation decision. Once you have chosen that best place, write the reason for your choice right on the arrow."

Independent Work During the first part of the independent writing session, individual conferences should focus on children's ending punctuation choices. Some students will be more articulate about this than others. Assigning partners to get advice from each other serves a double purpose; it creates a classroom buzz about different ways to end sentences and also provides support for writers having trouble.

Questions for individual conferences might include:

- Where is a place in your story you could have a character ask a question? Where might you ask a question to the reader?

- Is there a part that seems especially exciting?

- We know that authors usually have more sentences that end in periods than other ending punctuation. This means we want to choose only the very best spots to use question marks, exclamation points, or ellipses. What part or parts of your story make the most sense to put these less common marks in?

- When I read your story, where do you want my voice to sound different? What punctuation would make me do that?

Once students have begun to choose spots to put their sticky arrows, you may need to coach them in how to write the reasons for their punctuation choices. This might be done with what Lucy Calkins calls a "mid-workshop interruption" to briefly call children's attention to particularly clear explanations given by their classmates. These may or may not be the most sophisticated strategies; in fact, choosing one complicated idea to highlight and another clear but simple one could provide a useful and more inclusive contrast.

Some questions to ask as you confer about students' punctuation arrows could include:

- Where is a place you made an ending punctuation choice another writer might want to try? When might he or she try it?

- Now that you are looking over the different ways you ended your sentences in this story, are there any new things you might want to try in your next piece? Does it give you any ideas for how to change something you've already written?

You may also want to encourage students to go back to their writing folder and choose one older piece in which they made a good ending punctuation choice. This will give them an opportunity to use another sticky arrow. In the course of circulating, identify students for the share session. What in particular about a student's attempts would be beneficial for the whole class to think about? You might select one example of each type of ending punctuation, or several contrasting reasons for the same type (e.g., an exclamation mark for a loud noise, and one where something surprising happens).

Share Session

You can take one of several approaches to this share (and the final writing celebration that follows):

- Highlight one example of each type of ending punctuation.
- Show different approaches for the same type of ending punctuation.
- Connect different types of ending punctuation that all make our voice change in some way.
- Connect different types of ending punctuation that all make us feel a certain way (e.g., excited, curious, filled with suspense).

Whatever you choose to highlight, frame the share so students see the unifying theme or idea. Though there are times you want a more random feel, one of the objectives of this inquiry is to make generalizations about the types of things punctuation can do. Once students begin to see patterns, they will start to come up with new possibilities and think of punctuation as a tool for expressing themselves in different ways.

Ideas for a Final Celebration

Every writing cycle should end with a public celebration. Invite parents, administrators, and if possible another class to see the work students have been doing. It is a good idea for you or a student to introduce the celebration by explaining the nature of the study. Possibilities for how to structure this celebration:

- Have each student in the class share one example of ending punctuation with the whole group.
- Set up separate "punctuation stations" for all the writers who chose to highlight a particular kind of ending punctuation.
- Create a punctuation "museum." Each student displays his or her work, and visitors circulate from one to the next. (Providing a comment sheet on which guests can write complimentary feedback is a nice touch.)

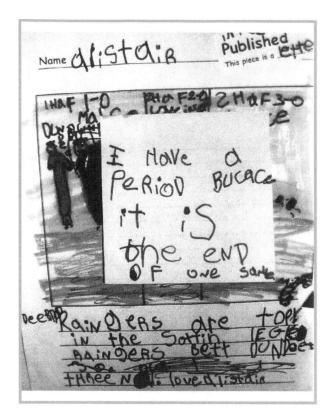

First-Grade Punctuation Noticings: "I have a period because it is the end of the sentence"

"I put the exclamation because I had fun"

Second-Grade Punctuation Wall

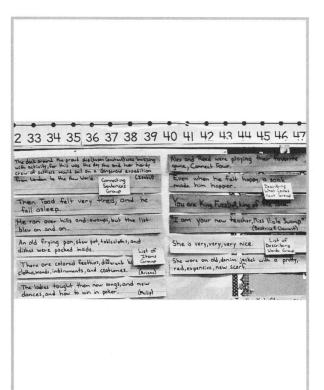

Second-Grade Comma Examples and Theories

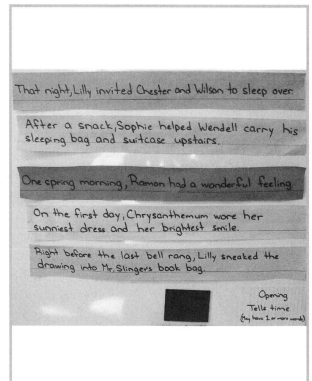

Nicky's "Am I Lost?!?" Second-Grade Writing, Focusing on Punctuation Experiments

One day, when I was on vacation
I was walking with my parents then
I decided to run!
I turned around...my parents weren't
there!!
I was sure they were still trying to
get to the corner of the street
I started to get scared!
I shouted up in the air "Mommy!!!
Daddy"!!!
I didn't hear them, I started to
get the shivers, then I thought what
will I do?
Always when I think I've lost
my parents I'm thinking inside how
will I survive?
Oh no. I've lost my mom and
dad I thought, it was so hard to think.
I was sure they were on the sidewalk!
No I was sure they weren't on
the sidewalk!
What should I believe I'm lost for-
ever... or I'm not lost for ever!?!
Then I thought how can I think
I'm not lost if I'm thinking I am
lost?
I started to calm down.

1

Page 2 of Nicky's Story

Page 3

Page 4

I ran to where I last saw mom
and dad.
They weren't there!!
I kept running back and forth!
I was crying also.
I kept running back and forth
and crying to see if a stranger,
would help me.
I was thinking what if I don't
have anything to eat?
Soon a stranger came... and asked
me "are you ok" I said "No."
The stranger came up with three
other ideas, the first idea was "When
did you last see your mom and
dad" I said "right here"
Then he said "well... what do they
look like" I said "It is too hard
to explain". He said..."do you know
your parents cell phone
number" I said "no".
While he was thinking... my mom
and dad came out of a
JEWELRY store!!!
I screamed!!
There They Are!!!

I ran to my mom and dad and
jumped up to hug them.
Before I could say thankyou
to the stranger...he was gone, I
was so sad!!
I couldent even say thankyou!
While I was walking home I was
thinking how he saved my life and if it
weren't for him, I would of never
seen my family again!
I also was thinking how someone
could care that much about me.

Ending Punctuation Revision Lesson
(Grades 2 and 3)

We have 26 symbols to work with as writers, but there are a whole lot more when you take into account the punctuation marks.
—Novelist Colum McCann

One of our most important objectives is for students to see punctuation as a tool of expression, not something to be repaired in the final stages of the writing process. Many authors see it as something to play with, and try out different possibilities before settling on an appropriate choice. More often than not, this involves rewriting the words as well. This is especially the case with ending punctuation; few if any sentences can be changed from a declarative statement to a question without revision.

Happily, re-punctuating is an opportunity to rethink exactly how we want the reader to experience our writing and try out new angles on the same idea. It is an ideal strategy for teaching revision, especially to second and third graders, who famously resist changing anything once they have finished a draft.

A revision lesson in which students try out new ending punctuation can easily be incorporated into just about any writing unit. In addition to being a valuable technique for re-imagining a text, it has the added appeal of seeming a little like a game. Often children who look at us blankly when we ask them to write a passage differently understand and take on the challenge of rewriting with new punctuation.

Messing Around with Ending Punctuation

Rationale/Purpose

Now that students have formed theories about different types of ending punctuation in the books they are reading, it is time for them to experiment with ending punctuation in their own writing. They need to see how the same idea can be expressed in new ways when punctuated differently. To do this successfully, words and phrases need to change along with the punctuation. This is a valuable lesson in revision, something second or third graders are not always keen to try. Remember too that at this grade level it is important to encourage experimentation; there will be time for "correct" punctuation soon enough. For now the object is to make your seven- and eight-year-olds passionate punctuators and convey the idea that it is OK to take chances.

Materials/ Preparation

Teacher:

- Overhead transparency of a piece of your own writing (preferably an example that students are familiar with from a previous lesson).

- Blank chart paper and markers.

- Prepared chart (see below).

Set up the meeting area so students can see both the projected transparency and blank chart paper, since you will be referring to one while writing on the other.

Students:

- Writing folders or notebooks, with samples of previous work to rewrite as they mess around with ending punctuation.

Sample Language/ Sequence

Once students have gathered in the meeting area, you might say, "Over the last couple of days, you have done a great job coming up with ideas about when authors choose to use periods, exclamation points, and question marks. Today we will have a chance to mess around with ending punctuation—to try using it in different ways, listening and seeing how it can change our writing. We will pick a piece from our folders and try changing the punctuation. To do this well might mean changing some of the words in the story. First, we will read it the old way to hear how it sounds. Then, we will mess around with punctuation and change some of the words. Last, we will read it the new way to see if our changes made it better. Watch as I show you how to do this, and listen as I think aloud about my punctuation choices."

Show students a transparency of your own writing, and think aloud as you rewrite it on chart paper with new punctuation. (Ideally this should be writing used in a previous lesson, so students have some familiarity with it and can concentrate on the rewriting.) You might begin, "You probably remember my story about my friend Dan's seventh birthday party and his older brother Pat the bully. It began like this:

> **Version One**
> It was my friend Dan's seventh birthday party, and he was all dressed up. Many older relatives were there making a fuss about how cute he looked, laughing and chatting. The other seven-year-olds at the party were being ignored. Off in the corner stood Dan's older brother Pat, who terrified me. He hit Dan when no one was looking and teased all the neighborhood kids.

"It seems to me that I could make this more interesting using different types of punctuation. Maybe I'll take that first line about the party and try making it a question." Write on the chart paper: *Who would have thought a birthday party could turn out to be so scary?* "That's a much better beginning. It grabs the reader's interest more than the other one. I took out some important information though, so I'll have to put it in the second sentence." Write on the chart paper: *My friend Dan was turning seven, and he was all dressed up. There were a lot of older relatives there making a fuss about how cute he looked, and the rest of us kids were being ignored.* "So now I've used two periods. Maybe I'll try making it exciting with an exclamation point."

Looking back and forth at the old version and then the new, you might write, *Unluckily, Dan's older brother Pat was there watching from the corner. OH NO!!*

"I'll try an experiment now and use both question marks *and* exclamation points. And then maybe those dots we called ellipses. Here goes." Write: *What if he tries to hit someone?!?! I remember thinking. Pat just kept on staring. . . .*

Now step back and say, "Let's see how this second way turned out, if all the new punctuation made a difference. I'm going to read it aloud, and then ask you to turn and talk about what you noticed me doing as a writer, and what I thought about as I wrote."

> **Version Two**
> Who would have thought a birthday party could turn out to be so scary? My friend Dan was turning seven, and he was all dressed up. There were a lot of older relatives there making a fuss about how cute he looked, and the rest of us kids were being ignored. Unluckily, Dan's older brother Pat was there watching from the corner. OH NO! What if he tries to hit someone?!?! I remember thinking. Pat just kept on staring. . . .

After you finish reading, ask children to turn and talk about what they have noticed. Then allow a few students to share. Alternatively, you can simply say, "Thumbs up if you noticed . . . ," or show students the following prepared chart:

Some Ways to Mess Around with Punctuation
- Go back and forth between different types of punctuation.
- Think about how you want the reader to feel.
- Change the words around from the first version so the new punctuation will work.
- Experiment.
- Read it to yourself and listen to how it sounds each way.

"When you get back to your tables you'll need to choose a piece from your writing folder. First, you will read it to yourself and listen to how it sounds. Next, you should mess around with punctuation as you watched me do, trying the things on the chart. Last, read it to a partner the new way to see if it works better. Whether you like it the new way or not, rewriting with new punctuation is one thing you can always try if you want to change a piece of writing."

Independent Work   As students begin to look through their folders for a story to work on, some will have a hard time choosing and others will choose too quickly. For those who can't decide, you might conduct a short, pop-in conference or quickly coach a small group in strategies for making this decision. Some questions you could ask are:

- Which story has the most exciting parts?
- Which story do you like but wish it had a more interesting beginning?
- In what place could you put in a question for the reader?

Reworking a piece of writing is sometimes a difficult notion for second and third graders; many feel they are "done" and will be resistant to the idea. You may need to do some line-by-line work as you confer with those having difficulty. Some ideas to get them started include:

- Is there a way you could start the story off with a question to the reader?
- Where is the part you want the reader to feel most excited? How would you change the words in that part so an exclamation point would work instead of a period?
- You've used two periods/exclamation points/question marks in a row here. What would be a different way to end the next sentence?
- Where is a place you'd like to ask the reader what he or she thinks?

When doing this sort of line-by-line work, remember to plant an idea but leave the student with a strategy for continuing on her or his own. For instance, you could end the conference by saying, "You did such a nice job putting a question/exclamation point at the beginning. When I leave, I'd like you to read through the rest of your story and mark two other places where a question/exclamation point could work, and then try writing the way those parts could go." It is a good idea to ask students to articulate their thinking about why they chose a particular type of punctuation, modeling the appropriate language whenever possible—"Are there certain places you especially wanted to draw the reader in/make the reader wonder?"

As you circulate, note contrasting examples of students' experiments and preselect those who will share. Let these students know in advance that they will be sharing and coach them on what to say about their "punctuation process," e.g., "I'd like you to be sure to tell the class how you decided that the beginning should start right in with an exciting part and then calm down. You can explain that this is why you chose to end the first sentence with an exclamation point and end the second with a period."

Share Session

Be sure that writers not only share examples of their experiments but also explain how they made their punctuation decisions. If students forget this part, you can chime in: "When I was conferring with Sonia, she told me that she thought it was important to slow down the action in this part. That is why she chose to put in those ellipses."

The critical lesson underlying today's work is that writers do in fact think about how they punctuate, and for any story there is more than one way it could go.

Possible Follow-Up Activities

- Have "punctuation partners" rewrite each other's pieces and explain the reasons behind their decisions.

- Ask students to take a favorite passage from the book they are reading independently and rewrite it trying new punctuation.

Ending Punctuation Glossary: Few Choices, Many Possibilities

Ending punctuation marks are in many ways the least complicated of punctuation families. They are clear, unambiguous. You always need one at the end of a sentence. There are a limited number of choices—three—and the basic function of each one is pretty easy to explain.

But on more careful examination it is clear there are subtle differences that go beyond knowing that an exclamation point makes it more exciting and a question mark means you are asking something. Children and even adults can get by knowing just the basic definitions, but familiarizing ourselves with the nuances of meaning when we use ending punctuation in different ways can enrich us as writers. And isn't it our job as teachers to know as much as we can about such possibilities, in order to guide students to go deeper and try new things in their writing?

The selective glossary that follows, adapted from Shaw's *Punctuate It Right!* (1993) and Stilman's *Grammatically Correct* (1997), gives these basic definitions and goes over some of the subtle differences in how ending punctuation is commonly used.

Period

The period is the most common form of terminal punctuation, indicating the end of a sentence or statement. As the most frequently used ending punctuation mark, the period can be applied to lots of very different grammatical situations, but is generally used to indicate a "stop" or to terminate abbreviations.

Exclamation Point

The exclamation point may be used in place of a period when the writer is trying to emphasize a point or demonstrate excitement or emotion. Though children tend to overdo them, most adult authors use exclamation points sparingly. "If the words don't produce the exclamation, what's the point?" asks journalist Jimmy Breslin (2007). "Why put *horse* under the picture?"

Question Mark

A question mark is used to turn a sentence into a question, or query. It may also be used to show uncertainty. It can sometimes be used interchangeably with a period to indicate requests.

Nuances of Ending Punctuation

Sentences fall into three broad categories—statements, questions, and commands. Depending on the context or author's intent, the three forms of ending punctuation can be used interchangeably, as described in the examples below.

Statements

Generally, a writer uses a period to indicate the end of a sentence; however, when replaced with a question mark or an exclamation point, the entire meaning of that sentence may be altered.

When to Use a Period

- Use a period to end sentences that are not emotionally charged or meant to ask a question.
- Use a period to indicate the end of a sentence that states a fact or condition: *She prefers asparagus to broccoli.*

When to Use an Exclamation Point

- Use an exclamation point to add emphasis to a statement. It is considered "incorrect" when used in sets (!! or !!!), should not be used often, and should not be used at the end of long sentences.
- Use an exclamation point to indicate that a statement is ironic or humorous: *With all his griping, he deserves his own personal complaint department!*
- Use an exclamation point to give a statement emphasis or to provide a feeling of extra emotion: *These rules of punctuation can really be confusing!*

Questions

When to Use a Question Mark

- A question mark is used to end most direct questions and should not be used regularly or within a set of two or more (??).
- Question marks should be used at the end of requests for specific information: *Where did you put the pile of punctuation books I left on the counter?*
- In some cases, a question mark may indicate that a particular type of response is expected: *You don't mean* she's *to be the one in charge?*

When to Use a Period

- Use a period for polite requests—for example, when the purpose is to "suggest an opinion or choice without requiring an answer" (Shaw): *Will you kindly fill out the application and send it in by April 15th.*

- A period may follow an indirect question when it occurs within a larger sentence (such sentences often include the word *when* or *what* and refer to *someone else* asking a question):

  My mother asked when we would be able to come for a visit.

  Let me know exactly what he said and which form he wanted us to send.

When to Use an Exclamation Point

- Exclamation points can sometimes be used to indicate instances in which questions don't need an answer. In these cases, a question mark or a period may be substituted just as well: *How can we ever repay you for your kindness!*

Commands

When to Use a Period

- A period may be used after a command that is not urgent: *Take as much time as you need and close the door when you leave.*

When to Use a Question Mark

- Question marks may be used to make a request appear more humble: *Would you mind taking a minute to fill out the feedback sheet?*

When to Use an Exclamation Point

- An exclamation point may be used after a sharp command or urgent request: *Come over here at once!*

And Then There Are Ellipses . . .

Like many stable families, the usually predictable and mostly rule-bound world of ending punctuation has a problem cousin. Depending on the guide you consult, ellipses, or ellipsis periods, may or may not count as a fourth type of ending punctuation. Many primary level read-aloud books employ the dot-dot-dot as a dramatic way to leave the young listener hanging on for more. "The big, hungry bear can smell a red, ripe strawberry a mile away . . ." write Don and Audrey Wood in *The Little Mouse, the Red Ripe Strawberry, and the Big Hungry Bear* (1984).

As a form of ending punctuation, ellipsis periods can indicate an indefinite ending to a sentence or a conscious trailing off. Confusing the issue is the fact that they are also sometimes used as internal punctuation *within* a sentence to show that information has been omitted or to create suspense (see the Internal Punctuation and Cadence Glossary at the end of Chapter 4 for more on this).

Ellipses have the dubious distinction of being the one form of punctuation that can either be put at the end or in the middle of a sentence. This being said, many writers consider them to be something of a cheap trick, a not-so-subtle way of letting readers know they are supposed to be on the edge of their seat. One thing is for sure—after young writers discover ellipsis periods, there's no stopping them. They are perhaps the most enthusiastically adopted and overused punctuation in writing workshops around the country.

According to Shaw's *Punctuate It Right!* when ellipses are used in the middle of a sentence, they generally come in groups of three (. . .) and are used to indicate omission or passage of time within quotations and lists. However, used as ending punctuation, ellipsis periods more commonly come in groups of four (. . . .), with the first one used to indicate the ending period.

As ending punctuation, ellipsis periods are primarily used in one of three ways:

1. To imply that more information should be reported on the written subject: *He loved her deeply, but something told him to go slowly, to take his time, to think* . . . (Shaw).

2. To give a statement a dreamy or poetic tone: *The waves crashed on the shore like a symphony, rising in a salty crescendo, falling off, then swelling once again.* . . .

3. To create an edge-of-the-seat feeling of suspense: *He turned around just in time to see the ball shooting right at her head, no time to duck.* . . .

CHAPTER 3

Breathing, Thinking, and Deciding What's Important

A Comma Exploration
(Middle Elementary Grades)

Give me the comma of imperfect striving,
thus to find zest in immediate living.
Ever the reaching but never the gaining,
ever the climbing but never attaining.
—Winston Graham

Commas help your reader figure out which words go together in a
sentence and which parts of your sentences are most important.
—The Writing Center Website, University of North Carolina at Chapel Hill

It had worked. The third graders in Barbara Rosenblum's class were becoming zealots. When I walked in, children would cheer, "Hooray! It's time for punctuation!" as though a class party were about to begin. At the end of reading workshop, students rose from their spots with independent books in hand, spontaneously pointing out punctuation they'd noticed that day to Ms. Rosenblum, or to each other. There was much talking and coming up with theories, usually accompanied by animated editorializing on why the author had used those particular marks. In *The Art of Teaching Writing* (1994), Lucy Calkins likens students' growing awareness of what writers do to her own experience of planning to buy a new car, "noticing the differences between Toyotas and Subarus, Pintos and Saturns. . . . Because I now view myself as someone who needs to know about cars, I see them everywhere." Enough conversation and debate around different types of punctuation had taken place in the room that these third graders not only were beginning to notice more but vied to be the first to make smart observations about what they saw.

It was time to harness this energy and curiosity toward a more focused study, to move away from general inquiry. A cursory examination of just about any text will tell you the most common form of internal punctuation is the comma. Barbara and I agreed that it made sense for students to focus on this ubiquitous punctuation. There were enough varied uses for students to continue their active observation, and learning to use commas for more than just lists and letter writing seemed a natural next step in their development as writers.

We knew that one essential element was to capitalize on the students' eagerness to one-up each other's theories, and comma use certainly loans itself to discussion. Besides, Louis and Maddie B.'s now famous classroom debate on the difference between commas and dashes had by now spread to other children; what punctuation to use for which kind of pause was a hot issue. With that said, a wide-open study of all sorts of commas seemed too broad. We wanted to focus on the particular comma uses that would give students the most bang for their buck as writers. Looking over the books they were reading, their writer's notebooks, and state standards, three types seemed most relevant:

- Commas after an introductory phrase.

- Commas used to combine two clauses.

- A pair of commas to tuck in information (apposition).

The tricky thing was that much of the students' enthusiasm so far had grown out of feeling that their ideas were the guiding force in the study. It would be easy to lead them to see that commas were the most common type of pause and the most useful to learn first. But how to get specific about these three particular uses of one type of punctuation and still give young writers a sense of ownership?

We opted to begin with another open inquiry in which we narrowed the focus; students would once again search through their independent reading books for instances of comma use, jotting down examples and briefly writing down their thoughts about why the author chose to use commas in these different ways. Now that our young writers had some experience with this kind of looking, we trusted that the level of their thinking and discussion would be more than superficial. And, as important, though we left the search open we knew that at least a few students would likely find examples of the types of comma use we wanted to teach during their independent work time. We would highlight them in the share session and narrow the study to suit our purpose. In this way, we could genuinely say the focus came from what students had noticed.

Is this manipulative? Stacking the deck in our favor? Absolutely. But good teaching, even in an inquiry-based/exploratory lesson, involves careful choreography. Sometimes we want to set things up in such a way that students are led to particular discoveries. Clearly there are lessons, such as in our initial punctuation explorations, where a teacher's primary job is to let students notice what they will and be responsive. But at other times we take the lead, laying bread crumbs for them to follow so they arrive at a teacher-planned destination.

This balance is at the heart of good workshop teaching. They say one of the things that made Duke Ellington a masterful jazz composer was his ability to set up the improvised solo. He would write beautiful melodies, chord progressions, and arrangements, which led to the horn player's sixteen bars in such a way that, though improvised, the solo nearly always fit the composition perfectly. In our planning we wanted to achieve that same quality, setting up the lesson so the children's individual angles, their particular choice of words as they defined a variety of comma use—like the horn soloist's unique style—led a certain way. Just as Duke drew on his knowledge of a player's musical personality to create his gorgeous compositions, we want to use our observations and assessments of children's understanding to plan focused inquiry lessons.

Weaving a spirit of inquiry together with particular teaching objectives should not be viewed as just an opening gambit. As the study continued, Barbara's students moved from noticing what other authors were doing with commas to messing around with these ideas themselves in their writer's notebooks. The payoff was not in the finished product but rather in the forming and testing of theories. Once they came up with clear ideas about how to use commas in reading workshop, our third-grade writers tried these strategies out in writing workshop—without the pressure of needing to publish a finished piece. Wisely, Barbara waited until the following unit to hold children accountable for correctly following comma conventions.

In this era of data-driven instruction and high anxiety over test scores, it is important to take the long view about this type of inquiry-based teaching. Over time, striking a balance between more exploratory lessons and those that lead to specific destinations results in deeper thinking.

The unit which follows is an adaptation of the one co-constructed by Ms. Rosenblum, her third graders, and me. As rich an experience as it was for the students of Class 3-221, it would be a shame to teach it exactly as written here. Some lessons might need to be stretched out over more than one class period; it may make sense to skip others entirely. Think of this unit as a guideline; adapt it according to the strengths, needs, and discoveries of the individual students you are teaching this year, today.

Punctuation Detectives, Part 1

Rationale/Purpose

A great shift occurs when a student moves from learning about ending punctuation (periods, question marks, exclamation points) to considering internal marks such as commas, colons, and dashes. For one thing, ending punctuation is governed by pretty strict rules; a question mark must always come at the end of a question, a period at the end of a declarative sentence, etc. The decisions a writer makes about ending punctuation have to do with the types of sentences they write in the first place—whether to begin with a question, where to insert an "exciting" sentence requiring an exclamation mark. This is quite different from considering whether to use a dash or a comma to create a shorter or longer pause.

Internal punctuation is more a matter of choice, less about rules. It is rare to find a passage where you absolutely could not use a pair of dashes in place of parentheses or a colon instead of a semicolon. Authors decide on which internal punctuation they want in order to angle their meaning; they may set off information with dashes to make it seem important or use commas to create a hurried pace.

This study begins with a general exploration of the difference between ending and internal punctuation. Then it guides students to the realization that of all the marks "inside the sentence," the comma is the one they see most often—and thus, the type of internal punctuation it makes most sense to concentrate on first.

Materials/Preparation

Teacher:
- A variety of preselected picture books (Big Books are ideal) or short texts that contain a variety of internal punctuation for students to look at in small groups—*Strega Nona* (dePaolo 1975), *The House on East 88th Street* (Waber 1962), *Click Clack Moo—Cows That Type* (Cronin 2000), and *The Cookie-Store Cat* (Rylant 1999)—are good choices.

- A preselected passage from one of these texts copied onto a transparency, chart paper, or a SMART Board.

- A prepared reflection on the middle punctuation in the passage (an example is shown below).

- Blank chart paper and markers.

Students:

- Reading notebooks and writing utensils.
- *Optional:* Blank graphic organizers to record examples/theories.
- Enough blank transparency sheets and overhead markers for partners to record passages they want to share.

Summary

The steps of today's lesson are to:

- Review what students know about ending punctuation and ask what is different about punctuation "inside the sentence."
- Read a text aloud and reflect on what different types of *internal* punctuation make our voices do—take a long pause versus a short one, slow down or speed up, draw out certain words, etc.
- Explain the procedure for choosing and copying examples to share.
- Send students off to look at examples of internal punctuation in preselected Big Books or short texts, then read the examples aloud to notice differences the punctuation makes in the sound of their voices.
- Have students copy examples onto an overhead transparency to share with the class.
- Help students share, discuss, and begin to make generalizations about what they've noticed.

The independent work and share sessions for this lesson require more time than in other lessons. You may want to allow a double period or carry the share over to the next day in order to fit it all in.

Sample Language/Sequence

"By now you are experts in how to use periods, question marks, and exclamation points. What these have in common is that they come at the end of a sentence. Some other punctuation marks happen *inside* the sentence, not at the end. Let's look at this passage from Lois Lowry's *Number the Stars* (1989) and see if we notice any examples."

> It was all imaginary, anyway—not real. It was only in the fairy tales that people were called on to be so brave, to die for one another. Not in real-life Denmark. Oh, there were the soldiers; that was true. And the courageous Resistance leaders, who sometimes lost their lives; that was true, too.

As students begin to volunteer examples (e.g., dashes, semicolons, commas), list them on chart paper, taking care to leave enough space next to each to record ideas. "Are there any *other* punctuation marks that happen inside the sentence, ones that are not in this passage?" Students will likely think of a few others, such as colons, ellipses, and parentheses, but may not know what to call them. While adding these to the chart, you can label them. "Now that there are a few things on our list, turn and talk to a partner about what each of these punctuation marks makes our voice do. Do we slow down? Do we pause? For how long? Come up with ideas for each mark." As students briefly discuss their thinking (no more than two or three minutes), listen in, noting commonalities, contradictions, etc.

Now introduce students to the lesson's main activity: developing theories and finding examples. "It was interesting to hear the ideas you were coming up with," you might say, "and how they were the same and different. Haskell thinks a colon makes your voice pause for longer than a comma, but Anzia believes it's the other way around. Ruth says a dash makes your voice speed up, and Abdo says it slows it down. Who is right? Today you and your group will be punctuation detectives and investigate.

"To demonstrate, I'm going to read a passage aloud from Bernard Waber's book *The House on East 88th Street* [1962]. I'll choose one punctuation mark *inside* the sentence and notice what it makes my voice do. I'll also think about how it helps me understand what is happening in the story. If I find two examples inside the same sentence, I'll need to do this for both of them. Listen to the sorts of things I think about, since you will be doing what you see me do when you are working on your own." As you read aloud, emphasize, even exaggerate, what the punctuation makes your voice do, pausing briefly at the comma and longer at the semicolon.

When a Citywide Storage and Moving man carried in their potted pistachio tree, everyone rejoiced; the truck was at last empty.

—The House on East 88th Street, by Bernard Waber

"There are two punctuation marks inside this sentence—a comma and a semicolon. I have ideas about both. The comma makes me take a short breath and pause just for a second. That breath lets me think back on the first part of the sentence, so I'm ready for the second. The semicolon is interesting, too. It makes a longer pause in my voice than a comma, and almost seems to end the sentence—but then there's a whole other part, which gives more information.

"Now that I've come up with ideas on what these punctuation marks do, I'll record them on a chart—as you will do in your reading journal. Since I made theories about *two* punctuation marks I'll need to write about each one separately. Once I've done that, I'll say something about how middle punctuation is different from ending punctuation." [*To save time, you may want to have this prepared ahead of time rather than writing in front of your students.*]

When a Citywide Storage and Moving man carried in their potted pistachio tree, everyone rejoiced; the truck was at last empty.

What the middle punctuation does to my voice:

The *comma* makes me take a short breath, which helps me remember the part that comes before.

The *semicolon* connects an extra part after the sentence seems over. Both parts could be sentences by themselves, but the author uses the semicolon to show me they are connected.

How is middle punctuation different from ending punctuation?

Ending punctuation stops a sentence.

Middle punctuation makes me pause during a sentence and connect ideas.

The comma makes a shorter pause than the semicolon.

"During your independent work today you will be punctuation detectives. There are Big Books/picture books/short texts at your tables. You and your partner will look for interesting examples of punctuation *inside* the sentences and think about what that punctuation makes your voice do—and how it helps you understand. Find at least three passages to write about in your journal as you've watched me do. We will pick the most interesting ones to copy on transparencies for the whole class to see. I'll be coming around to ask what you are noticing."

Independent Work

As partners begin to read texts at their tables and come up with theories, encourage them to think about how punctuation inside the sentence affects the sound of the language as we read it (aloud or to ourselves) and helps us to understand. This should not be a silent lesson; it is important that students read passages aloud in order to think about what the punctuation inside the sentences makes their voices do. Some questions to push their thinking may include:

- How long do you pause after that comma? How long after the dash/colon/semicolon? Why do you think the author wanted you to pause for different lengths of time?

- How would the sentence sound if the dash were a comma? If the colon were a dash? If the comma were an ellipsis? Read it aloud to show how it would be different.

- What are the different parts of the sentence about? Is one part more important than another? How does the punctuation divide them?

The goals for the beginning of this unit are two. First, you want students to begin to reflect on the general nature of internal punctuation; second, you want them to notice the frequency of the different marks, eventually coming up with the idea themselves that commas might be the most useful ones to learn about first. Though this second objective is dealt with directly in coming lessons, it may be useful to foreshadow it in today's conferences. Ask:

- Are any of these punctuation marks used in more than one way? How are they different? Which would be most useful for an author to know how to use?

- Are there any places where the author could have used a different kind of punctuation instead of the one she or he chose? What could be used instead?

Once students have chosen at least two passages and written down their theories about middle punctuation, direct them to copy the most interesting one onto a transparency for the share. Copying these examples and theories will take time; if necessary, delay the share to a later period or to the following day. As students copy their passages, circulate and note common threads in their thinking, grouping examples (e.g., students who have examples with semicolons, or commas after an introductory phrase, etc.) in order to plan for the share.

Share Session

In order to focus the conversation, plan ahead which examples to share. The aim is to group passages using the same type of punctuation; reading more than one example of a dash or comma or colon in a row helps children make generalizations. Though you should not discourage attempts to define punctuation marks in a broader way, the emphasis today is to notice the difference in how they make the text *sound*. Encourage students to:

- Develop theories about what particular punctuation marks make our voices do—slow down or speed up, vary pause lengths, rise or fall, etc.

- Make general statements about how punctuation inside the sentences is different from what comes at the end.

Using the overhead transparencies so others can follow along, have students who are sharing read their sentence aloud and tell what the punctuation makes their voice do. Following each series of examples (e.g., three passages using dashes, two with commas in a list), lead a brief conversation, guiding students to come up with a generalization ("Is there a way we can put together what Nathan, Andrea, Sara, and Carl each said about how colons sound?"). Write these generalizations down and refer to them when you create charts defining each type of internal punctuation.

At the end of the lesson, collect students' transparencies and reading journals, to prepare a sheet of examples for Lesson 2.

Possible Follow-Up Activities

The question of how ending and middle punctuation differ has no exact answer, and students may benefit from hearing what a variety of people have to say on the subject. A possible homework assignment is to have them interview three separate adults on the subject, asking:

- What does punctuation inside the sentence do?
- What does punctuation at the end of the sentence do?
- How are they the same?
- How are they different?

Punctuation Detectives, Part 2

Rationale/Purpose This lesson shifts from noticing what punctuation makes our voices do to reflecting on why authors *choose* particular punctuation marks. As students share their theories, it is critical for them to construct definitions for each type of punctuation *in their own words*. Inventing their own terminology allows children to understand in a more invested way and will likely spark their curiosity to learn conventional definitions later.

Materials/ Preparation

Teacher:

* Passages collected during Lesson 1—one copy for each student, plus a copy on an overhead transparency. These should include several examples each of commas, dashes, colons, semicolons, and ellipses. Below each set of examples, allow space to record students' definitions of why an author might choose each punctuation mark. (If necessary, add additional passages so each type of internal punctuation is well represented.)
* Blank chart paper and markers.

Students:

* Reading notebooks and writing utensils.
* Sticky notes.

Summary The aim of this lesson is to come up with co-constructed class definitions for each type of punctuation inside the sentence. You can frame this process by asking students to consider *why* an author might choose a particular mark, thus encouraging them to think about punctuation strategically—how a comma or a dash or a colon can affect the way a reader understands.

Begin by modeling coming up with a definition for one type of punctuation in your own words. Partners then examine the sheet of examples and mutually decide how to define each type of punctuation. The share session will be longer than usual as the class compares definitions and comes to a consensus on how to describe each type of punctuation.

Sample Language/ Sequence "Now that we've thought about what punctuation inside the sentence makes our voices do," you might begin, "it's time to go further and figure out why authors choose to use these marks in their writing. In other words, when might an author want to put in a colon? When would she think about using a dash instead? I've put together the examples we collected in class to remind you of different ways authors use these punctuation marks. Today you and a partner will look at these passages and come up with ideas about why an author might choose to use each one. To do this you will need to come up with definitions of each, in your own words. Watch as I demonstrate thinking aloud about dashes."

> 1. Ants are not bugs—they're insects.
> 2. Luckily, there are still miracles in this world—sometimes in the shape of a little cat.
> 3. As summer slips into fall, grandma and Sama share a rich golden harvest—and their sweet, sweet memory.
> 4. Get the bag of flour—the unopened one—from the pantry.
> 5. You will have to find a notebook—red or green or black.

"The dash in these sentences makes a pause that gets us ready for extra, important information. For example, in the first part of sentence 1 we hear that ants *aren't* bugs, which makes us wonder what they are instead. Then, after the dash, we learn they are insects—which answers the question. In sentence 2 the author tells us there are miracles in the world—and then adds that the miracle comes in the shape of a cat, which is the main point. I'm not sure *all* dashes do this, but in both of these examples it seems like a *get-ready-for-something-important mark*. I'll record this definition on my sheet."

> **Why an author might choose to use a dash:**
> Authors put a dash in when they want us to pause before an extra piece of information. The dash lets us know something important is coming. It is a *get-ready-for-something-important mark*.

Once they have watched you model the process, give students an opportunity to come up with a definition as a group before they go off to work independently. Read an example such as the one below aloud, emphasizing the pauses made by both colon and commas.

> They thought of the things that matter most to them: friends, family, supper.

"Turn to a partner for a moment and see if you can come up with an idea about the colon in this example. What is it doing? I called the dashes get-ready-for-something-important marks. What would you call this colon?"

As partners discuss the example (no more than a minute or two), listen in, noting their thinking and adding brief comments or questions to help clarify an idea. Though the focus is on the colon, don't discourage ideas about the commas in the sentence or what either punctuation mark makes our voices do. In summarizing student conversations, stress that there is no right or wrong and all thoughtful ideas are worth considering.

"I heard some great ideas coming up in your conversations," you might say, calling students back to attention. "Haskell thinks a colon is used only before a list, but Anzia believes it can call attention to any important information, list or not. Tess and Ann-Marie agree that we could call it a pay attention! sign. All of these are good ideas, and would be interesting things to record on your sheet. When you go off for independent work, your first job will be to look over the examples on your own and make notes in your reading journal on what to say about them. After a few minutes I will give you a signal to meet with a partner and agree on how to fill in the definitions. You should explain what the punctuation does, and then give it a name as you saw me do for the dash and as we did together for the colon. By the way, the names we came up with already might not be the best ones—see if you can't make up your own for those as well! Once we have thought of names for these different types of punctuation, we will come together as a class to agree on which definitions to put up around the room on chart paper."

Independent Work During the first five minutes or so, circulate and make sure students are reading through the examples and making notes in their journals. Once they have begun partner conversations, listen in, asking questions and making brief comments to push their thinking. You might ask:

- Have you checked to see that the name you are giving this punctuation mark makes sense for all the examples?

- It's important that the name we give to each type of punctuation belongs just to that one and could not be true of the others. Could your definition of dashes also be true of colons? How are those two types of punctuation different from each other? When might an author choose one rather than the other?

- This punctuation seems to be doing different things in different sentences. Should we give it more than one name, depending on how it is used?

The important idea that one punctuation mark can do different things may also be expressed more specifically:

- The dash in this sentence seems to be getting us ready for important information, but this other example, with two dashes, is more like parentheses; it inserts information in the middle of the sentence. Could dashes do more than one thing? Perhaps we can have more than one name for what a dash does.

While circulating and listening in on conversations, identify particular students to lead today's share session. In making these selections it is important to find several with contrasting definitions, to stimulate conversation.

Share Session The aim today is to compare students' thinking about different types of punctuation inside the sentence and agree on class definitions. It is important that these definitions are in the students' own words; you want children to construct their own understanding. This process will take longer than the usual share, so plan accordingly. As they agree on terminology, students are likely to notice the same punctuation doing different things (e.g., a pair of dashes used like parentheses, a single dash used to add important information at the end of a sentence). In these cases they may want to come up with more than one definition.

Your role in facilitating the conversation is to connect students' ideas and help the class agree on how to describe particular punctuation marks. "Benjamin and Christina think a dash should be called a stop-look-and-listen sign," you might say, "and Joanne and Taylor described it as a don't-forget mark. We could combine these and say that a dash is a stop-don't-forget-this signal."

Another important role to play in guiding the share is to encourage the class to accept more than one definition, where appropriate. "In the sentence from *The House on East 88th Street*, Barbara and Nathalie noticed that the comma separates a part telling *when* something happened from a part telling *what* happened. They decided to call that a when-what comma! But Cara and Kiri pointed out that in the 'Still, life goes on' sentence, the comma comes after just one word—and seems to be connecting the new sentence to the last one. They called it a quick-connector comma. These names both describe a comma very well—but they are very different ways to use a comma. Here we might want to agree on two definitions."

Filling in charts as you go may slow down the conversation. You may want to visibly take notes on a pad about what the class agrees on and make the chart later. "Now that we have come up with these definitions," you might sum up the share, "we will post them around the room to think about as we look at more and more examples. One thing is for sure—it's clear writers don't want to bore their readers with dull sentences, like 'I went to the park.' Punctuation inside the sentence helps them connect ideas and write longer, more interesting sentences."

After the Lesson Begin displaying charts of children's theories about particular punctuation. (To prepare for Lesson 4, you'll want separate charts for each type of punctuation—one for commas, one for dashes, etc.) These charts should summarize ideas discussed in class but ideally will be living documents that you add to and change as new thoughts come up in subsequent lessons and conversations.

Punctuation Theory

Sample Format 1:
Punctuation Theory
(adapted from Barbara
Rosenblum's third-grade
class)

© 2008 by Dan Feigelson, from
Practical Punctuation: Lessons on
Rule Making and Rule Breaking in
Elementary Writing. Portsmouth,
NH: Heinemann.

Commas

1. Before lunch, when Harriet was painting a picture, she dripped paint onto the carpet.

2. There were donuts, bagels, cookies and three different cakes.

3. Everyday, when Felicity came home from Miss Manderly's, Nan was waiting for her.

4. Still, life goes on.

Why an author might choose to use a comma:

Colons

5. The following day there was a new message: Please stay!

6. And each day Charlie saw the same thing: a blue whale.

7. This is what we saw: the farms in Iowa.

8. They thought of the things that matter most to them: friends, family, supper.

Why an author might choose to use a colon:

Dashes

9. Ants are not bugs—they're insects.

10. Luckily, there are still miracles in this world—sometimes in the shape of a little cat.

11. As summer slips into fall, grandma and Sama share a rich golden harvest—and their sweet, sweet memory.

12. Get the bag of flour—the unopened one—from the pantry.

13. You will have to find a notebook—red or green or black.

Why an author might choose to use a dash:

Ellipses

14. Mama says my stories go on . . . and on . . . whenever I'm at the beginning of one, she just tells me "Get to the point, Jamaica!"

15. At 86th and Main she goes down . . . and down . . . into the subway station.

16. The scarecrow is thinking his long, slow thoughts . . . and soon, birds will be coming by.

17. We'll play cards until the lightning bugs shine in the trees . . . and we won't mind that we forgot to keep score.

Why an author might choose to use ellipses:

Semicolons

18. You don't need to be rich; you just need someone to care about you.

19. They wouldn't ride with me; they just rode behind me and whispered things I couldn't hear.

20. Sticks and stones can break my bones, but that heals; it's hard to heal a broken heart.

21. I was the only child; and my father having died two years after my birth, we two were alone in the world.

Why an author might choose to use semicolons:

Parentheses

22. The Indians thought that they (the Europeans) were just giving them a present.

23. The month of March (as in the old saying) had come in like a lamb.

24. She had moved to Epiphany and taken a job with my father, who is the best dentist in town (fact).

25. The round face of the lass (her eyes big with curiosity) peered down at him through the iron bars.

Why an author might choose to use parentheses:

Sample Format 2
(adapted from Nathalie
Mac's third-grade class)

Sentences We Found	Theories About This Punctuation Mark
Commas Before lunch, when Harriet was painting a picture, she dripped paint onto the carpet. And that, for your information, is how to get famous in Brooklyn. When I look though my window, I see a brick wall. There were donuts, bagels, cookies and three different cakes. However, the sisters did agree on one thing.	
Dashes This heartfelt story is a celebration of life, friendship and most of all—hope. She dashed down the stairs—and up again—with the maple syrup. These words—*borrow your tackle box*—gave me a weird feeling in my belly. You'd better pull a rabbit out of your hat tomorrow night—or else! There was no particular reason for Cara to cry— she just felt sad.	
Colons There were plenty of sweet things to eat: cake, cookies, ice cream and cupcakes. She always started her homework routine the same way: pouring a glass of milk, sharpening her pencil and kicking off her shoes. His kitten especially loved to play with one thing: a tiny little stuffed Cat-in-the-Hat doll.	

Listening to Punctuation

Rationale/Purpose   Once students have investigated punctuation "inside the sentence" and discussed their thinking with classmates, they will naturally want to see whose ideas were closest to the truth. Rather than fight the competitive spirit, use this curiosity as motivation to continue exploring.

In this lesson the class turns its attention to the *sound* of punctuation. Students are challenged to read sentences aloud to partners and have them guess the punctuation mark. They are encouraged to:

- Listen for lengths of pauses.
- Notice the sorts of ideas a particular mark connects or separates, making connections to their theories from last lesson.

**Materials/
Preparation**   Teacher:

- Excerpt from a familiar children's book with interesting internal punctuation, copied onto chart paper or an overhead transparency.
- A classroom aide (or a student) briefed in advance to model the guessing game.

Students:

- Independent reading books with examples from last lesson.
- Reading journals and writing utensils.

Summary   This lesson has two objectives: *procedural* (laying out the steps of what students are to do) and *conceptual* (modeling what they are to notice and think about). Begin by demonstrating how to read passages aloud to a partner expressively so he or she can guess the correct punctuation. (It is best to have practiced with your adult or student partner ahead of time.) Next, model thinking aloud about the ideas and how they are connected, looking for further evidence of theories students came up with in Lessons 1 and 2.

"Today we will test some of the theories we came up with yesterday," you might explain. "We'll listen carefully to the way punctuation inside the sentence makes the words *sound*. What does it make your voice do? By reading aloud with expression and listening carefully, we should be able to hear which punctuation marks make longer or shorter pauses and get some idea of how authors use punctuation to connect different parts of a sentence. To do this we will play a game. You will first find examples from your independent reading that use some of the punctuation we looked at yesterday, and mark them with sticky notes. Then when I give the signal you will take turns reading these examples aloud to your partner and guessing what punctuation is being used. The tricky part is, you will also need to explain *why* you made your guess. Watch as we demonstrate how it's done."

It may be a good idea to have your partner do the expressive read-aloud so that you can demonstrate guessing and explaining your thinking. You may want to guess one punctuation mark correctly and another incorrectly, to underscore the idea that punctuation is often subjective. As you model the game, students should be able to see the text as it is read aloud, so they'll notice what the punctuation makes the reader's voice do. (The person doing the guessing should not be able to see the text until afterward.)

To frame the demonstration, you can point out upfront what students should be listening for. "As you watch us play the game," you may explain, "notice how my partner first reads the example aloud clearly and with expression. Notice what the punctuation made her voice do. Then listen to how I explain my guesses according to the way she read it aloud. The object is to try to show the correct punctuation with your voice. Remember, you are working together with your partner, not against each other. The team gets one point for each correct guess."

> In the background, he heard the cows busy at work:
> Click, clack, **moo**. Click, clack, **moo**. Click, clack, **moo**.
> —Doreen Cronin, from *Click, Clack, Moo—Cows That Type*

"It seems to me," you might think aloud, "that there is probably a comma after 'in the background.' I think that because there is only a *short* pause, and we decided last time that commas make the shortest stop. I also remember from last lesson noticing how authors can use commas right after short opening phrases that tell *where* something is happening. So since 'in the background' tells *where* the noise is coming from, a comma makes sense."

"The next place I hear a pause is after 'busy at work.' This is a longer pause, so I'm not sure exactly which punctuation mark goes there. Since the pause is to get us ready for the sound of the cows clicking and clacking and mooing, I'm going to guess it is a dash. That creates a longer pause, and gets us ready for something coming next in the sentence."

At this point, you can look at the text (on chart paper or an overhead transparency) to check the accuracy of your guesses. "I was right about the first comma, but not about the dash. It seems the author chose to use a colon there instead. A colon and a dash both make a longer pause, so to guess this one I need to think of what the sentence is saying.

In our last lesson some of us noticed that colons *announce* something, and in this sentence they are announcing the sounds the cows make when they are busy. A dash tells us a little bit and then gets us ready for a little more information, and a colon stops everything to make a big announcement. I guess the author wanted to give the sense that this was a big announcement, and then surprise us with the 'click-clack-moo.' Silly sounds like that after the idea that a big announcement is coming make it funnier, and this is certainly a funny book. So I guess the author made a good choice. And our team got one out of two points!"

"Before you try this game yourselves," you might continue, "turn and talk to a partner about the sorts of things you saw me listen for and think about as I made my guesses." As students talk briefly (no more than a minute or two), eavesdrop and gauge their understanding, listening for comments that take into consideration how the punctuation *sounds* and the way it affects the *meaning* of the sentence.

"Danilo and Seth noticed that I thought about the length of the pauses, which ones were long and short," you might sum up before sending students off to play the game. "This is paying attention to the way the sentence *sounds*. Sophie and Kyla noticed I talked about what the author wanted us to think and feel. This is how the punctuation affects the *meaning*. As you make your guesses, be sure to notice what the punctuation makes your voices do, and also how it helps you understand the sentence. Remember, you will need to explain your thinking if you want your team to get a point." (You may want to list these two qualities on chart paper or the board to remind students what they should be thinking about as they play.)

"When you get back to your seats, you will have a few minutes to go through your independent reading book to choose passages for the game. It's OK to look over the examples you collected during the last lesson; you may choose some of those to use as well. Remember, although you are working together, your partner should not see the examples yet; he or she is supposed to guess the correct punctuation from the way you read it out loud. The team gets one point for each correct guess. I will give a signal when it's time to start playing."

Independent Work   As students prepare to play the game, circulate and check in on the passages they are choosing. It is important that:

- Examples use a variety of punctuation.
- Students rehearse in their head how to read the passages aloud—which pauses will be the longest, where their voice should slow down or speed up, etc.
- Students think about why authors chose one particular punctuation mark over another.

While circulating, you might ask:

- Is there more than one type of punctuation inside these sentences, or do they only use commas?
- Where will you pause as you read this example aloud and for how long? Which pause will be the longest/second longest, etc.? Why?

- Why do you suppose the author chose to use a dash/comma/colon here instead of some other type of punctuation?

After five or ten minutes, signal for students to begin playing the game. Your role should be that of silent researcher, circulating once again and listening to their guesses and explanations. In particular, take notes (partly to assess student understanding and partly to use in the share session) on how students describe the characteristics of particular punctuation marks. For example, how do they explain what commas/colons/dashes make our voices do? What do they say about the differences between types of punctuation, and why an author would choose to use one rather than another?

Share Session

Today's share session has two parts:

1. Begin by checking in with the class on how the game went. What was easy? What was hard?

2. Once they have shared their feelings about the process, either call on preselected students to report what they have noticed about particular punctuation marks or simply report what you overheard. Highlight both differences in opinion (e.g., whether a dash or a colon creates a longer pause) and places where the class has reached consensus (e.g., a comma is the shortest pause). Following the share, these new insights should be added to the charts of student theories created after the last lesson.

"It's interesting to notice," you might sum up, "how punctuation inside the sentence makes our voices do certain things. Some of our ideas about what a certain mark makes our voices do are the same, and in some cases we disagree. It's the same for authors in the world; even though there are some things they agree on, each writer has his or her own way of using punctuation. Two goals for us as writers are to learn how to use the marks most people agree on and to develop our own personal style of how to use punctuation."

Possible Follow-Up Activities

In this lesson, students will notice differences in how long each punctuation mark makes us pause as well as the reason an author might choose it (to announce something, to give extra information before going back to the main part of the sentence, etc.). You may want to ask a student committee to take the ideas discussed in class over the last two lessons and make a chart listing the different types of punctuation in order from shortest to longest pause. This chart can then be displayed alongside those created after the last lesson about children's theories of particular punctuation.

Assessment

As you get deeper into the unit, keep an eye on the writing students are doing in their notebook and in other subjects to gauge whether they are internalizing some of these punctuation ideas. To reinforce the importance of what they are learning, it's a good idea to celebrate and call attention to such experiments when they occur. Take a moment between lessons, after lunch, or before transitions in the school day to share examples of new punctuation students are using in all of their writing, whether in their writer's notebook, a math procedure, or a set of science notes.

Trying Another Way

Rationale/Purpose

This lesson is fairly sophisticated but if approached correctly can be enjoyed by even the most resistant student. It may be done with a small group, presented as an extra activity during free time, or even assigned for homework once introduced and modeled. The idea is simple; rewrite a sentence by changing its internal punctuation—an ellipsis instead of a dash, a colon instead of a semicolon, etc. Experimenting with possibilities, students begin to see how punctuation choices shade their writing in different ways.

Materials/ Preparation

Teacher:
- A passage from a children's book using one particular type of internal punctuation, copied onto chart paper or overhead transparency.

Students:
- A variety of passages containing one particular type of internal punctuation; these may be examples gathered from previous lessons, sentences from their writer's notebook, or new passages from their independent reading.
- Writer's notebooks and writing utensils, brought to the meeting area.

Summary

Though the idea of today's activity—to rewrite a sentence using different punctuation—is fairly simple, students may have difficulty understanding what to do without a concrete demonstration and think-aloud.

Sample Language/ Sequence

"Today's activity is a sort of game," you might begin. "Now that we have come up with so many ideas about why authors choose different types of internal punctuation and the different things these marks make our voices do, we are going to experiment. The idea is to take a sentence from our independent reading or from a passage in our writer's notebook that uses one type of punctuation—let's say a comma—and rewrite it with another punctuation mark. To do this, we will probably have to change other things in the sentence as well. Once we have tried it a couple ways, we can compare the different versions and decide which works best for what we want to get across to the reader. As I demonstrate rewriting a sentence from my writer's notebook, listen to the sorts of things I think about."

> *Original sentence:*
> If I ever get chased by a dog again, I will calmly walk away.

"The comma in this sentence connects what happened before—getting chased by a dog—with my thoughts on what I would do next time. It makes my voice pause, to get ready for the next part, but it doesn't really create any suspense. I know that an ellipsis is one way to do that, so I'll try using that instead."

> *Ellipsis:*
> If I ever get chased by a dog again I will . . . walk away!

"The ellipsis works pretty well here. It makes a longer pause in the middle so you feel a little suspense, and when the "walk away" part comes in it makes you laugh. The exclamation mark helps with that, too.

"For the ellipsis I didn't have to change too much—just remove the word *calmly* and change the period to an exclamation mark. To try it with a colon, I'll need to rewrite a little more. Since a colon *announces* something, I'll change my tone so it seems like I am talking to the reader, giving a warning."

> *Colon:*
> There is only one thing to do if you are chased by a dog:

"Then, instead of using the same words as before I'll change *calmly* to *slowly* and switch its position to the end of the sentence. It might also make the reader laugh if I add another short pause just before the end. I'll do that with by adding a comma."

> *Colon:*
> There is only one thing to do if you are chased by a dog: walk away, slowly.

Once you have demonstrated rewriting a sentence without changing much and also by making substantial changes, children need an opportunity to work through the process before they try it independently. "Turn to a partner," you might suggest, "and see if you can think of a way to rewrite the original sentence, this time using a dash. If you come up with an interesting way, copy it into your writer's notebook."

As students talk over possibilities (no more than two or three minutes), listen in, gauging their understanding and noting comments to share when the group is called back to attention. You'll want to highlight their strategies for rewriting—what they decided to change and why in order to add new punctuation.

In summing up be sure to tie together contrasting examples, to emphasize that there is always more than one solution."Judith wanted to use the dash to make it feel like the sentence was being interrupted, so she chose to rewrite the whole beginning: *When a dog is chasing you, many things may pop into your mind—but just stay calm and walk away.* Ralph made the second part longer, because he wanted it to feel like a how-to book: *When a dog is chasing you—take a deep breath, walk slowly, and whatever you do act calm.* There are lots of ways that would work, and when writers play around with punctuation they often try different marks before deciding which to go with. When you go off to work on your own, first choose a few sentences to rewrite. They may be from your writer's notebook or independent reading, or they could be examples we've looked at in class over the last few lessons. Then try rewriting each one at least two or three different ways, using different punctuation."

Independent Work

As students get into rewriting their sentences, cheer them on and spontaneously share examples with the class. You're trying to get across the sense that writers sometimes *play* with punctuation; to reinforce this idea, the atmosphere of the lesson should be a joyful one in which experiments are encouraged.

If students are having difficulty rewriting using a particular type of punctuation, it may be a good idea to pair them with classmates who have used it successfully. The whole activity could be done with a partner. Apart from being a support for strugglers, the resulting conversations are a concrete way for students of all levels to articulate their strategies for rewriting.

You may want to ask:

- Which punctuation mark might you use if you wanted to create more suspense? Which would you use to make the reader laugh?

- How long a pause does this punctuation make? What would it do to the sentence to make it longer/shorter? How might you do this?

- What happens if you make the first part of the sentence shorter/longer? How does it change the way we read it?

As always, choose students ahead of time to ask to share. Look for contrasting examples of the same punctuation to encourage the idea that there are many possibilities and a writer should experiment.

Share Session

Since the priority is to play with punctuation, you should encourage a sense of humor and camaraderie. Tolerating incorrect attempts is critical; in the likely event that a student uses a type of punctuation incorrectly, gently correct him or her, but only after first applauding the effort and the thinking behind the rewrite.

"From now on, when you write something with one type of punctuation," you might say to sum up, "take a minute to consider what would happen if you did it another way. Maybe you'll come up with something even better!"

Which Punctuation Should We Look at More Closely?

Rationale/Purpose
Though until now students have investigated any and all internal punctuation, the objective is to lead them to the realization that commas are the most widely used—and probably make the most sense to learn about first. This lesson involves copying and tallying examples of interesting punctuation students have collected so far and determining which mark occurs most frequently. On one level it is a simple counting exercise, but in the course of looking over these passages with a partner students will reflect on many examples and how they compare. This is a necessary step in guiding young writers to think about the importance of the comma relative to other internal punctuation.

Materials/ Preparation

Teacher:

- Charts (from Lesson 2) detailing students' theories about particular types of punctuation, displayed around the room.

- Two examples (on chart paper) of how students should copy their examples onto sticky notes, one with a single type of punctuation, the other with more than one (see lesson below).

- Steps of today's activity copied onto a chart, a transparency, or whiteboard.

Students:

- Independent reading books.

- Reading journals and writing utensils.

- Sticky notes to use in copying examples for display.

Summary
This lesson is largely procedural and does not involve thinking aloud. Students will be working with partners and should be encouraged to discuss the different punctuation examples as they copy, display, and count them. Begin by explaining the point of the activity (starting with the *why* is always a good idea), and then tell students the steps they must follow:

- Gather examples from reading journals, books, etc.

- Copy them onto sticky notes.

- Display the sticky notes on the appropriate chart—comma examples on the chart with student theories on commas, dash examples on the chart about dashes, etc.

- Count the number of sticky notes on each chart to see which punctuation occurs most frequently.

The share session will be a bit longer than usual and structured somewhat differently. In order to guide students to the realization that commas are the most important form of internal punctuation and should be studied first, have them count the instances of each type of punctuation and then facilitate a class discussion to draw conclusions.

Sample Language/ Sequence

"We have done some good work looking at the differences between ending punctuation and punctuation inside the sentence," you might begin. "We've also come up with smart theories on what those punctuation marks make our voices do and why an author might choose one over another. Those theories are posted on charts hanging around the room. With so many interesting punctuation marks to choose from, it makes sense to figure out which one authors use the most and then become experts on that one. Today, working with a partner, we will gather as many examples as possible from the last few days and copy them onto sticky notes. These sticky notes should have the full sentence, not just the part with the punctuation, and the name of the book and author, like this example."

> Lottie slept beside her bed, curled in a soft circle, and Nick leaned his face on the covers in the morning, watching for the first sign that Sarah was awake.
>
> —Patricia MacLachlan, *Sarah, Plain and Tall*

"This passage has three commas, so we can stick it on the chart about commas. But what if an example has more than one type of punctuation inside the sentence, as in this one from the other day?"

> In the background, he heard the cows busy at work:
> Click, clack, **moo**. Click, clack, **moo**. Click, clack, **moo**.
>
> —Doreen Cronin, *Click, Clack, Moo—Cows That Type*

"In a case like this, where there is a colon *and* some commas, you'll need to copy the example twice and put it up on both the colon chart and the comma chart. You and your partner can each copy it one time, to share the work. Before you copy an example, discuss with your partner whether it is a good one to put up, and why. The two of you must agree before copying, and each of you should be working—so be sure to agree on two at a time! There is no limit—copy as many as you can until it is time for sharing. When we are done, we'll tally all the examples the class has found to see which punctuation inside the sentence authors use most."

Independent Work   As students go off to work with partners, circulate and listen in on their decisions. Rather than conferring with individuals, stop by briefly, making comments and asking questions to extend and (in some cases) jump-start conversations. Examples of such questions and comments include:

- Why do you think the author chose to use a comma/dash/colon/ semicolon there rather than some other type of punctuation?

- What is another way the author could have punctuated this sentence? How would it have changed the way your voice sounds as you read it?

- I see you have more than one example that uses commas. Do you think the author uses them in the same way each time? What is different about the way they are used in some of your examples?

- What punctuation inside the sentence do you notice writers use most often? Why do you think they use that one more often than others?

As students have these conversations, they will likely come up with new theories on particular punctuation marks and the differences in what they make our voices do. Take notes on these ideas so you can introduce them during the sharing session and also to include them in part of your long-range assessment.

Once the class starts copying examples, putting them up on charts, and returning to their desks, a buzz of excitement will begin. Don't discourage this feeling—allow children to have fun while at the same time keeping things focused. You can periodically interrupt the proceedings to call attention to a particular example or share an interesting idea that has come up in conversation.

Your job today, then, is to play several roles at once:

- Conversation facilitator, asking questions and making comments to push conversations further.

- Cheerleader, celebrating children's ideas and sharing interesting examples of punctuation they have found.

- Researcher and recorder of ideas, taking notes on students' theories, understandings, and misconceptions about particular punctuation marks.

- Referee, keeping order and focus without dampening enthusiasm!

Since the ultimate objective is to call attention to the fact that commas are the most frequently used type of internal punctuation, it is important to check the progress of the count as sticky notes accumulate on charts. This outcome will almost certainly occur naturally, but just having more comma examples is not enough; you also want to be sure there are a variety of comma uses (commas in a list, commas after introductory phrases, commas separating two clauses, etc.) that can be investigated in future lessons. So notice what passages students are selecting and, if necessary, gently suggest certain sentences over others.

Once there are a convincing number of sticky notes on display and you have taken notes on student observations, call students to the meeting area for a discussion. You might choose a student or group of students to be official counters or do the tallying with the whole group.

Share Session

There are two main objectives: to lead students to the realization that commas are the most frequently used type of internal punctuation, and to make them curious about its different uses.

Begin by counting off the sticky notes children have copied and displayed. The simplest way is to tally the sticky notes on each chart. A more complicated variant is to count every comma in every sticky note (a sentence like the previous example from *Click Clack Moo*, for example, contains seven commas). Allowing students to have fun with this activity is critical; cheering and laughing should not be discouraged.

Once students are satisfied that commas do in fact appear most frequently, you want to set them up for the next phase of the unit, i.e., to wonder about the different ways in which it is used. "Since commas appear in so many sentences," you might ask, "would you agree that they are an important type of punctuation to learn about? As we've studied all these different examples, many of you have noticed commas being used in very different ways. Josh told us earlier how his passage had commas separating things on a list, and Molly shared an example where a pair of commas was used to put extra information in the middle of a sentence. We've all seen commas at the beginning of letters after "Dear So-and-So," and of course they are used when writing the date. How many ways are there to use commas anyway? Turn and talk with your partner about this."

Allow students to talk briefly, and listen in on their conversations. Having piqued their curiosity, you can end the lesson by saying: "Think about this question, and perhaps ask a few adults how many uses they can think of for commas. We'll begin investigating this in our next lesson!"

Possible Follow-Up Activities

There are several possibilities for homework assignments. The suggestion to ask an adult at home could become an "official" interview, with answers recorded in reading journals. As an alternative foreshadowing of the next lesson, you might ask students to go back over their nightly independent reading to come up with examples of at least three (or two, or four) different ways authors use commas.

Which Commas to Study? Narrowing the Focus

Rationale/Purpose

It has been said there are thirty-two uses of the comma, and clearly some are more complex than others. In a beginning comma study, it is important to narrow the focus to a few types. The criteria for choosing should of course come from the needs and experience of children in the class—you want to concentrate on those that will be most useful to them as writers and readers, and that they are most likely to see in the texts they read. During the early stages of the unit, you should decide which types of commas will be most useful to study and set up your lessons in such a way that students will agree these are the ones they should learn.

The outcomes of a successful inquiry are partly planned in advance. The hard part is making students feel their observations and ideas are guiding the lessons—that it is not all predetermined. This is a subtle art. On the one hand you are manipulating the situation so the class comes to a certain conclusion. On the other you are taking cues from them and choreographing your inquiry so it will lead to targeted instruction. You need to be open to changing your best-laid plans if your writers come up with a different, better idea or if evidence begins to mount that you were not on the right course in the first place.

The purpose of this lesson then is for students to begin thinking about which types of commas to look at more closely and which they will be held accountable for knowing by the end of the study. Start by asking children to search through texts looking for as many different types of commas as they can find. At least a few are likely to find examples of the types you plan to teach. By noting these examples as you circulate and confer during independent work, you can highlight them at the share session and further narrow the study—and at the same time genuinely say the focus comes from what students have noticed.

Be aware that narrowing down and naming the types of commas you want to study will take time. Here it is a two-part process. In this first lesson students find examples and have conversations about different types of commas as they collect sentences to share. Your role is to guide their discoveries so that the selected passages fit the pre-elected categories. In Lesson 6, the class puts these sentences into groups and names what makes the groups different. The definitions they come up with become the categories the class "agrees" to study.

Materials/ Preparation

Teacher:
- Prepared examples of two sorts of comma use, copied onto chart paper or a transparency.
- The book these examples came from.
- Sticky notes.

- *Optional:* Reproduced copies of short texts with various types of comma use. (Students should be able to do this lesson successfully using just their independent reading books, but you may want to have prepared texts for students having difficulty.)

Students:

- Independent reading books.
- Sticky notes.
- File cards on which to copy examples.

The decision about which commas to study should depend on the needs of your particular group of students. However, experience teaches that the following tend to be most useful for elementary school readers and writers:

1. Commas in a list. *We went to the store, the park, the school, the bank, and my friend's house.*

2. Introductory commas—ones that come after an introductory word or phrase. *Still, life goes on.*

3. A comma separating two independent clauses. *I wanted to say more, but I was afraid I'd start crying.*

4. A pair of commas taking the place of parentheses. *Arthur's teacher, Mr. Ratburn, explained the homework.*

5. Commas taking the place of a period before a closing quotation mark. *"Yes," he said.*

These are recommended for most classes and are the basis for the lessons in this unit. Variations based on observations of your students as readers and writers are strongly encouraged!

Summary

In this lesson you will:

- Model looking at two contrasting types of comma use and defining them in your own words.
- Have partners search through their independent reading (or prepared short texts) for passages that illustrate different types of comma use.
- Guide students to find the five types of examples listed above, and copy them onto file cards.
- Share and discuss what these students have found.

When students have gathered in the meeting area, independent reading books in hand, you might begin by saying, "In our last lesson we agreed that commas are the punctuation most often found inside a sentence and that to become better writers we should learn all we can about them. We also noticed that even though commas always signal a breath, or pause, authors seem to use them in lots of different ways. The idea of today's lesson is for you and your partner to find as many of those different ways as possible in your independent reading books and think about exactly what makes them different. When you find a good example, mark it with a sticky note and jot down what you think the commas are doing. After a while you will choose a few to copy onto file cards, to share. Once we have examples of many different ways authors use commas, it will be possible for us as a class to choose which to concentrate on and begin to use in our own writing.

"To see what I mean, listen as I think aloud about a sentence from the book I am reading, *Fig Pudding*, by Ralph Fletcher. I'll say what I think the commas are doing and write that on a sticky note." Holding a copy of the book and referring to the example you have copied onto chart paper, begin thinking aloud.

> He's okay, as babies go, but most of the time I don't pay all that much attention to him.

"This sentence uses two commas, which come before and after those three words *as babies go*. It's like they are taking us away from the main sentence, to whisper something in our ear before going back to the main point. In fact, this sentence would still make sense if you took out that whole part. So I'd say Ralph Fletcher is using these two commas to add extra information in the middle of a sentence. I'll jot that down on a sticky note: *Two commas to add extra information in the middle of a sentence—whisper in the reader's ear.*

"Now let's look together at another example from this book and see whether the commas are doing something the same or different—just as you will do with your partner when you are working independently."

> He spent all afternoon in there surrounded by bowls, mixer, figs, eggs, molasses, lemon, buttermilk, walnuts, cinnamon, nutmeg, brown sugar and confectioner's sugar.

"Turn and talk to a partner about what you might jot down on a sticky note to explain."

As students talk, listen in to gauge their understanding of the task, as well as to choose an explanation to share. After a few seconds, report on what you overheard. "Sophie and Lena noticed there are quite a few commas in this sentence—ten, to be exact—but these commas are doing something very different than in the other example. The sentence is about someone cooking, and the author is listing all the ingredients he is using. Caleb and Harley said they would write, *Separating things in a list*, on their sticky note, which seems like a good idea."

In order to allow students to focus on comma use without distracting them from comprehending or enjoying their independent reading, it is important they look for passages in chapters they have already read rather than moving ahead in the book. "As you and your partner go off to find interesting sentences in your books," you may remind the class, "choose different types and not several examples of the same thing. For example, if you already have commas in a list, look for a different type of comma use. We'll spend the first part of our independent work time looking back on what we've already read on our own and putting sticky notes on examples. After a few minutes, when I give the signal, you and your partner will compare what you have found and agree on examples to copy onto file cards to share. Remember, by finding lots of different ways authors use commas, we will learn how to be smarter readers and writers ourselves."

Independent Work   As students read and look for examples on their own for five or ten minutes, look over their shoulders to get a sense of what they are noticing. Though this is not the time for full-fledged conferences, it is important to stop in for quick check-ins and, where appropriate, gently steer students to the five preselected types of comma uses. You may want to ask:

- Where in the sentence does your author use commas?

- Here's an example where a comma comes near the beginning, after just one word. Why do you suppose the author did that?

- Here's a sentence where the comma comes in the middle, dividing the sentence in two. What's in the first half, and what's in the second? Why do you suppose the author divided the sentence like that, and how does the comma help?

- Does your author use commas in lots of different ways, or just a few? What are they?

Once partners begin to compare notes, your role shifts slightly: you'll listen in on conversations and guide students to choose certain examples; push them to articulate what they think the commas are doing; and when necessary send them back to look for more (or different) sentences. By the end of the partner discussions, students should have selected examples to copy onto file cards for the share session. Possible comments or questions include:

- In this sentence the author puts a comma right near the beginning, after just one word (e.g., *however, finally, sometimes*). Is that something you've seen before? Might it be a useful sort of comma to learn about?

- Here the comma comes right in the middle and divides the sentence in half. The second part gives more information about the first part. That "comma in the middle" might be an interesting one to study.

- This sentence has two commas, and inside them is extra information. Would the sentence still make sense if you took out those words between the commas? That information is extra—you don't really need it. This could be useful to us as writers, if we ever want to add extra, interesting stuff in the middle of a sentence.

- Look at how the author uses a comma right at the end of the character talking, before the ending quotation mark! It seems like a period should go there. Are there other examples of that? Since we use dialogue in our writing, it would probably help us to learn when we need to use a comma instead of a period.

After five or ten minutes, direct students to copy their passages onto file cards. To prepare for the next lesson (i.e., putting sentences into groups), circulate and guide the class so that you end up with several examples each of the five preselected types of comma use. As students are copying, choose several sentences to use during today's share and put them on chart paper or a transparency.

Share Session

Since defining categories is the focus of the next lesson, the purpose of today's share is to begin discussing and comparing ideas about different types of commas without necessarily coming to consensus on class definitions. The objective is to set the stage for putting examples into groups. In order to do this you might choose four students ahead of time—two who have found similar types of comma use, and two with types that clearly do not go together. The discussion could then focus on which sentences seem alike, which seem different, and why.

"We are beginning to come up with interesting ideas about these comma categories," you might conclude. "Tomorrow we will play a sorting game, to help us put our sentences into groups. This will help us decide which ones would be most useful to study to make us better writers and readers."

Sorting Commas

Rationale/Purpose This lesson, conceived by master teacher Barbara Rosenblum, calls on students to sort the comma examples they have found into five groups. It requires some preparation; you must carefully go through the collected passages yourself first and prepare numbered sentence strips for students to sort. (You may need to add extra sentences to be sure each type of comma use is well represented.) Naturally, the groups should be those you have determined ahead of time are important for these particular children to learn.

Materials/ Preparation Teacher:

- Sets of numbered sentence strips with each of the five comma uses well represented (see examples below), one for each pair of children. (A work-saving option is to give students the sheets of examples and have them cut the sentences into strips as the first part of the lesson.)

- A set of these numbered sentence strips copied onto chart paper or a transparency.

Students:

- Reading journals and writing utensils.

Summary There are several steps to this lesson, which culminates in students identifying five categories of comma use to study:

- Explain the sorting activity.

- Demonstrate the activity by thinking aloud.

- Allow partners time to sort and explain their groupings.

- Have a class share session to agree on definitions for the comma uses you will concentrate on during the remainder of the unit.

"In our last lesson," you might begin, "each of you found examples of different ways to use commas in the books you are reading. We compared these commas and came up with our own explanations of how writers use them differently. For us to become better readers and writers, we need to decide which of these we want to start trying out in our own writing.

"Today's lesson is a sorting game, similar to things we have done in math class. You and your partner will each get a set of sentence strips showing examples of comma use the class has collected. Below each sentence you will see a number. Your job today is to separate these sentences into five groups. Each sentence must go into one group, and you and your partner must agree on how to explain the rule for each one. When you have decided, list the sentences in each group, using the number of the sentence, and write the rule above each list."

At this point model the process, taking care to show one instance of sentences not going together, and another where they do fall into the same group. "To show you what I mean," you might continue, "I'll demonstrate how to play the game. Your job is to notice the sorts of things I think about. Here are three sentence strips."

At first, he couldn't believe his ears.
15

We bought spaghetti, milk, cheese, pasta, and cookies for dessert.
26

Still, life goes on.
6

"To begin with, the comma in example 15 comes right at the beginning of the sentence. In fact, there are only two words before it. It seems the author is telling us that when it happened—*at first*—is very important. That's why this information comes first, and it stands out because the comma makes us pause before going on to the rest of the sentence.

"The next sentence, example 26, has three commas. They are separating the things on a shopping list. It's a good thing, too—without the commas it would certainly be confusing! That's a very different way of using commas than in the other example. Obviously these two sentences wouldn't go together in the same group.

"The last one, example 6, reminds me more of number 15. It's not exactly the same—for one thing, the comma comes after only one word, not two. Also, the word *still* does not really say when something happened. But the comma does come right at the beginning, and it does make that word *still* seem very important, since we pause right after reading it. These two examples, numbers 6 and 15, may go together. If I had to guess now, I'd say the rule for this group is that the comma comes right at the beginning, after just one or two words, and the author wants us to know that the first part is very important. Before I decide for sure, I will need to see if there are other sentences that follow this same rule."

Before sending partners off to sort their comma examples into groups, have them turn to a partner and briefly discuss what they noticed you were thinking about in your demonstration. This might include:

- Considering the "why"—the author's reason for using a certain type of comma.

- Seeing how the pause affects your understanding of the sentence (pointing out how the first part is very important, not getting confused about the items in the list).

- Waiting to decide on groups until you see whether more than one example fits the rule.

Before students go off to begin sorting, you might remind them, "Be sure to read through all the examples as you make your groups. And remember the two rules: each sentence must go into one of the five groups, and both partners must agree on the rule for each one."

Independent Work   As students begin to sort the sentence strips into groups, listen in on their conversations before answering questions or offering to help. Are they able to connect what the comma *makes our voices do* to the author's purpose, that is, *how it affects the way we understand* a sentence? You might tell students, "Pretend I'm invisible for the first five minutes," since it is so important to take notes on what they are thinking.

After listening in on student conversations, ask questions that push student thinking and encourage them to be clear and specific in their definitions. These might include:

- These two sentences both have more than one comma. In what other way do they go together, if any? How are they different?

- How does the pause affect the way we understand the sentence?

- Does the comma [Do the commas] make any part of the sentence seem more important?

- Does the comma [Do the commas] make any part of the sentence seem less important?

- Are there any sentences that you thought at first should go together but then decided against putting in the same group? What made you decide?

- Are there any sentences that you thought at first should *not* go together and then decided to put in the same group? What made you decide?

Take notes on particular students' definitions, and ask them ahead of time to be prepared to explain their thinking. It is not cheating to stack the deck in your favor and preselect children to share who have identified groups clearly, in words that reflect how we want the class to think of them.

Share Session

This share session is critical and will certainly take time. Your objective is to identify the five categories of comma uses the class will concentrate on for the remainder of the study and to agree on definitions using student terminology.

To facilitate and contain this process, you may want to ask students to share who have similar or complementary definitions. These may be combined to make a more comprehensive rule, so the class feels the final list is a product of consensus rather than just one or two students' work. "Naomi and Elizabeth define this group as a pair of commas that stick extra information in the middle of a sentence," you might say. "Kiri and Cara call that same group oh-by-the-way commas, to show how the information in the middle is helpful but not necessary for understanding the sentence. Evan and Nora went even further, saying you could take out the words between those two commas and the sentence would still make sense—though it wouldn't be as interesting. We may want to put all these ideas together, and agree that our class definition will be: *a pair of oh-by-the-way commas that stick in helpful information to make it more interesting.*"

Once the class has agreed on definitions for each of the five comma groups, sum up by reminding students of their larger goal: to become experts in using commas to be better readers and writers. "From now on," we might conclude, "we will want to notice when authors use commas like these as we read. Since they are the ones we mostly found in our books, it makes sense they will be the most useful for us to become experts in. Moving forward, we will also want to practice using them in our own writing."

Possible Follow-Up Activities

Following this lesson, it is critical to publicly display the definitions of comma use the class has agreed on. Students need to be able to revisit and refer to these definitions frequently, in order to internalize them and continue to notice examples that fit into the five groups.

- You could assign small groups of students—one group for each type of comma use—to create posters displaying the definitions, along with examples illustrating each one.

- You might compile all the class comma definitions on a "punctuation theory sheet," to put into students' notebooks for quick and easy reference.

- As homework, students could find additional examples of the five types of comma uses in their independent reading and record them in their reading journal (or simple mark them with sticky notes to share the following day). As a variation, assign different groups of students to find examples of one particular type of comma use.

Encourage students to bring up exceptions to the rules and tweak the definitions; punctuation in the real world evolves, changes, and adapts as authors try new things, and your approach in the classroom should reflect this reality.

Sample Sentence Strip Sheet

(adapted from Barbara Rosenblum's third-grade class)

A dog is a big responsibility because you have to walk, feed, bathe and play with it.

24

"You poor baby," he said.

22

I wanted to say more, but I was afraid I'd start crying.

8

At first, he couldn't believe his ears.

15

We bought spaghetti, milk, cheese, pasta and cookies for dessert.

26

Still, life goes on.

6

After that, the guest room must be made ready.

3

Arthur's teacher, Mr. Ratburn, explained the homework.

16

I'll tell you but you've got to listen to the whole story, not just a part of it.

2

We read the story together, out loud, and when we finished we started a second one.

10

On Earth, water boils at 212 degrees.

18

I found it in the desert, close to the truck stop.

17

"I think we're ready to go now," her mom said.

1

On his birthday, which was right after school began, his mom and dad gave him a box of 64 Crayola crayons.

19

I felt very proud, but also scared.

5

"It's the most beautiful place in the world," she said.

25

My grandmother's house is big, but it's crowded.

11

© 2008 by Dan Feigelson, from *Practical Punctuation: Lessons on Rule Making and Rule Breaking in Elementary Writing*. Portsmouth, NH: Heinemann.

The house has a high fence around it, and a wooden gate with a lock on it that my grandmother locks every night.

14

Although the people in town talk about her in whispers, they all went to see her if they had troubles.

20

When World War II broke out, the Patersons left China and returned to the United States.

23

Sam, my brother, goes to basketball practice at the Y.

4

In a town in Calabria, a long time ago, there lived an old lady everybody called Strega Nona.

7

We went to the store, the park, the school, and my friend's house before we went home.

13

However, I still disagree.

12

"I'll be right up," said Martha.

3

Every day, when Felicity came home from Miss Manderly's, Nan was waiting for her.

21

It was flaming red, shiny, and perfectly round like a marble.

27

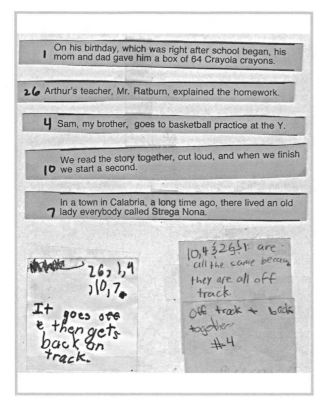

I | On his birthday, which was right after school began, his mom and dad gave him a box of 64 Crayola crayons.

26 | Arthur's teacher, Mr. Ratburn, explained the homework.

4 | Sam, my brother, goes to basketball practice at the Y.

10 | We read the story together, out loud, and when we finish we start a second.

7 | In a town in Calabria, a long time ago, there lived an old lady everybody called Strega Nona.

26, 1, 4
10, 7

It goes one & then gets back on track.

10, 4, 3, 2, 6, 1 are all the same because they are all off track.

Off track + back together #4

11 | My grandmother's house is big, but it's pretty crowded.

5 | I felt very proud, but also scared.

2 | I'll tell you but you've got to listen to the whole story, not just a part of it.

8 | I wanted to say more, but I was afraid I'd start crying.

sentence # 11, 5, 2, 2 and 8 we think are in the same group because they both are the opposite after the comma. example: I was proud, but also scared.

Lesson 6: Sorting Commas (third grade)

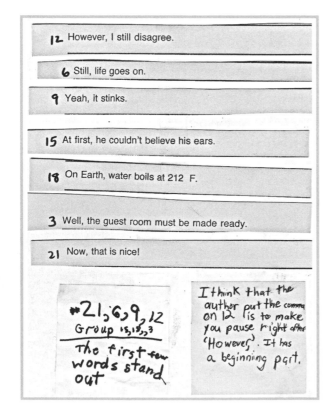

12 | However, I still disagree.

6 | Still, life goes on.

9 | Yeah, it stinks.

15 | At first, he couldn't believe his ears.

18 | On Earth, water boils at 212 F.

3 | Well, the guest room must be made ready.

21 | Now, that is nice!

#21, 6, 9, 12
Group 15, 18, 3

The first few words stand out

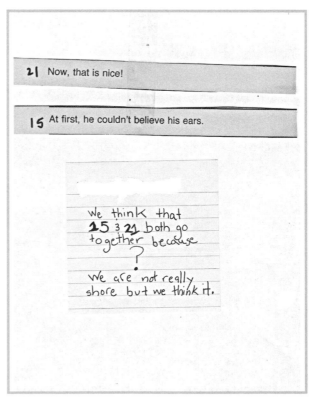

21 | Now, that is nice!

15 | At first, he couldn't believe his ears.

We think that 15 3 21 both go together because ?

We are not really shore but we think it.

> (See Saw Sentences)
> • My grandmother's house is big, but it's pretty crowded.
> • I wanted to say more, but i was afraid I'd cry.
> • I felt very proud, but also scared.
>
> These sentences have 2 parts. The first part of the sentence tells you something. The second part says the opposite of what you would expect. It's like a see saw. The comma separates the 2 parts. The word but comes after the comma. When we say the word "but" we stretch out our voices.

Third-Grade Comma Theories, Using Student-Invented Terminology—See Saw Sentences

> (DETOUR SENTENCES)
> • Sam, my brother, goes to basketball practice.
> • Arthur's teacher, Mr. Ratburn, explained the homework.
> • We read the story, out loud, and started to cry.
>
> The sentences have 3 parts: a beginning, a middle and an end. After the first part, there is a comma. Then the writer gives you information about the first part (a detail). Then there's another comma. Finally, the sentence comes back together.
> * You could read these sentences without the extra information and they would still make sense.
>
> In a town in Calabria, a long time ago, there lived a woman.
>   beginning   detail   comes together
>   (detour)

Detour Sentences

Claire's "Punctuation Knowledge Story," Third-Grade Notebook Experiment

Zipporah's "My Problems," Third-Grade Comma Writing

> Puncuation Knowlage Story
>
> Last year in second grade we were in the middle of a minilesson, and the window was open. All of a sudden.....A fly the size of a peanut she'll! Everyone was screaming at the top of their lungs because they thought it was a bee, but it wasn't. Everyone was acting like-like.... MONKEYS!!!! We had a teacher named Ms. Rios. She didn't know why we were screaming. When she bent down to get something the fly flew right over her head! Everyone stopped screaming and started laughing!

> My Problems
> by Zipporah Gatling
>
> My famliy is good, my friends are good, my church is good, even my neighbors are good. But my famliy has a problem. Yes, my famliy. My dreams, my famliy, my home, my life. But I know this to-it will be all over the anger, the problems, my life. Yes, my life. My dreams, my famliy, my friends. That's why, I can't waste any precious time of my life.

Messing Around with Commas

Rationale/Purpose   Once students have spent time thinking about comma choices made by other authors, the next step is for them to make these choices themselves. In this lesson they have the opportunity to experiment with the five comma uses they have identified, without worrying about coming up with new topics. By reworking passages from their writer's notebook in a before-and-after format, they get to enjoy messing around with commas. This reinforces the notion that punctuation can be a tool writers play with to express meaning in powerful ways.

**Materials/
Preparation**

Teacher:

- An entry from your writer's notebook copied onto chart paper or transparency.

- Blank chart paper or transparency to model experimenting with commas.

- Charts displaying the five types of commas the class is studying.

Students:

- Writer's notebooks and writing utensils.

- Examples of the five comma uses to look at as models for their own writing.

Summary   The objective is to give students a chance to use commas in the different ways they have noticed over the last several sessions. Keep in mind that some attempts may seem forced, incorrect, even humorous—intentionally or not. This is nothing to worry about, and an experimental atmosphere should be encouraged. You want students to see playing with punctuation as something enjoyable and as a means to an end; by doing so they will become more expressive writers.

The steps of this writing lesson are:

- Demonstrate reworking passages from your own writing as you experiment with commas.

- Have students try this in the meeting area with another passage from your writing.

- Send students off to experiment independently with the five comma uses, rewriting sections of their own writer's notebook entries.

"Now that our class has thought so much about how authors use commas," you might begin, "it's time to mess around with them in our writer's notebooks. We'll look for parts of entries that would be fun to revise and try out the different sorts of commas we have discovered. We will certainly have to change the words as well, or the commas will never work. As I do this with a section from my own writer's notebook, notice the sorts of things I think about." In order to model effectively, your notebook entry should be visible to students as you rewrite. While thinking aloud, be sure to demonstrate going back and forth between the old and new versions of the entry, to call attention to new ways you are using commas. "OK, here's my original."

> Frizzy-haired Kiri is riding her bike up the street as I turn down our block. "Hi Dan!" she shouts as she whizzes past. It is six o'clock and any minute now her mom will be calling her in for dinner. The flowered shirt she is wearing rustles in the wind and makes a rainbow in the corner of my eye. Her voice sounds a little like singing.

"The first sentence," you might begin, "is a little confusing. I'm not sure my reader will know who Kiri is! That is information I can add using a pair of commas, as we noticed authors doing in our research. Since I am adding some new words, I may have to take some out as well."

> Frizzy-haired Kiri, the nine-year-old girl next door, rides her bike up the street as I arrive home from work.

It is a good idea to try to integrate some of the class terminology for different types of commas as you are thinking aloud. "That works better. I've used those oh-by-the-way commas we named in class. The next part shows Kiri calling out to me. This may be a good place to practice the comma-in-place-of-a-period—but I'll have to rewrite some words to make it work. I want to keep the exclamation mark after she calls out my name, since it shows her excitement, so I'll add another sentence after it, one that would end in a period. This way I'll be able to use the comma in place of the period right before I write *she shouts*."

> Frizzy-haired Kiri, the nine-year-old girl next door, rides her bike up the street as I arrive home from work. "Hi Dan! You're home early," she shouts.

"It seems to me the *whizzes past* part might work better if I use the dividing comma we talked about—the one that separates two halves of the sentence. I can separate *she shouts* from *whizzes past* with a comma, which will make the writing move faster—just like Kiri on the bike. But I'll need to change some words again to have it work out."

> Frizzy-haired Kiri, the nine-year-old girl next door, rides her bike up the street as I arrive home from work. "Hi Dan! You're home early," she shouts, whizzing past.

"Now that I've put in the comma, I can add some interesting description—*like a tornado*."

> Frizzy-haired Kiri, the nine-year-old girl next door, rides her bike up the street as I arrive home from work. "Hi Dan! You're home early," she shouts, whizzing past like a tornado.

Once you have modeled how to think through this process, it is a good idea to let students practice it together, using one piece of writing as a common text. "Before you experiment with commas in your own writing," you might say, "let's try one together. Open your notebook and write a new line for my entry, using one of the types of commas we are studying. You may look at the comma charts to remind yourself of the choices. Remember that you might need to change words from the old version and even make up things that weren't there before."

As students do this quick-write, look over their shoulders and note which comma types they are trying. After two or three minutes, call for their attention and briefly share some of the ideas you've noticed.

"Marco tried using commas in a list," you might say, "by writing a sentence about what Kiri was wearing: *She is wearing a flowered shirt, purple tights, light green slippers and a yellow scarf in her hair*. Jackie tried out the comma-after-a-short-intro: *Any minute now, her mother will be shouting out of the window for her to come to dinner*. So you see there are all sorts of ways you can have fun, just messing around with different sorts of commas.

"When you go off to your independent work today," you might conclude, "your first job is to find an entry in your writer's notebook you'd like to mess around with. Then pick a part to rewrite, experimenting with some of the commas we've studied. Feel free to change words, add ideas, even if it makes the entry completely different. The idea is to go a little wild with commas, so we can learn to use them in different ways."

Independent Work Students are going to need support making choices in one or more of the steps in this activity. Deciding on a notebook entry to work with may be a challenge for some, while choosing which types of commas to try could prove daunting to others. Many children will have a hard time letting go of the earlier version of their writing, and they'll resist adding new ideas or changing words. Be on the lookout for such issues as you confer, and make suggestions that will help students move past the problem. Some possible questions and comments include:

- Do you have an entry where you liked the idea but think you could write it better now?

- One way to try out commas in a list is to look at a part of your writing where you have introduced a character or place, then think of three adjectives to describe it. For instance, a restaurant could be *dark, dirty and loud,* or a person might seem *tall, quiet and skinny.* Try putting these words in as you introduce the character or place.

- What extra information could go in the middle of this sentence to make it more interesting? Could you use a pair of commas to add it in?

The eventual goal of this and every lesson in a punctuation unit is for writers to reflect on how adding or changing punctuation affects the way a reader understands the piece. Individual conferences are an ideal place to begin pushing students to reflect on ways they can use commas to make their pieces richer. You could ask those having some success in their experiments questions such as:

- How does separating the first and second half of the sentence with a comma change the way we read it? Does it make either part seem more or less important?

- How would putting in a comma after the first word or two (like *however, naturally, anyway, in any case*) make the sentence more interesting?

- How does adding this comma change the way a reader reads the piece?

- Commas divide sentences into parts. How do they help us keep track of the different ideas in the sentence?

To prepare for the share, choose a few students in advance, each of whom has tried a different kind of comma in his or her rewriting. Since it will be a before-and-after share (students will show how their writing looked before they rewrote it and again after they incorporated their comma experiments), they will need time to copy both passages on to a transparency or chart paper for classmates to see.

Share Session

In addition to having students show how they have rewritten their passages, you'll also want them to tell the thinking that went into their decisions. (For example, "I decided that adding a sentence where a comma comes right at the beginning—*Naturally, we thought it would be safe to go to pet such a friendly looking dog*—made it seem more conversational, like I was talking to the reader.") You may need to coach them beforehand in how to explain their thinking clearly.

Once each student shares the before-and-after versions of their writing as well as the thinking behind the comma use, the rest of the class may comment from a reader's perspective on the effect of the comma. For this follow-up to be successful, you may need to ask specific, leading questions about:

- The way the comma calls attention to different parts of the sentence. For example: "Ruby added information in the middle of a sentence with a pair of commas. Since we pause before and after the commas, how do they make us think of the beginning, middle, and ending parts? Is one more important than another?"

- The way the comma affects the sound of the sentence. For example: "By dividing that sentence in half with a comma, Carl makes us slow down as we read the first part. When we come back to the second part, we read it quickly. It seems as if the comma first slows things down, then speeds them up."

"Now that we've begun experimenting with different sorts of commas," you might conclude, "the goal is to make our writing more interesting by using them. From now on, whenever we want to add information in the middle of a sentence, divide a sentence in two parts, say something short before the main part of a sentence, or list things, we know that a comma can help us do it. I'll be looking to see which writers in our class try adding these sorts of comma sentences to their notebook entries and published pieces from now on."

Commas from Scratch

Rationale/Purpose The objective moving forward is for students to use commas thoughtfully and inventively in their everyday writing. In order for a writer to make appropriate choices about comma use, there must be opportunities to experiment. These opportunities must feel safe, without the pressure of worrying about a finished piece. You also want to give students a variety of *ways* to experiment.

In the last lesson, students rewrote excerpts from old notebook entries in order to try out new comma possibilities. The next step is to invent comma sentences from scratch using the specific comma uses the class has chosen to study. Some may want to write full entries, others separate sentences or paragraphs; some may work on serious stories, while others try to make their classmates laugh with silly sentences. It is important to accept all efforts and establish an atmosphere of experimentation. For certain writers this may be intimidating, for others liberating; the objective here is to try both rewriting and inventing, perhaps reflecting along the way on how the two feel different. In either case the tricky question is how to hold students accountable for learning specific comma uses, while at the same time making them feel comfortable enough to go out on a limb and try new things.

Materials/ Preparation Teacher:
- Mentor sentences from familiar texts, authors, or previous lessons to illustrate each of the five comma uses—commas in a list, commas after introductory words or phrases, commas dividing sentences in half, pairs of commas setting off added information, and commas at the end of quotations—displayed so they can be referred to easily during the lesson,
- Blank chart paper, a SMART Board, or a transparency to use in model writing.
- Markers.

Students:
- Writer's notebooks and writing utensils.

Summary Begin as always by discussing the *why* of the lesson, that it is important for writers to experiment with commas in different ways—that is, by rewriting and also making up sentences from scratch. To demonstrate, model and think aloud through the process of trying two contrasting types of comma use. Modeling more than one possibility sends the message that students are encouraged to try their own variations and experimenting is encouraged.

"Rewriting parts of our notebook entries helped us see some of the choices commas give us as we change and revise our writing," you might begin. "But it's also important to see how commas can help us when we think of sentences and stories for the first time, in notebook entries and first drafts. By experimenting both ways, we can think of commas as tools to help us express ourselves better whenever we write. To demonstrate this idea, I'm going to do some new writing. Notice how I think about using commas as I think of ideas for what to write about."

Turning to the chart paper or a transparency, think aloud about what to write and how commas can help get meaning across. Show how you rule out one idea in favor of another. "The routine of waking up in the morning and getting to school at my house is a little crazy," you might begin. "It always feels rushed, I usually feel like I'm forgetting something, and it's difficult deciding what to do first. I think I'll write about that."

> Getting to school in the morning is not as easy as you might think at my house.

"The next part is where commas might help. I want to go through the different things I have to do in the morning, showing step by step how much there is to do. One way would be to use commas in a list, listing everything in order. The problem is, if I list them too quickly, then I can't tell any of the details of the morning, which is what makes it interesting. A better idea would be to try commas after an opening word or phrase; that way I can tell the order of one thing at a time with a phrase like *first of all*, and then tell a little about what it is I'm doing each step of the way."

> Getting to school in the morning is not as easy as you might think at my house. First of all, there's remembering which books and things I need to put in my backpack.

"*Now* commas in a list might work, since I can tell some of the different things I pack each day and get across how much there is to remember."

> Getting to school in the morning is not as easy as you might think at my house. First of all, there's remembering which books and things I need to put in my backpack. I usually throw in notebooks, pencils, a hairbrush, my cell-phone, and a snack.

Along the way, you might also refer to some of the mentor sentences for ideas. These should be displayed so students can see them easily. Don't imitate these examples precisely but rather encourage using them as a jumping-off point for playing with punctuation.

"This is one thing I might want to write about using some of the comma types we have studied," you might continue, "but since my purpose is to experiment, I am also going to try something totally different. I've always been interested in the way people talk to their pets. I'll admit it, when no one is listening I sometimes get pretty silly myself saying things to my cat, Fabala. This could be fun to write about. First, I'll get down an opening line, maybe starting with a question to the reader."

> Have you ever noticed the different ways people talk to their animals?

"Next, I want to use some type of comma sentence. Looking over some of the examples we've collected from books to get an idea, I noticed this one from *Anastasia Krupnik*, by Lois Lowry."

> Her parents said, very kindly, that perhaps she should choose a profession that didn't involve her feet.
>
> —Lois Lowry, *Anastasia Krupnik*

"It seems to me a sentence like that, where the author puts in extra information between two commas about *how* people say things, could work well to write about the way people talk to animals. I'm going to try writing a sentence like this one to describe the way I talk to my cat."

> Have you ever noticed the different ways people talk to their animals? I sometimes ask my cat, just like I'm talking to a baby, if she would like another treat before bedtime.

"Next, I can put in some exact words I'd say to Fabala," you might continue to think aloud, "practicing the rule about using commas in place of a period with quotation marks. This could be a place to have some fun."

> Have you ever noticed the different ways people talk to their animals? I sometimes ask my cat, just like I'm talking to a baby, if she would like another treat before bedtime. "Have a little treaty-weetie, Fabala honey," I coo as she runs and hides under the sofa.

"What are some things you want to try writing about as you experiment today? Like me, you may want to try out a couple of different things, or perhaps just stick with one. You might want to be serious, or you may want to try making people laugh. As long as you try out some of the comma types we have been studying, you can do whatever you want. Turn and tell your partner what you plan to write about and how certain comma types might help you with your idea."

As students discuss possibilities, eavesdrop on their thinking to gauge their understanding. After one or two minutes, briefly share with the class some of what you've overheard before sending them off to work on their comma experiments independently.

Independent Work   Once students are back at their desks working on new notebook entries and comma possibilities, circulate and note the range of things they are trying. In your conferences you can:

- Ask students to articulate their thinking about how a particular type of comma use will help get across a particular meaning or idea.

- Have students explain reasons for using one type of comma over another.

- Suggest new possibilities to try, after listening carefully to what the writer is trying to express.

While making your way around the room, look not just for students who are writing interesting passages, but also for those who can share their reasons for using a certain type of comma to get their meaning across. Looking ahead to the share, ask these writers in advance to share their thinking with the class, and perhaps practice how they will explain it. Be sure their passages are copied onto the board, a transparency, or chart paper so classmates are able to see the examples being discussed.

Share Session   Though it is always good for students to hear, see, and ask questions about one another's writing, it's especially important in this lesson. By listening to other writers articulate their thinking about comma choices, students may consider some of the ideas they have heard but not otherwise thought to try in their own work.

Speaking about their thinking is not always easy for young writers however, and it falls to you to help students learn to do so. Most likely you've had a chance to listen in advance to what they plan to say and make any necessary suggestions to help them express their thinking. You don't want to interrupt them or undermine their feeling of ownership. You *do* want to facilitate these conversations so that the whole class benefits, to make sure students' explanations are clear. It is also your job to connect what one writer is sharing to what other students might try. Therefore, you might carefully paraphrase students' explanations after they have finished and suggest how their classmates may use the idea in their own writing. "Sophie did a great job of using divide-the-sentence-in-half commas here: *My play dates with Clara almost always begin with some sort of argument, but by the end we usually make up and see things the same way.* It seems that she is doing it for a very particular reason—to tell how something begins, and then ends. To use a comma to show that time has passed is a very smart idea we haven't thought of before. When you are writing about something that changes from the beginning to the end, you may want to try using a comma the way Sophie did."

To end the share, you might ask for a show of hands of those who are planning to try one of the comma strategies a classmate has explained.

Possible Follow-Up Activities

Since this series of lessons focuses on learning comma conventions and experimenting rather than going through a complete publishing cycle, it makes sense to provide several opportunities for messing around before sharing the most interesting of these experiments during the culminating celebration. You might suggest the following activities for students to try at home, in class, during transitions, and when working in classroom centers:

- Rewriting passages from their independent reading books to try out different comma uses.

- Trading notebook entries (or passages from entries) with another student and rewriting each other's work with new comma choices.

- Imitating particular sentences from favorite texts that contain interesting comma uses.

Students should begin thinking about which of their experiments they will share and explain during the celebration. You will also want to think ahead about how students will reflect on and articulate what they have learned about commas, and explain how this knowledge will help their writing.

Preparing to Celebrate Experiments

Rationale/Purpose   At the end of most writing units, there is a publishing party to recognize the hard work students have done to produce a finished piece. To send the message that process is also important, it makes sense to find opportunities to celebrate their experiments, not just finished work. This study is one of exploration and discovery, and its culminating celebration should be about just that—students should share their comma experiments, think about their thinking, publicly articulate what they have learned, and set goals for their next steps as writers.

      The two parts of this lesson, each followed by a brief period of independent work, help students prepare for such a celebration. First, you'll think aloud about what writing to choose for the share, then model filling in a reflection sheet about what you have learned. (The example here is adapted from second-grade teacher Deborah Hartman, whose seven- and eight-year-old writers have displayed impressive metacognition in their writing celebrations.)

Materials/ Preparation   A celebration of process must fit into a long-range plan that makes sense. To teach these lessons well, you need to think strategically about what to teach next. While it is important to celebrate student reflections and appreciate comma experiments for their own sake, you want to be sure students apply what they have learned. This means setting up the expectation that they use commas thoughtfully in their next finished piece and plan your next unit accordingly. A nonnarrative genre study, for example, provides lots of opportunities for lists, two-clause sentences, and commas after an introductory word or phrase; a realistic fiction unit could work too, since it involves incorporating dialogue and using pairs of commas to insert extra detail. Whatever you choose to cover next, be thoughtful in your planning. Also, set the stage for the following unit at the end of this one by indicating how their new knowledge of commas will help students with their next piece of writing.

Teacher:

- A selection of your own comma experiments on chart paper or a transparency. The examples may be new or ones used in previous lessons.
- A class set of reflection sheets for students to fill out in preparation for the celebration (see the example at the end of this lesson).
- A filled-out reflection sheet on a transparency or chart paper.

Students:

- Writer's notebooks and pens/pencils, which they should bring to the meeting area.
- Sticky notes to use to mark comma experiments they want to share.

Summary

Since the culminating celebration will be about process rather than product, it is important to model how to prepare. Students need to know what is expected of them in choosing comma experiments to share and in recording their reflections. First demonstrate how to get ready for the celebration by modeling your decision-making process as you select comma experiments to share. Once students have had some time to do this themselves, call them back to the meeting area to watch as you think aloud and fill out the reflection sheet, then send them off to do this on their own.

Sample Language/ Sequence (Part 1)

Once students have gathered at the meeting area with their writer's notebooks, explain what they will need to do to prepare for the celebration. "Now that we are coming to the end of our comma study," you might announce, "it's time to choose writing we've done throughout the unit to share. This celebration will be different from the usual ones, since we are not showing off finished pieces. Instead we'll share a few of our most successful comma passages. You may want to choose some before-and-after examples from when you rewrote notebook entries, or parts of the new writing from last lesson. If you imitated comma sentences from other authors, you might choose one of those and show the original sentence next to the one you created. All of these or a combination of several would be great. The experiments you choose should be those that are the most interesting ones to read, of course, but also those that taught you the most as a writer. Watch as I decide which of my own comma experiments to share."

Direct students' attention to the charts or transparencies displaying samples of your own writing. The charts can be hung across the wall next to one another; transparencies will need to be examined one at a time.

"Looking over all the comma writing I have done," you might begin, "the first thing I notice is this entry about waking up in the morning."

> Getting to school in the morning is not as easy as you might think at my house. First of all, there's remembering which books and things I need to put in my backpack. I usually throw in notebooks, pencils, a hairbrush, my cell-phone, and a snack.

"Although showing a typical morning was a good idea, I'm not sure it is the most interesting passage to share at the celebration. For one thing, I used commas in a list pretty well before, so it doesn't really show what I have learned. For another, though the idea was good, I don't think the writing is that much fun to read—not enough action. I am going to rule this one out and not read it at the celebration.

"This other example, from when I rewrote my notebook entry, is a different story."

> Frizzy-haired Kiri, the nine-year-old girl next door, rides her bike up the street as I arrive home from work. "Hi Dan! You're home early," she shouts, whizzing past like a tornado.

"Writing this one, I really began to understand how to add information in the middle of the sentence, using oh-by-the-way commas. I'm talking about when I added *the nine-year-old girl next door* after *frizzy-haired Kiri*, using a pair of commas. I also love the way this passage paints a picture of Kiri *whizzing past like a tornado*, with the comma calling attention to that description. Plus, it will be interesting to show the difference between how I wrote it the first time and then after I changed it. I am going to rewrite the before-and-after versions on a separate paper to share at the celebration.

"Now that you've watched me making some decisions," you could continue, "take a few minutes right here and now to do the same. Look through what you have written and choose one passage you'd *like* to share and another you *don't* want to share. Then turn and tell a partner why you made those choices."

As students make their choices, circulate and watch what they are doing. Are some flipping through pages randomly? Are others carefully going back and forth between certain passages, weighing their options? Coach students to learn from one another. When students begin explaining their choices to partners, your role switches to that of listener; note how easy or hard it is for them to explain their thinking and decide which overheard conversations to share when you call them back to attention.

"Sam has decided to share a sentence with list commas that he modeled after Roald Dahl," you might sum up. "Even though he already knew about using commas in a list, he had never thought about using them to describe the way something feels, as Roald did. It was also the first time he had ever learned about punctuation from imitating an author, which he may try again. Ellen is going to share her crazy sentence about her younger brother that made us all laugh, to show that commas can be used for comedy. During your independent work, continue making choices about what to share at our celebration. When you find passages you like, mark them with a sticky note, and when you've settled on at least three, begin copying them onto separate paper so you'll be able to display them. In a little while I will call you back to talk about how to explain ways commas have made you a better writer."

Independent Work (Part 1)

As students make their choices, encourage them to read passages aloud to classmates in soft voices, testing the pauses made by their commas and making sure the sentences work the way they want them to. Also start them thinking about how their comma experiments have made them better writers by asking quick questions rather than holding full-length conferences:

- Which experiment made you think the hardest?
- What is one passage you liked so much, you'd like to write one just like it in your next piece?
- In your opinion, which comma use will be the most helpful for your future writing? Why?

Once students have made at least one or two choices, call them back to the meeting area to discuss the reflection sheet, which will also be shared at the celebration.

Sample Language/ Sequence (Part 2)

It is important to model what students must do in order to fill out the reflection sheet before asking them to do this on their own. "One of the reasons we are celebrating our experiments rather than full, finished pieces," you can explain, "is to reflect on how learning about commas has helped us as writers. In choosing which experiments to share, we have begun to think about what we have learned. I have called you back to catch you in the middle of this thinking and ask each of you to take a few moments to fill out a reflection sheet. On this sheet you'll tell which experiments worked well and what you'd still like to learn about using commas. As you look at the sorts of things I've included on my sheet, think about what you might say on yours."

Reflection: Comma Study

Congratulations, punctuation experts! Now that you've explored, defined, and messed around with different types of commas, the time has come to share what you have learned. This means deciding which of your experiments to share with the class (AND WHY!) and jotting down your thoughts about how commas will help you be a better writer.

1. Think of some of the ways you used commas during this study. Which worked best, and why? List them here.

Learning to use a pair of commas to add information in the middle was especially helpful, since it saves you from having to write a whole extra sentence just to add one fact. An example was the passage about Kiri, where I wrote, "Frizzy-haired Kiri, the nine-year-old girl next door, rides her bike up the street." Another experiment that worked well was, "Hi Dan! You're home early," she shouts, whizzing past like a tornado." I like the way I described the action by putting a comma after the word shouts.

2. What are your goals for using commas in your future writing? How has this study changed you as a writer?

I am still a little confused about when to separate a sentence in the middle with a comma. It's hard sometimes to know when it makes sense to put in a pause. This study has definitely made me think more about where I want the reader to take a breath and how putting in commas can make one part of a sentence really stand out and seem important.

To prepare for our celebration, practice reading your comma experiments aloud, making sure your voice does what the commas tell you to do. Aside from reading to a classmate, be sure to practice at home by reading to an adult or older sibling. Write the name of this person on the line below.

I read my comma experiments aloud to: _____

In reading through your sample, point out things you expect all students to include. For example:

- An explanation of what you tried and why it worked well, followed by the quote itself.

- At least one thing you would like to get better at.

- At least one way you will use what you have learned in future writing.

Independent Work (Part 2)

Stopping to go over the reflection sheet while students are in the process of choosing experiments to share is intentional. You want to encourage them to think carefully about which to celebrate rather than picking the first one they come across. However, students don't need to stop everything and begin working on their reflection immediately. Some may prefer to wait until they have finished making their choices; others may use filling in the sheet as a way to help decide what to share. As you circulate, let the class know that whatever way they wish to proceed is OK, as long as the sheet is completed in time for the celebration.

Reflection: Comma Study

(adapted from the classroom of second-grade teacher Deborah Hartman)

Congratulations, punctuation experts! Now that you've explored, defined, and messed around with different types of commas, the time has come to share what you have learned. This means deciding which of your experiments to share with the class (AND WHY!) and jotting down your thoughts about how commas will help you be a better writer.

1. Think of some of the ways you used commas during this study. Which worked out best, and why? List them here.

   _____

   _____

   _____

   _____

   _____

2. What are your goals for using commas in your future writing? How has this study changed you as a writer?

   _____

   _____

   _____

   _____

   _____

To prepare for our celebration, practice reading your comma experiments aloud, making sure your voice does what the commas tell you to do. Aside from reading to a classmate, be sure to practice at home by reading to an adult or older sibling. Write the name of this person on the line below.

I read my comma experiments aloud to: _____

A Comma Celebration

Rationale/Purpose

This celebration is an opportunity for students to share their process and reflections, as well as examples of their comma experiments. Since the focus is on what they have learned as writers rather than a published piece, place special emphasis on how they will use commas in future writing. In order to solidify their understanding, convey the expectation that in their next piece of writing they will continue to experiment with commas, this time in the context of a published piece.

Materials/ Preparation

Teacher:

- Refreshments!

- A chart explaining the five types of commas the class has studied, to use during the introduction.

Students:

- At least three passages of writing per student, reflecting the types of commas they have studied.

- Filled-in reflection sheets.

You will of course want to invite parents and/or students from other classes to attend and create a party atmosphere (refreshments, music, etc.). Think about how the work will be displayed. Should it be laid out on desks for guests to circulate and read? Should groups of students read their work aloud to guests who move from station to station? Do you want each student to read aloud one at a time? There are pros and cons to each arrangement. Allowing the students a voice in how the celebration is run will of course increase their engagement and sense of ownership.

Sample Language/ Sequence

Since you are celebrating explorations and experiments, it is important to begin with a brief introduction to give guests a sense of the study. You may present this explanation yourself or have it prepared and read by students.

"Welcome parents and friends," you might begin, "and thank you for coming to our celebration. In this study we began by looking at all sorts of punctuation that does not come at the end of the sentence; we decided that commas would be the most useful ones to learn about. Since there are so many different ways to use commas, we narrowed our study to those that seemed most useful for us as writers." Refer to the chart explaining the comma uses you have studied. Asking different students to read aloud and explain each comma use is one way to get many children involved. "After looking closely at the way authors use these commas, we experimented with them ourselves. What you will be seeing today are some of our attempts."

The next order of business is to celebrate what students have learned. An arrangement that worked well in second-grade teacher Debbie Hartman's class was to have the class seated in a circle in the meeting area. Following the introduction, each shared how learning about commas helped him or her become a better writer. (Students can read from their reflection sheets or speak without notes; whatever approach is taken, they will need time to practice presenting their thoughts.)

Another approach is for class members and guests to circulate and look over everyone's work. Two structures that work well are:

- A *museum share*, in which each student's work and reflection sheets are laid on tables, and guests move around the room reading and writing brief comments.

- A *station reading*, in which writers stand alone or in groups reading their most successful comma experiments, taking care that their "voice does what the commas tell it to do." If you use this approach, assign students to an "a" or a "b" group, and switch the groups from listeners to presenters midway through the celebration.

Comma Comma Comma Comma Comma Chameleon: One Mark, Many Uses

The commas are the most useful and usable of all the stops. It is highly important to put them in place as you go along. If you try to come back after doing a paragraph and stick them in the various spots that tempt you you will discover that they tend to swarm like minnows in all sorts of crevices whose existence you hadn't realized and before you know it the whole long sentence becomes immobilized and lashed up squirming in commas. Better to use them sparingly, and with affection, precisely when the need for each one arises, nicely, by itself.

—Lewis Thomas, "Notes on Punctuation"

Next to the period, the most ubiquitous punctuation mark is the comma. Even authors who disdain the use of other internal punctuation grudgingly turn to commas now and then to create pauses, separate ideas, and make sentences less confusing. Clearly students need to know about them, and yet they remain one of the most complicated things to teach a young writer to use well.

There are several reasons for this. For one, like most punctuation "inside the sentence," the decision to use a comma or not is often a judgment call on the part of the writer. In many instances, while it may be a good idea, a comma is not mandatory. For another thing, its effect on a reader's understanding is not always obvious. Lynne Truss, in her bestseller *Eats Shoots and Leaves* (2003), has cited passages where meaning is completely altered when a comma is added or removed, but we are seldom conscious of its importance as we read along in a text.

In order to teach students to use commas effectively, we must:

- Be familiar with the wide variety of ways commas can be used, and provide examples for students to see and discuss.

- Demonstrate how to make choices about comma use, and think aloud about the reasons for these decisions (placing emphasis, inserting information, making something less confusing, etc.).

This highly selective (and subjective) reference guide highlights some of the most common uses of this most common of punctuation marks—those that seem most useful for student writers. It would not be a good idea to teach more than a few at a time, and which we choose to study may vary from class to class. Nonetheless, we should be prepared to answer the questions of young writers as they explore and make theories about any and all commas.

The seven broad categories that follow are loosely adapted from Lederer and Dowis' *Sleeping Dogs Don't Lay (And That's No Lie)* (1999). Within these categories are twenty-six specific uses.

1. Divide It in Two

Use a comma to separate independent clauses in a compound sentence.

Students have described these as divider commas, cut-'em-in-half commas, and other colorful phrases that get at the idea of *a sentence with two parts, similar in length*. As one third grader aptly put it, "The second part tells you more about the first part." Typically the two parts of the sentence are connected by a single word (a conjunction, to be precise) such as *and, but, nor, or, neither, yet, for,* or *so*.

- A comma should be used to separate independent clauses connected by a conjunction (e.g., *and, but, nor, or, neither, yet, for, so*).

  She did not return their phone calls, and it became clear that the party should be cancelled.

  The presidential election was two weeks away, but the candidate decided he would make time for a weekend retreat.

2. A Little Something Before It Starts

Use a comma to set off a short (or long) introductory phrase from an independent clause.

This is the sort of comma used when the second part of the sentence could stand by itself, and is not connected to the first part by a conjunction. Sometimes the introductory phrase explains or prepares us for the second part.

- A comma should set off an introductory phrase that explains an *action* important to what follows (i.e., a *modifying* phrase). To justify a comma, the introductory phrase must contain a verb.

  By finishing her work and cleaning her room, Sonia was able to make time for a movie and dinner.

- In other instances the comma sets off a single word (e.g., *however, anyway, nonetheless, otherwise, anyway, coincidentally*) or short phrase (e.g., *in any case, in spite of this, this aside, with this in mind*) from the main part of the sentence.

  Coincidentally, his mother showed up at the same time.

  Money isn't everything. However, it does help.

  They may or may not have food for us when we arrive. In any case, it's best to have a snack before we leave.

3. Putting Stuff in the Middle

Use a pair of commas to set off words and groups of words inserted within a sentence.

Here a pair of commas acts much like parentheses, enclosing extra information in the middle of a sentence. Though this information may or may not be critical to understanding the piece of writing as a whole, the sentence itself could stand perfectly well without it. Students usually find this to be one of the easier comma categories to understand, and often come up with interesting names to describe it. Some choice definitions have been *oh-by-the-way commas* (a fourth grader), *detour commas* (a third grader), *extra-in-the-middle commas* (another third grader), and *excuse-me marks* (a second grader). Though all these uses are similar in function, there are some subtle differences.

- *Explaining the first part of the sentence:* Sometimes a writer will use a pair of commas to insert a phrase in the middle that tells about the words that came *before* it in the first part of the sentence. A pair of commas should be used to enclose words in *apposition* (i.e., words that follow a word or group of words and that identify or give important information about what comes before).

  Kate Montgomery, who works in New Hampshire, is a brilliant editor.

- *Specifying which is which:* A variation of this same type is used to enclose explanations that start with the word *which*. Use a comma before clauses that begin with *which*.

  The subway, which was often late, came on time that day. She arrived early, which gave her time to stop at the toy store.

- *Bringing out the main idea:* A pair of commas may also be used to emphasize a main point. While the basic information of the sentence is conveyed in the first and last clause, the extra stuff in the middle stands out and calls attention to the big idea. Often the voice in a reader's mind pauses a little longer for these sorts of commas. A pair of commas may be used to set off elements that are important to understanding the full meaning of the sentence. Typically the sentence may be understood without them, but they do serve to emphasize interesting and/or important information.

  She is an inventive teacher, a professional with an extraordinary knowledge of reading and writing, and I would not hesitate to put my own child in her class.

- *Telling something interesting that isn't really needed:* In contrast to the last sort, we use this pair of commas to insert *nonrestrictive* phrases or clauses; while interesting, this information is *not* necessary for meaning or emphasis.

  Dizzy Gillespie, who was originally from South Carolina, is one of the most important trumpet players in the history of jazz.

- *Referring to what was said before:* A pair of commas may also be used to insert a word or phrase that refers back to information not in the sentence. This information may or may not be somewhere earlier in the text, *before* the sentence. Use commas to enclose words, phrases, or clauses that might otherwise be put inside parentheses.

  He arrived, as always, a half hour early.

4. Listing Things

Use commas to divide elements in a series.

- Commas are used to separate items in a list. Whether it is a list of *things, people, objects, ideas,* or *descriptive words such as adjectives,* when there are more than two of them, they are usually separated by commas.

- *Comma before "and"? Depends who you talk to. . . .* Here we come to our first example of a contradiction in what different punctuation guides say is the "correct" way. According to the *Chicago Manual of Style* (2003), a comma *should* be placed before the word *and* in a list (e.g., *apples, oranges, and grapefruits*). According to several other guides (e.g., Lederer and Dowis, Shaw), there should be *no* comma before the *and*. As in many cases, the ultimate rule should be clarity and consideration for the reader; in other words, do whatever makes it clearest.

    At least three things on the list, but no *comma before the word* and. Not as complicated as it sounds. As long as there are three things on the list, a comma comes after each of them—up until the second to last, where the word *and* replaces the comma. So the names of the four Beatles would be John, Paul, George *and* Ringo.

    Cara and Allen went shopping for food, clothing and furniture.

    Kiri's pets include a dog, cat, guinea pig, frog and fish.

    At least three things on the list, and put *a comma before the word* and. When a conjunction joins the last two elements in a series, a comma should appear before the conjunction. *Chicago* strongly recommends this widely practiced usage, since it prevents ambiguity.

    The meal consisted of soup, salad, and macaroni and cheese.

    Paul put the kettle on, Don fetched the teapot, and I made tea.

- *Adjectives and adverbs—commas can separate words that describe.* Typically a writer describes a thing (i.e., noun) with one adjective, and an action (i.e., verb) with a single adverb. Now and then he or she may go further and use two or more. This series of adjectives (or adverbs) falls into the same category as other lists, and must be separated by commas. If the adjectives come *before* a noun, then there is a comma between each one; if they come after the noun, the last comma is replaced by the word *and*. (Remember, the *Chicago Manual of Style* feels differently, so one could argue this is a judgment call on the part of the writer.)

    She lives in a huge, well-designed, comfortable house.

    Simone is beautiful, smart, charming and sarcastic.

    A list of adverbs typically comes *after* the verb, and the same rules apply; the last comma is replaced by *and*.

    Wanda ran quickly, quietly and stealthily through the night.

    When a list of adverbs comes *before* a verb, the word *and* usually replaces the last comma once again.

    The young orphan greedily, hungrily and quickly reached for the cupcake.

On rare occasions, a list of adverbs comes before and is separated from its verb by another word or set of words; in these instances the word *and* may not replace the comma.

Beautifully, gracefully, the dancer glided across the floor.

- *Conjunctions—lists with connector words in between.* At times authors connect each item on a list with another word *in addition* to the comma (see examples below). This is a literary device to show the importance of each separate item on the list.

Jamie has no inspiration, or motivation, or hope left.

Cyrano has wit, and strength, and a healthy appetite for danger.

5. Stating Names, Numbers, Titles, Dates

These sorts of comma uses are typically among the first children learn in school.

- Use a comma between the name of a city and a state and after the state.

  Brooklyn, New York, is the place where the hippest young people look for apartments.

  The hippest young people find apartments in Brooklyn, New York.

- The year should be set off with commas when a month, day, and year are used in a sentence.

  Sonia was born on September 22, 1992.

- Do not use a comma between the month and year when the *day* of the month is not used.

  He remembered September 1992 like it was yesterday.

- Use a comma (or commas) to separate thousands, millions, etc. when writing large numbers.

  35,274

  6,000,000

- Use a pair of commas to enclose initials or titles after a person's name.

  Maurice Cohen, Ph.D., and Maya Solnick, M.D., served as the chairs of the committee.

6. Avoiding Confusion

Use a comma or commas to prevent misreading.

- In certain instances, authors use commas to prevent a reader from misunderstanding the meaning of the sentence.
- It is a good idea to use a comma to separate repeated words.

  If you want to go, go before it gets dark.

- On rare occasions, authors may use a comma to replace other words which the reader may infer. This helps avoid wordiness.

  Certain students are always on time; of those, Sonia and Lily stand out.

- Use a comma to separate elements in a sentence when the point is to show contrast.

  The show began with a monologue, not a song.

7. Addressing Someone Directly

Use a comma to make dialogue and letters easier to read.

This category contains one of the trickiest comma conventions for student writers to master (*replacing the last period in dialogue*) and one of the easiest to understand (*putting a comma after the opening greeting in a letter*). One way to frame these comma uses is to say they all have to do with talking or writing to people.

- When the last piece of dialogue within a set of quotation marks ends in a period and is followed by other text (usually an identifier such as *he said, she asked, the captain shouted*, etc.), we put a comma before the closing quotations. The comma replaces the *final* period. (In contrast, when the last sentence of the dialogue ends with any other punctuation—a question mark or exclamation point, for example—the comma does *not* replace it.)

  "I'll come back to pick you up by 5:30," the driver reassured us.

- Use a comma after the opening greeting (*Dear _____,*) of a friendly or informal letter.

  Dear Grandpa,

  Dear Abby,

- Use commas before and after the names of people you're talking to.

  "Goodbye, Mom, Dad, and don't forget to write," she said.

CHAPTER 4

Writing as Good as It Sounds

Internal Punctuation and Cadence
(Upper Elementary Grades)

> She went out to stand in the drizzle. It was cold but the water felt good, like punctuation.
> —Anne Lamott, *Blue Shoe*

We had already spent a good ten minutes on the rug, using nonsense syllables to illustrate the rhythm and the rise and fall of our voices. Some passages were short: *the boy slept late* became *de-duh dut duh*. Other examples were longer; tapping out the rhythm of multiline descriptive passages from Ralph Fletcher's "The Last Kiss" (1993) caused several students to giggle nervously, anticipating their turn. A few of the boys in Jackie Levenherz's fifth-grade room began to drum along, which seemed somehow less embarrassing than using nonsense syllables, and encouraged more to participate. It was at this moment that Sho Hashizume, normally soft spoken, had his inspiration. "Hey!" he called out spontaneously. "This is like drum language!"

Consciously or not, all writers think about the way the words on the paper sound. There is the awkward phrase that, correct or not, simply feels wrong. We might notice a paragraph in which each individual sentence works perfectly well, but put together they seem clunky and confusing. Randy Bomer (2006) has written of how *prosody* helps readers make sense of a text, whether it is read aloud or they are hearing it in their head. Listening "with one's mental ear . . . [to] the melody of the sentences" gives a sense of what is important and what might come next and may shape the way we respond to what the author is saying. The truth is, when writing feels off rhythmically it is less clear, whether or not any rules are broken. Mark Twain famously described Wagnerian opera as "better music than it sounds." His point was that when melodies don't fall naturally on the ear, with appropriate breaths and other signposts, they are at best difficult—and at worst, not worth hearing. Wagner's operas have stood the test of time, and many would say they are worth the effort, but how written text sounds is still an important idea. On some level every writer must develop strategies for composing prose that flows naturally, in a way that makes its meaning clear. The notion of what Sho called drum language—rendering a phrase in nonsense syllables in order to concentrate solely on the way it sounds, momentarily putting aside content—is one such strategy.

And yet we rarely address the idea of how writing *sounds* in our writing workshops. In teaching poetry, it is common practice to consider rhythm but usually as something related to a rhyme scheme or a particular form, like haiku or sonnet. We seldom consider how the rhythm and intonation of words help us understand in a particular way. "Every text in a reader's native language," writes Bomer, "has voice because the reader can always speak the text internally as he or she reads. A news article, a poem, an entry in the encyclopedia, even the driest administrative memo—any text can have a voice. To listen is to make oneself conscious of that voice."

The purpose of this unit is to make students conscious of the sound writing makes as it speaks to a reader—the cadence of the text—and how that sound can be shaped to create shades of meaning. It would be a mistake to say there is a right or wrong way to do this. The important thing is to make students aware of it and teach them the tools authors use to get there. Developing this awareness is the natural next step following the earlier ending punctuation and comma studies. Once writers are convinced that punctuation is a tool of expression, not, as eleven-year-old Morris Reeves observed, "just something you do to make the sentence correct," they are ready to explore the way it can make a text sound.

One of the primary ways a writer creates "the melody of the sentences" is through artful use of internal punctuation. Where the pauses fall and how long they last, which parts of a phrase seem louder or softer, faster or slower—all of these can be manipulated with commas, dashes, colons, semicolons, and ellipses. Unlike ending punctuation, there are few absolutes when it comes to which marks we put in the middle. Going with a colon to make a full stop before announcing something or a dash for a less prominent pause is a judgment call on the part of the author. It has more to do with the desired effect than a "correct" way of doing things.

In a broad sense the function of internal punctuation is to break up parts of sentences, creating pauses within them. Where these pauses happen relative to one another in large part creates the rhythm of the passage. Similarly, where the sentences end—their stopping points—adds to the overall music of the writing. When an author wants to achieve a pleasing cadence over a longer stretch of text, she or he must also consider the lengths of the sentences. "Varied sentence length" is listed in many rubrics as a standard for good writing, but a more accurate measure might be an *awareness* of sentence length. Sometimes a series of short sentences is the right way to get across quick, separate movements. Think of a squirrel scurrying across a field. Stopping. Sniffing. Darting a few feet. Stopping again. A group of long sentences with sections connected by commas may work well to show flowing action, like a dancer in a pas de deux, twirling across the stage, dipping forward, one leg rising as the other bends, coming to rest in the arms of her partner. As students begin to experiment with the way internal punctuation affects the sound of their writing, it follows they should also think about the sequence of sentences overall.

All this said, a skilled writer seldom considers rhythm apart from meaning. When we connect what an author is trying to get across to the notion of cadence and rhythm, it makes sense that the way words *sound* can affect how a reader understands them. The purpose of this unit is for students to explore that connection.

Are these ideas too abstract for ten- or eleven-year-olds to grasp? As we tried the lessons with several fifth and sixth grade classes, it became apparent that considering the sound of text and how it affects meaning was not so complicated for writers who had never been taught *not* to think about it. Lily Colburn, a fifth grader planning the lead for a story about colliding with her friend on the street, explained, "I'm going to use commas to make it all la-di-da and loose. Then a dash or ellipsis to make it tense for the CRASH!" Her classmate Max

Litvack-Winkler commented more generally about how he was beginning to use punctuation differently: "I am thinking now of the mood I want to create," he wrote in his final reflection, "and the best punctuation mark to use. I think about strategy now in writing—almost like I think of it in baseball."

Max's words sum up the main objective of this unit—to turn children into punctuation strategists. Though the focus is on internal punctuation and different sentence lengths, we are really looking for something more ambitious. In the end, whether a student understands all the subtleties of the semicolon or knows each use of a dash by heart is not so important (though the likelihood is they will be more invested in learning these rules for having experimented with different possibilities). What we are after are classrooms of students who pay attention to the balance and flow of text and see it as something that can help them become better readers and writers.

In this series of lessons, even more than the earlier units, it is important to check in frequently to gauge student understanding and adapt instruction according to what we observe. Some lessons might require more than one session to sink in fully (Lesson 5, on drum language, is an example), and extra time may have to be built in for drafting and revision. As in the other units, sample texts and think-alouds are woven throughout. Ideally, teachers will come up with their own and truly model the process. Donald Graves has said that if we don't try what we are asking students to do, we can never know the obstacles they may encounter in the process. Not inconsequentially, through this unit we may heighten the awareness of rhythm and melody in our own writing as well.

What Do We Notice About Internal Punctuation?

Rationale/Purpose   Upper elementary students have seen examples of internal punctuation all through their lives as readers. Most however have not stopped to think about the way commas, dashes, colons, and semicolons affect the meaning of a passage and how they make a sentence sound and feel. In this lesson they start to notice some of the reasons writers use internal punctuation, focusing on how it helps them express different feelings and ideas.

Materials/ Preparation

Teacher:

- Two passages from *Fireflies* (1986), by Julie Brinckloe (or other examples from a writer of your choice), copied separately on chart paper or a transparency.

- Blank chart paper and markers.

- Enough blank overhead transparencies and overhead markers for partners to record what they notice (i.e., half the number of students in the class).

- *Optional*: A selection of passages with interesting internal punctuation, copied from classroom library books or read-alouds and duplicated so partners may use them in their independent work.

Students:

- Reading notebooks and writing utensils.

- Independent reading books.

- Sticky notes for marking passages.

Summary   You begin this unit by:

- Defining what is meant by internal punctuation.

- Pointing out that unlike ending punctuation, there are few precise rules authors follow in the way they use commas, dashes, colons, and semicolons.

- Modeling the way a reader might notice and think about interesting examples of internal punctuation.

Sample Language/ Sequence

"We spend a lot of time in reading workshop thinking about how authors express feelings and ideas," you might begin. "Most often our conversations have to do with the words they choose to use or the information they decide to put in so we will understand what they are writing about. In this unit we are going to look at another thing authors make choices about—internal punctuation. I am not talking about periods, question marks, or exclamation points. Those come at the end of sentences, and most of the time there are strict rules about how to use them correctly. When I say *internal* punctuation I am talking about commas, dashes, colons, semicolons, and sometimes ellipses; all the punctuation that can come in the middle of a sentence. Often authors make choices about internal punctuation just like they do about words and descriptions, making up their own rules so it will sound and feel the way they want.

"To show you what I mean," you might continue, "I am going to look at a passage from Julie Brinckloe's book *Fireflies* and think about how she chose to use internal punctuation so we would understand the story a certain way. After I do that, I'll write down what I think the different punctuation marks are doing. Then I am going to ask you to do the same thing with another passage."

As you read the first Brinckloe excerpt aloud, pause where appropriate, speed up and slow down, and emphasize the rise and fall of your voice to illustrate the effect of the internal punctuation. Students should follow along with the text, which is displayed on a chart or transparency, so they see what the punctuation looks like.

> I blinked hard as I watched them—*Fireflies!* Blinking on, blinking off, dipping low, soaring high above my head, making white patterns in the dark.

Next, model how to notice and think about the author's punctuation choices. "In the first part," you could say, "she uses that dash before the word *fireflies* to set it off from the rest of the sentence. When you read it you pause for a second, and then say the word *fireflies* quickly, which makes it seem like seeing them is a big surprise and the narrator is really excited. In the next sentence the commas coming one after another—*blinking on, blinking off, dipping low*—make the words seem to swirl around like the fireflies. When I read it my voice goes up and down, like I imagine the fireflies are doing. Since the last part, *making white patterns in the dark,* is a little longer than the rest, I want to stretch it out more. It seems like after she gets excited about the fast movement of the fireflies, the narrator starts to slow down and notice more about what they are doing.

"Now that I've thought about the way the internal punctuation works in this passage," you can explain, "I'll want to record my thinking." [*To save time, you may want to have a chart prepared ahead of time rather than writing in front of the students.*]

> **Dash**
> Makes you pause for a second, to set up a surprise (the fireflies), and create a feeling of excitement.
> **Commas**
> Separate the different things the fireflies are doing, make the words swirl around like the fireflies.

Ask students to listen and follow along as you read the second passage from *Fireflies* aloud.

> Then we dashed about, waving our hands in the air like nets, catching two, ten—hundreds of fireflies, thrusting them into jars, waving our hands for more.

Have them turn and talk with a partner about how the internal punctuation helps them read the passage and understand it, as you demonstrated in your earlier think-aloud. As students discuss the passage, listen in and gauge their understanding. After a moment or two, call for students' attention and share some of what you've overheard. (It's not necessary to call on volunteers to share—they will have a chance to reveal their thinking during the share session.)

Wrap up the minilesson by linking it to today's independent work. "When you go off to read independently today," you might say, "notice passages where your author uses internal punctuation in an interesting way and mark them with a sticky note. After reading for a while, meet with your partner to share passages and talk about how the punctuation helped you understand them, just as we've done with the sentences from *Fireflies*. Then, agree on one passage to share with the class and write down your thinking about its punctuation, just as I did earlier. I will give you an overhead transparency and marker to copy the passage and record your thinking, so the class can see it."

Independent Work   Circulate as students search for examples. In your conferences, discuss internal punctuation in terms of comprehension and meaning rather than rules of usage. *To set the stage for future lessons in which you will concentrate on the way punctuation affects the sound of language, have students read their passages out loud and point out what you hear their voice doing.* (For example: "I notice your voice rose up on the word just after the comma. Did that comma give you a signal to stretch out the word that followed?")

Not all texts will have passages suited to your purpose, and not all learners will be equally adept at finding examples. One variation on this activity is to collect appropriate passages from familiar class library books or read-alouds so students can consider the context of the piece as they discuss its use of internal punctuation. Make copies of these, and distribute them to students.

Some things you might bring up during your conferences are:

- How does this passage sound in your head as you read it? What is the punctuation that made it sound that way?

- Can you think of any places in the book where sentences are very long? What sort of punctuation did the author use?

- Think of parts where the story gets complicated. Let's look at how the author uses punctuation in those parts. What do you notice?

Once partners meet to discuss passages, listen in and coach them in their efforts:

- Which of these examples uses internal punctuation in a way that's different from what you've seen before? How is it different?

- Imagine this passage without the commas/colons/semicolons/dashes—how would you read it differently?

- Why do you think the author chose to put the comma/colon/semicolon/dash here?

- Does the internal punctuation make your voice speed up/slow down?

- What sort of pause does this punctuation create, long or short?

- What feeling is created by this pause (e.g., suspenseful, confused, funny)?

Seeing the way internal punctuation looks is critical to understanding how it works. Once partners have shown you their examples and brief written descriptions of their thinking, give them an overhead transparency and marker so they may recopy their work to display during the share session. Remind them that they should be prepared to read their passage aloud and explain why they think the author chose to use internal punctuation in this way.

As students prepare to present, circulate and preselect partners whom you will ask to share. (Remember that sometimes hearing peers explain their ideas can give less confident students a push to take chances in their own thinking.) One of your objectives is to create an environment in which students feel safe airing their theories, "correct" or not. This will become especially important later in the unit, when students begin to mess around with internal punctuation in their own writing. To that end, you may want to pick a handful of students with diverse, even contradictory ideas about the effect of a comma, semicolon, colon, or dash.

If possible, select students to share passages that illustrate each of the following:

- Slowing down/speeding up.

- Rising and falling of the voice.

- Different types of pauses (long, short, suspenseful, funny, etc.).

Share Session

Ask partner teams to read their examples aloud as the rest of the students follow along on an overhead transparency. After each such share, help students make generalizations and comparisons. "Brett and Aisha pointed out that the commas seem to slow down the sentence," you might say, "and give it a calm feeling. Notice the difference from Juan and Sonia's example of the dash making the second part of their sentence go faster, so it feels more exciting."

To end the share, you could recap some of the questions that came up along the way, setting the stage for further investigation. "As we continue looking at internal punctuation, it will be interesting to see how often a dash calls attention to the part that comes after it, as in Juan and Sonia's example, and how often it shows an interruption, as in Aidan and Sadie's passage."

Possible Follow-Up Activities

- For homework, have students find another example of interesting internal punctuation in their independent reading and again write a short description of their thinking. This could be an open, whatever-you-notice assignment, or you may choose to narrow the focus, such as:

    - Find an example of punctuation that is the same as/different from the punctuation you found in class.

    - Find an example of punctuation that slows down/speeds up the way you read.

    - Find an example of punctuation that creates long/short pauses.

- In order to provide opportunities for students to see and reflect on as many examples of internal punctuation as possible, display students' transparencies and/or homework in the classroom.

Testing Theories

Rationale/Purpose Now that students have begun exploring the way punctuation affects a reader's understanding, it is important for them to see whether what they've noticed holds true across several texts. In this lesson, they will test theories they have developed so far by looking for supporting examples in their independent reading.

Materials/ Preparation

Teacher:

- Two passages from *Judy Moody Was in a Mood* (2000), by Megan McDonald (or passages of your own choosing), copied separately on chart paper or a transparency.

- First passage you used in Lesson 1.

- Blank chart paper and markers.

Students:

- Reading notebooks and writing utensils.

- Independent reading books.

- Sticky notes for marking passages.

- Overhead transparencies and markers from the last lesson.

Summary You'll begin by testing one of your own theories about internal punctuation from last time, then have students do the same, working independently or with a partner. After finding at least two passages to illustrate their thinking, students will copy them into their reading journals.

Sample Language/ Sequence "We've come up with some theories about why authors use different types of internal punctuation," you might begin, "but can't be sure they are true unless we test them. To do this we will have to search for *other* passages in our reading where a writer uses punctuation the same way. If we can find more than one example, it's likely our theory is a good one.

"To demonstrate," you can continue, "I'm going to look back at my theories about the passage in *Fireflies*." Display the chart from last lesson with the passage and your theories. "The second one, about the commas making words swirl around, seems so specific to *this* story that I don't think it'd be a good one to test—after all, how many stories talk about things swirling around? My first theory, about the dash, would be a better one to look for in other books. The idea of using a dash to set up a surprise and create excitement is one I believe may be used in lots of writing."

Now call attention to the new chart containing the passages from *Judy Moody Was in a Mood.*

Example 1 (p. 7)

"I made sunny-side up eggs for the first day of school," said Dad. "There's squishy bread for dipping."
There was nothing sunny about Judy's egg—the yellow middle was broken.

Example 2 (p. 15)

Now, on the first day of third grade, he gave her a birthday party invitation. Judy checked the date
inside—his birthday was not for three weeks!

Students might not realize they sometimes need to rule out an example before finding one that matches a particular theory. To help model these steps, conceal the second passage while thinking aloud about the first.

"As I was reading this Judy Moody book," you can begin, "I noticed this example of using a dash, on page 7. It says, 'There was nothing sunny about Judy's egg—*dash*—the yellow middle was broken.' The part after the dash explains more about the part before it; we know something was wrong with the eggs from hearing there was nothing sunny about them, and then we find out what the problem was, the yellow middle was broken. It's not really a surprise, the way it is when Julie Brinckloe follows her dash with the word *Fireflies!* in the last book. So far my theory doesn't hold true. But I know that authors use the same internal punctuation in different ways sometimes, so I'm not giving up on my theory just yet."

Then call attention to the second passage. "As I continued reading, this other example caught my eye. Here Megan McDonald *does* seem to use the dash the same way it was used in *Fireflies.* You get the feeling that when Judy looks at the invitation she isn't expecting the party to be so far off, and when she sees it's three weeks away, she feels surprised—just like when the narrator realizes about the fireflies.

"So now that I've found another example using a dash the same way I noticed before, I'm ready to copy it into my notebook. I'll need to tell what book it's from, and be sure I know which theory it goes with. When I'm done it will look like this."

I blinked hard as I watched them—*Fireflies!*

—*Fireflies*, Julie Brinckloe

Judy checked the date inside—his birthday was not for three weeks!

—*Judy Moody Was in a Mood*, Megan McDonald

Dash

Makes you pause for a second, to set up a surprise (the fireflies, the birthday party being in three weeks) and create a feeling of excitement.

"Take a minute to think about which of your theories from last time would be the best one to test, then turn and share it with the person sitting next to you." As always, listen in on these conversations, noting the punctuation theories students plan to test. Before sending them off to work independently, you may briefly want to share some of these theories and point out similarities, or pair students who are looking for the same thing.

"As you read your independent books today, be on the lookout for examples of your theory. The only rule is you will need to find at least two examples, including the one you already have, to prove the idea works. Be sure to share with a partner and ask his or her opinion as well. After you've found your passages, copy them in your reading journals so you can teach the class something new about how authors use internal punctuation in their writing."

Independent Work   Give students about twenty minutes to read and search for examples that support their theories about internal punctuation. Then have them meet with their partner and copy down examples. Since the point is to continue thinking deeply about this subject, it is fine for children to revise their ideas or come up with a completely new theory. It is a good idea to have texts on hand that are rich with examples of internal punctuation to help students who are having trouble, especially struggling readers. But for those who are up to the challenge, it is important to notice these examples in their regular independent reading.

Questions you might ask when conferring with students include:

- How does this dash/comma/semicolon, etc., work differently from the one you wrote about last time? What about it is the same?

- How does this new example make you change your theory?

- Are you noticing any new ways of using internal punctuation in today's reading?

- What sort of mood does this internal punctuation create? Does it make the reader feel excited, surprised, nervous, happy?

After students begin working with partners, listen carefully to their conversations to be sure their theories make sense. *It is also important for them to read examples aloud to each other to see if they agree on how it should sound, and the shades of meaning created by the punctuation.* When coaching partners, you can use the questions from the last lesson as well as these additional ones:

- Do the two examples make your voice speed up/slow down in the same way or differently?

- What about the punctuation makes the passage convey this particular feeling? How does it affect the way we understand the story?

As you circulate, be on the lookout for partners with interesting and diverse examples and theories. In particular try to choose students to share who have revised their original theory in some way (e.g., "the ellipsis creates suspense but *also* a sense of surprise") or whose work contradicts or affirms ideas raised during the last session. It is more important at this stage that students debate possibilities for how internal punctuation can affect meaning than to come up with "correct" answers, or even agree on the same point. Once again, be sure examples are on transparencies and that children who are going to share practice reading them aloud and explaining their thinking ahead of time.

Share Session

Partners again read their examples aloud, beginning with an explanation of what theory they were trying to prove and how today's findings support or contradict their original thinking. Your job is to make connections across theories and highlight instances in which students have altered an idea. "It's interesting," you might say, "how Emilio was looking for examples of commas slowing things down, but ended up finding a passage where a comma made us first pause and then speed up."

To conclude, comment on how some of the ideas discussed last session have changed or broadened. "It seems as though our question about dashes is still up for debate," you might point out. "Today Lucia and Kyra found a place where the words after the dash explained the first part, and then there was another dash afterward. It was as if the dashes acted like parentheses. That's a use we hadn't thought of before, which may be important to think about."

Possible Follow-Up Activities

- Have students prove or disprove their own or a classmate's theory by looking for more examples in their independent reading (or in books from their home libraries).

- Widen the discussion to include parents or older siblings. Students could interview them ("What do you think are the reasons a writer might use a dash instead of a comma?") or simply ask whether they agree with a particular theory and why.

Marinating Ourselves in Punctuation: Filling the Classroom with Examples

Rationale/Purpose Discussing the teaching of poetry, Georgia Heard (1989) stresses the need to "marinate" children in examples—to create opportunities to read, see, and think about as many different types of poems as possible. In this unit, you want to create the same sort of opportunities by surrounding your students with examples of interesting internal punctuation. Now that they have spent time looking for such passages in texts, students choose particularly intriguing ones to copy onto sentence strips or posters for classroom display. They will also include short written explanations of "what the author was trying to do" in using internal punctuation that way.

Once the passages have been selected, copying them from the reading journal onto sentence strips or posters may be done as a transitional activity or when other assignments are completed. As with any project, final products can be more or less elaborate depending on time and inclination. The important thing is that in the end the classroom is filled with examples of internal punctuation for young writers to see and think about.

Materials/ Preparation Teacher:

- Blank chart paper and markers.

- Prepared examples of texts; passages from "The Last Kiss" (Fletcher 1993) and *The Cello of Mr. O* (Cutler 1999) are used here.

- Poster paper or sentence strips for students to use in preparing their examples and theories for display.

Students:

- Reading notebooks containing several examples of interesting punctuation and written descriptions of their thinking about why the punctuation works well.

- Pencils.

- Markers.

Summary In this lesson, students:

- Choose a passage they have found that shows a particularly interesting use of internal punctuation.

- Copy the example and accompanying explanation/theory onto a sentence strip or poster so it can be displayed in the classroom.

"Over the last couple of days," you might begin, "you have collected several different examples of interesting internal punctuation and formed theories about how the punctuation makes us read and understand the passage a certain way. Now that you've done all this work, it's time to show it off to your classmates! One way to think hard about something is to surround yourself with it. So today partners will choose their best examples and copy them onto sentence strips to display all over the classroom for others to think about. It is important to choose examples that show interesting ways of using internal punctuation and to include clear explanations. After all, we want our fellow readers to learn from our examples. Watch as I choose one of mine and show you the sorts of things you will want to think about as you pick your own example."

Anticipate stumbling blocks students may run into and model ruling out passages before making a successful selection. You will want to avoid choosing passages that are very difficult to explain, include too many kinds of punctuation, or illustrate very common rules (e.g., commas in a list).

You might say, "I think I could use the last sentence from this part in 'The Last Kiss' for my sentence strip—the part that starts with 'Just this.' The whole passage includes a lot of sentences with pretty standard punctuation. But this last sentence has a couple different types."

> I was grateful to go next to my father. His goodnight kisses were more formal affairs, but that was all right. Formality was exactly what I wanted just before bed. And no accompanying body hug, either. *Just this: his male scent, the faintest remnants of morning aftershave lotion, and the whisker-stubbly contour of his proffered cheek—a textured surface that made a satisfying contrast with my mother.*

"I like the way the colon after the first phrase—*just this*—makes my voice go up, as though something important is about to happen. Then the commas after each thing in the middle section—the male scent, the faintest remnants of aftershave, the whisker-stubbly cheek—make me read it quickly, leading up to that last dash. After the dash, it feels like you should draw out the textured-surface part to show that's the most important thing."

Then pause and troubleshoot your choice. "As I read it over," you might continue, "I'm worried that it doesn't make sense without the sentences before it. That will make it hard for someone reading it on a sentence strip to understand what Ralph Fletcher was trying to do. It would also be hard to explain all the different parts in a clear way. I'd better look for another example."

"Another one that might work better," you may reflect, "is this example from *The Cello of Mr. O*, by Jane Cutler."

> My father and most of the other fathers, the older brothers—even some of the grandfathers—have gone to fight.

"This example stands by itself—you don't need to know what came before to understand it. The punctuation does interesting things too. I like the way Jane Cutler uses the comma after the word *fathers* to add the information about older brothers—it makes my voice go quickly, like that information isn't as important as the first part. Then when she uses the two dashes to set off the bit about the grandfathers, it seems important and surprising, like, "Oh, my gosh, even *grandfathers*!" The last part, *have gone to fight*, makes my voice go down. Coming in after the second dash, it feels very final, like there's nothing more to say. The question is, can I explain that clearly in writing, to put underneath my sentence strip?"

Thinking aloud, try writing an explanation on chart paper or a transparency to test how clear you can be.

My father and most of the other fathers, the older brothers—even some of the grandfathers— have gone to fight.

—Jane Cutler, *The Cello Of Mr. O*

Comma Before Dashes
The comma makes you say the next part (about older brothers) quickly, and then the dash makes you stop suddenly. The part *inside* the dashes, about grandfathers, seems surprising and important— your voice stretches it out. The last few words, after the dashes, feel very final. Your voice gets lower as you say them.

"When you go off today," you can conclude, "you and your partner should look over the examples you have collected so far and choose two. Then, do as you watched me do— rule one out and pick the one that will work best for our display. As I go around the room conferring I'll ask you to tell me about the one you didn't choose and the one you did pick—and your reasons for each."

Before the children go off to work on their own, explain the logistics of making the sentence strip/posters. One way is for you to approve their choice before giving students the blank sentence strip/poster. Also, it is a good idea to have children first copy their passage and explanation in pencil. Once you or a reliable peer editor has proofread the entry, the words may be gone over with a marker.

Independent Work As students look over the passages they have collected so far, circulate and check in on their decision making. Do your best to be sure that a variety of observations will be displayed on the classroom walls, based on different types of internal punctuation. Your other role is that of proofreader/facilitator—examples must be copied accurately, and the accompanying observations must make sense and be easy to understand.

Some questions you may want to ask include:

- What is surprising about the way the author used internal punctuation in this passage?

- Which example did you rule out, and why?

- What can we learn about commas/colons/parentheses/semicolons from the way they are used in this example?

You can have partners read their examples and explanations to other students, to be sure their thinking (and writing) is clear.

Share Session

Since this lesson is not a workshop activity in the pure sense, you may or may not allow time for students to share their selections at the end of the first day. If interesting trends have emerged (many examples of dashes used to set off information, a lot of short phrases at the ends of sentences following a comma, etc.) this is a good time to point them out. Once the sentence strips/posters are finished and on display, you will certainly want to have a "museum" session, in which students go around the room reading and commenting. If another class is doing the same unit, the students could visit each other's room and compare notes on what they are coming up with.

Possible Follow-Up Activity

For a greater challenge, students may copy both of their supporting examples for display.

Assessment

After the display has been put up, look over students' observations to gauge their understanding. For example, are they beginning to compare the lengths of pauses suggested by different types of punctuation? Are they commenting mostly on the rise and fall of the voice (cadence), speed (pacing), emphasis (which information is most important)? Students can and should be enlisted in this assessment. Ask what things they notice the examples have in common, and discuss how they might categorize their observations so far. Such a conversation would be a natural lead-in to the next lesson.

Categorizing Our Ideas (A Guided Share)

They were having ideas about punctuation but they weren't organized. Rodini and Marisa said the comma in their sentence made it nice and smooth, kind of dramatic. They were noticing the way punctuation makes your voice sound— touching on mood—but their ideas weren't very explicit. I wanted to give them categories to help organize some of what they were noticing. I also wanted them to see that some of what they were finding was contradictory—for example, they'd say a sentence was sad, but also exciting. So we met on the rug and they shared what they were thinking. I helped them group the ideas as they spoke—a sort of guided share. This is where, as a class, the children developed their strongest ideas about internal punctuation.

—Alexandra Marron, fifth-grade teacher

Rationale/Purpose

Up to now students have made observations about internal punctuation and the way it affects a reader's understanding, but they haven't structured their thinking. Their theories have for the most part been applied only to the particular examples they have found. They need to go from the specific to the general—pull back and take stock of what they have noticed so far, make generalizations about the *types* of things internal punctuation can do, and put their thoughts into categories. For them to be able to do this effectively, you need to steer the conversation carefully, allowing students to express their thinking but at the same time helping them group their examples.

Materials/ Preparation

Sentence strips/posters prepared during earlier sessions should already be on display in the classroom.

Teacher:

- Three examples of internal punctuation, two that belong in the same category and one that does not.
- Notepad or clipboard on which to record important ideas that come up in the conversation.
- Blank chart paper and markers.

Students:

- Reading notebooks containing the examples of interesting internal punctuation they have found so far.

Summary

This lesson does not follow the normal time allotments. You'll begin by tying your purpose to the children's recent work and modeling your thinking. Independent work will be brief, because the share is the focal point. Students will return to the meeting area after a few minutes of partner work to participate in an extended conversation. Your objective is to use the examples the students have found so far to form categories and make generalizations about ways authors use internal punctuation.

Sample Language/ Sequence

"Now that we have found so many examples of ways authors use internal punctuation to make writing interesting," you might begin, "it makes sense to put them into groups. If we can figure out from what we have noticed so far exactly what types of things internal punctuation can affect, it'll help us become better readers—and may give us ideas for our own writing as well. To show you what I mean, I will look at a few examples and think aloud about how I might group them."

Example A

Allegiances are forged and broken, titles change hands, indelible moments are created—in short, history is made.

—*Smackdown Magazine*, April 2006

Example B

Roger felt strangely secure, like an infant in a cradle. True, he was exhausted; true, his life hung by a thread.

—*A Barrel of Laughs, a Vale of Tears*, by Jules Feiffer

Example C

Some, like Mama's friend Marya, stay because they have no place else to go. And some, like my mother, have decided to stay—no matter what.

—*The Cello of Mr. O*, by Jane Cutler

"In this first example," you might reflect, "the beginning phrases, divided by commas, sound the same. Your voice doesn't really change as you read them. They lead up to the dash, which sets off the final, short part, which sums it all up. It's clear the author wants us to know this last bit—*in short, history is made*—is the most important part, the big idea, and the dash coming after those flowing commas tells us to get ready and say the last part in a strong voice. So in this example, I'd say the punctuation shows which part is most important."

Turning to the next passage, you continue thinking aloud. "This next example is quite different. That second sentence is an interesting one—the two sections before and after the semicolon are about the same length, and they have the same sort of rhythm, with the word *true* followed by a medium-length phrase. So it's very balanced, with your voice rising, then falling, rising then falling. Neither half of the sentence feels more important—they are equal, and the punctuation dividing it makes it feel kind of musical. So this one wouldn't be in the same group as the second example.

"In the third example, the second sentence, about the mother deciding to stay, seems a little like the first example. It begins with some phrases divided by commas, and then the big climax—*no matter what*—is set off by the dash. Again, the punctuation tells us to say the last part in a strong, final kind of voice. I'd put those two in the same group. Both of them use punctuation to let us know which parts are most important—and both end with short, final-sounding sections. I'll call this the lets-us-know-which-part-is-important-with-short-final-ending group.

"Take a look at some of the examples you have collected, and those hanging around the room," you now suggest. "Turn to your partner and talk about which ones you would group together." As students briefly (two minutes, max) discuss, listen in to gauge their understanding and briefly share what you have overheard.

"Today you will have a shorter time than usual to work with your partners," you might conclude, "just long enough to start looking at examples and grouping them into categories. In ten minutes I'll be calling you back to the meeting area. Together we'll agree on some big ideas about how authors use internal punctuation."

Independent Work

As partners start grouping examples, briefly pop in on as many of their conversations as possible. Making generalizations (i.e., coming up with names for categories) will most likely be difficult for them; don't hesitate to jump in with suggestions. Also, remind students to make notes in their reading journals to prepare for the share, and decide ahead of time which students to call on first to get the discussion rolling.

Share Session

Today's share is more guided than usual. You will need to take an active role in naming categories and suggesting which examples should go together. This requires a sensitive balance of listening and leading. While remaining open to children's ideas, you'll need to guide them to think about internal punctuation in specific ways, including:

- Where we pause, and for how long.
- The length of different parts of the sentence (two long phrases, then a short one; a short phrase at the beginning followed by one slightly longer; etc.).
- Pacing (how quickly or slowly we say particular parts of a sentence).
- Dynamics (how loudly or softly we say certain words or phrases, and the way the voice rises or falls).
- Mood (scary, calm, tense, exciting, etc.).
- Emphasis (which part is most important).

You'll want to record children's ideas from this conversation in order to make a We've Noticed Internal Punctuation Can Affect . . . chart for the classroom. While you are leading the discussion, take notes on a clipboard or notepad. Later, after the share is over, create the chart, concentrating on wording things clearly, writing legibly, etc. Remember to give credit to as many students as possible by putting their names next to their ideas. This chart plays an important role in future lessons, as you refer to and add to it in order to come up with ideas for your own model writing.

Drum Language and Cadence: Breaking Sentences into Parts

Rationale/Purpose In the earlier lessons, students began thinking about how internal punctuation affects the way we read and understand. Most of these conversations had to do with pauses and voice modulation. They are now ready to go further, focusing on the way internal punctuation breaks sentences into parts of different lengths, some longer, some shorter. When we read these separate parts, sometimes slowly and sometimes quickly, together with pauses and a rising and falling of the voice, the words take on a rhythm. This rhythm, or *drum language*, is often what we are noticing when a sentence or passage flows clearly and naturally or "just doesn't sound right." It is one of the most important things a writer must think about, and one of the most important reasons to experiment with internal punctuation.

Looking at how punctuation breaks sentences into parts will lead naturally to a discussion of varied sentence length—the way a short sentence sets us up for a longer one, etc. This attention to the sound of language is what writers refer to as *cadence*, or *prosody*.

Materials/ Preparation

Teacher:

- Blank chart paper and markers.
- Two passages (see next page), one from "The Last Kiss," by Ralph Fletcher, the other from *A Barrel of Laughs, a Vale of Tears*, by Jules Feiffer (or other passages from books of your own choosing), copied separately on chart paper or a transparency.
- A few blank overhead transparencies and markers, to be used by students selected for the share.

Students:

- Reading notebooks and writing utensils.
- Independent reading books.
- Sticky notes for marking passages.

Summary

You will first acknowledge the good work students have done reflecting on internal punctuation and how it affects our reading. The next step is to examine the way it breaks sentences into parts, creating a rhythm that "sounds right" and helps a reader understand.

Sample Language/ Sequence

"We have begun thinking about what internal punctuation makes us do as readers," you might begin. "It causes our voices to rise and fall, makes us slow down or speed up, and tells us to pause in certain spots, for different lengths of time. When an author puts in these pauses, it breaks up the sentences into parts. Today we are going to look at how breaking sentences into parts, together with all the things internal punctuation makes our voice do, gives writing a rhythm. It may sound funny, but learning about this will help us notice good writing when we read it. It will also give us a tool to make our own writing sound better."

Read aloud the first passage from "The Last Kiss" as students follow along, calling attention to the final sentence.

> My childhood had symmetry. Teeth brushed morning and night. Good deeds and sin. The bus to school and the bus back home. Chores and play, light and dark, inside and out.

"Notice the first few sentences are pretty short, just four or five words," you can point out. "Then the second to last one, about the bus, is a little longer. It's sometimes helpful to imagine the rhythm of a sentence without the words, using what I like to call *drum language*. In drum language *the bus to school and the bus back home* would be *da dut-de-duh, de-de dut-de-duh*. This rhythm gets us ready for the last sentence, which has three sections—*chores and play/light and dark/inside and out*. The commas tell us to pause between each section, which gives it a singsongy feeling—*dut de-duh/dut de-duh/dut-dut de-duh*. So you see when authors use different sentence lengths and break sentences into parts with internal punctuation, it gives their writing a certain rhythm. That rhythm, together with the rise and fall of your voice as you say the words, is what writers call *cadence*."

Next, ask students to think with a partner about how breaking sentences into parts creates a rhythm as they look at another passage, this one from Jules Feiffer's *A Barrel of Laughs, a Vale of Tears*.

> To and fro he swung in space, in a rhythm that was syncopated with the clicking of his teeth. To and fro, back and forth, body swinging, teeth clicking. In the blackness of the night, knowing nothing of where he was—how high, how low?—Roger felt strangely secure, like an infant in a cradle.

After reading the passage aloud as students look at the chart or transparency, ask them to turn and talk with a partner about the second sentence, specifically noticing:

- How many sections is it broken into?

- How would this sentence sound in drum language (the rhythm of the sentence without the words)?

- What do you notice about the way the different sections sound in drum language? Are they the same, longer, shorter?

- What do you notice about the length of the sentences that come before and after? Do they affect the way we read the second sentence?

Once again, circulate and listen in as students have brief discussions (one or two minutes), in order to weave some of their observations into your instructions for today's independent work. "David and Georgia counted four sections!" you might say. "Lily and Kofi noticed that the first two sections—*to and fro, back and forth*—sound exactly the same in drum language—*dut de-duh, dut de-duh*. Joanne and Ralph said the same thing, but also pointed out that the third section, *body swinging*, is just a little longer, which changes the rhythm—*dut de duh-duh*. They also said the commas create the same-length pause, a short one, between each part. Interesting how Jules Feiffer chose not to use any other sort of internal punctuation, only commas—he must have wanted it to feel like it was repeating.

"Today as you read," you might conclude, "be on the lookout for the rhythm of the words. Of course, you will want to focus on internal punctuation, but also notice how long and short the sentences are before and after. When you find a passage where sentences are broken into separate parts, mark it with a sticky note. You and your partner will get a chance before the end of today's workshop to try it in drum language and think about how it sounds."

Independent Work Observe students carefully as you confer, gauging their understanding of the concepts addressed in today's lesson. Some readers take more readily to the idea of rhythm in writing than others, and no doubt a number of students will need coaching to reinforce the unusual notion of drum language. You should differentiate students' independent work accordingly—some students may just look for sentences with two, three, or four sections, while others go the next step and try saying the rhythm of the sentence out loud. Trying this drum language out loud along with your students reinforces the notion that there is no one correct answer.

Questions you might ask during your independent reading conferences include:

- Which parts stick out in your mind when you think back on the story so far? Let's look carefully at the sentences in those parts. Which ones have more than one section? What is their rhythm?

- Are all the pauses in this sentence the same length? How can you tell if one is longer or shorter? What does that tell you about the difference between a comma/colon/semicolon/dash?

Questions you might ask partners who are sharing their findings include:

- Are all the sections in this sentence equally long? How does the difference in length affect the rhythm of the sentence?
- What is the feeling of the drum language, or rhythm, in this sentence/passage? Is it happy? Does it show nervousness/fear/surprise? Why?
- What do you notice about the sentences leading up to the one you are focusing on? How do they get us ready for this sentence?

Choose particular students in advance to share. Be inclusive: include students who just talk about the number of sections in their sentence, and others who feel comfortable talking about the rhythm, or drum language. To prepare for the share, you will need to:

- Ask them to copy their passage onto a transparency so that other students can follow along as they discuss their thinking.
- Have them rehearse what they will say to the class, including reciting the drum language of their sentence/passage. (You may want to do this along with them.)

Share Session

Ask partners to read their examples aloud as their classmates follow along on a transparency. Vocalizing the rhythm of sentences without the words is a new idea, and it's a safe bet there will be giggling along the way. Your job is to create an environment where students feel safe to share; stress that there is no one correct answer, applaud their efforts, and put yourself on the line by trying out the drum language as well.

End the share session by urging students to be conscious of the rhythms used by authors of the books they are reading and to start thinking about these ideas in their own writing. "When you come across internal punctuation in authors you are reading," you might say, "notice how they break up their sentences. Do they mix up long and short sections? Do some parts sound smoother than other parts? Once we start to think about this in our reading, we should get ideas for making our own writing sound more interesting."

Possible Follow-Up Activities

For homework, students may look back over their favorite books for passages that use internal punctuation to break sentences into parts. They can reflect on the effect this has on the way they read the passage, noticing:

- The balance of long and short sections.
- Whether the sound of the sentence is choppy, singsongy, upbeat, drawn-out, etc., and how this affects our understanding.

Messing Around in Your Writer's Notebook

Rationale/Purpose   Lucy Calkins (1994) has said that our goal as teachers of literacy is to help children learn to write like readers and read like writers. The first several lessons of this unit, in which students examine the effect internal punctuation has on the comprehension of text, take place in reading workshop. At this point you will switch gears and continue the study in writing workshop, incorporating the reflections undertaken as readers and making new connections. As in most writing units, students begin by first experimenting in notebooks, the goal being to use internal punctuation in new ways.

Materials/
Preparation   Teacher:

- A chart, Reasons Writers Mess with Punctuation, summarized from class conversations (see example on the next page).

- The chart from Lesson 4.

- Posters, sentence strips, and charts of internal punctuation the class has noticed so far, displayed in the classroom.

- An old entry from your own writer's notebook (copied onto a chart or transparency or scanned onto a SMART Board).

- Blank chart paper and markers.

Students:

- Writer's notebooks and writing utensils.

Summary   You will make generalizations about the internal punctuation noticed so far and then model:

- Reflecting on how to use what you have noticed about internal punctuation in your own writing and setting goals for what to try.

- Reworking an entry from your writer's notebook with new punctuation.

Students then:

- Come up with punctuation goals for themselves.

- Choose an entry from their notebook to use in experimenting with internal punctuation.

- Rewrite this entry, trying out new ways of using punctuation.

Sample Language/ Sequence

Once students are settled in the meeting area with their writer's notebooks, begin by acknowledging the good work they have done in filling the room with examples of interesting internal punctuation. "Now that we have surrounded ourselves with posters/ sentence strips," you might say, "we are ready to use them as inspiration and try out new ways of using internal punctuation in our own writing. In our chart from Lesson 4, we came up with several different reasons writers mess around with internal punctuation. This list summarizes what we've talked about."

Ideally, you want the wording of the list to reflect previous class conversations. Here's an example of how it might look:

Reasons Writers Mess Around with Internal Punctuation

1. To divide sentences into parts.
2. To emphasize or set off certain parts.
3. To play with the rhythm of words—*drum language*.
4. To affect the sound, or *cadence*, of the words (how we read it out loud):
   Pacing—slowly, quickly.
   Dynamics—loudly, softly.
   Rise and fall of the voice.
   Smooth, choppy.
5. To create a certain mood—scary, romantic, excited, etc.

While reading through the list, point out passages displayed around the room that illustrate each idea. "Since we've identified these different categories and surrounded ourselves with examples," you might say, "it's time to experiment with internal punctuation ourselves. By practicing this way, we'll get better at using punctuation in our writing— not just knowing the rules, but working with rhythm and mood and sound and meaning. Since we want to be able to concentrate just on our punctuation experiments, it makes sense to choose an old notebook entry to work on—that way we won't have to come up with a whole new subject to write about. First I'll show you how I do this, then you'll try it on your own."

Model choosing an entry from your own notebook, taking care to rule one or more out. "There's not enough action in this entry," you might say, or, "This already has a suspenseful mood, and I can't think of a different way to write it." The important thing is to demonstrate looking and evaluating, not just picking the first entry you come to. (Of course, you'll preselect an appropriate passage to work on and plan the think-aloud in advance. If possible, have transparencies of several entries prepared, so you can replicate the process of flipping through your notebook as you decide.)

After settling on an entry, continue to display it as you think aloud and experiment with its internal punctuation. (Ideally, although you'll plan this out ahead of time, act it out in class for students to observe; a less effective option is to use prewritten passages and explain what you've already done.) *Emphasize that changing punctuation involves changing the text as well; in most cases it is difficult or impossible to alter punctuation without largely rewriting.*

> **Original Writer's Notebook Entry**
> Mrs. Whipple walks slowly, like it takes such effort to move one leg, the other. Her dresses are long and ancient, her face is wrinkled and timeless, shopping every now and then on the avenue like it is a big social occasion, all alone. Her creaky porch is a dirty, dark green with paint chips flaking. It seems hundreds of years old, spider webs tangled from the doorway to the supporting columns.

"This entry, about my neighbor Mrs. Whipple," you might say, "should work well for rewriting. I wrote it a long time ago and really overdid the commas. In fact I didn't use any other types of internal punctuation at all! Besides, it would be fun to show how slowly Mrs. Whipple moves, and the way my thoughts about her seem to pop up, using some of the ideas we've talked about."

Using chart paper or an overhead transparency, write a new version of the notebook entry, thinking aloud as you go. "First of all," you might say, "I'd like to show how Mrs. Whipple's walking stops and starts. To do that, I'll start with short sentences—some of the words can come from my old entry. I'll use a comma when I explain the walking, to show how my thoughts follow one after the other—like the way her feet move!"

> Mrs. Whipple walks. Slowly. It takes such effort, so much work.

"Next," you could continue, "I'll use ellipses to give the reader a feeling of how slowly she moves."

> Mrs. Whipple walks. Slowly. It takes such effort, so much work. First one leg . . . then the other leg . . . then the first, again.

"I like that comma after the word *first*—it shows she has to keep working at it! Now I want to give some information about how she looks and make it seem like I'm thinking of things first, and explaining them after. Colons could work well for that. I'll definitely have to rewrite some of the words, though."

> Mrs. Whipple walks. Slowly. It takes such effort, so much work. First one leg . . . then the other leg . . . then the first, again. Her dresses: long and ancient. Her face: wrinkled but also beautiful, like a wise woman from a mysterious tribe.

"Now I want to list some of the things she does so a reader can picture the way she moves—so I'll use commas. It could be interesting to start that way and then interrupt the description with my thoughts. A dash is good for making it feel like an interruption."

> Mrs. Whipple walks. Slowly. It takes such effort, so much work. First one leg . . . then the other leg . . . then the first, again. Her dresses: long and ancient. Her face: wrinkled but also beautiful, like some wise woman from a mysterious tribe. Shopping on the avenue, walking to her mailbox, watering the plants on the porch—you always wonder if she's going to make it to the finish line.

"Now that you've watched me do this work," you continue, "take a minute to look over the entries in your writer's notebook. Pick at least one that would *not* be a good choice for messing around with punctuation. Then look carefully and find another entry that *would* be a good one to rewrite, trying out new internal punctuation. When you've found it, make some notes about the type of punctuation you'd like to try."

Observe students as they work and ask questions about their decision making ("Why would this one *not* work?" "What new punctuation will you try here?" etc.). After a few minutes, briefly share one or two of these conversations. "Remember," you might say, calling attention to the chart from earlier in the lesson, "the important thing today is not to use punctuation perfectly. We want to try using it in ways that affect how our piece is read aloud, its rhythm, its mood, and how it is broken into parts. Doing this will give us new tools to use as writers."

Independent Work   It is likely that some students will still be deciding which entry to work with while others are ready to begin writing. Questions you might ask in conferences with students who have not yet chosen include:

- Can you find an entry that has some very fast action? Which part describes that action? How could different punctuation make it feel even faster?

- Show me an entry where you tried to make a part really suspenseful. How could different punctuation put the reader even more on the edge of his or her seat?

- Which entry describes an instance where you had to wait a very long time and were impatient or bored? Could you use punctuation in that part to really make the reader feel your pain?

Once all the students are writing, remind them that to experiment effectively they must change the words, not just insert new punctuation. Possible prompts or questions include:

- Where's the least interesting writing in this entry? Let's try rewriting it three different ways, each time using other punctuation.

- Is there a certain place you'd like the reader's voice to get louder/softer/smoother/choppier?

- Which pauses in this entry are you least satisfied with? Try rewriting those parts.

- Where's a place in this entry (or elsewhere in your notebook) you succeeded in writing some nice rhythms, or drum language? Where's a place you didn't do as well? What did you do in the more successful part? Can you try doing something similar with this passage? Try it a couple different ways in your notebook and decide.

- Are there any passages on the wall that we studied and made theories about that you particularly like? Try writing a passage where the punctuation works the same way.

You may want to read some students' experiments aloud, to create buzz in the classroom and give ideas to writers who are stuck. (Remember to include the before-and-after versions, to reinforce the notion that writers are rethinking their language and punctuation.) While circulating and conferring, note the types of things students are trying in order to better determine which areas to address in future minilessons or small-group work (e.g., if all students are attempting to speed passages up, we might model slowing down; if many are trying to change mood we may want to call attention to rhythm).

Select students to share who are trying a variety of ideas, in order to open up possibilities for others. If you choose one student who is experimenting with mood, you'll also want to hear from another who is working on pacing, etc. These experiments need to be seen as well as heard, so ask the writers who are going to share first to copy their passages onto transparencies or chart paper. To build momentum in this first writing lesson, it helps to choose students who can read aloud expressively (alternatively, you can ask permission to read aloud for them). In either case they need to share not only their writing but also what they were trying to do as writers (slow it down, speed it up, make it more suspenseful, make the reader's voice rise or fall on a particular word, etc.).

Share Session

In order to make this share as valuable as possible:

- Take an active role in naming the work writers are trying.

- Record and display ideas students have shared, for their classmates to refer to as the unit progresses.

- Create (insist on!) a safe environment in which students feel comfortable reading their work aloud expressively, illustrating rhythm, cadence (rise and fall), pacing (speed), and mood created by internal punctuation.

As students show their writing on transparencies or charts and explain their thinking, name and record their ideas on a list or chart. For example, if a student describes an attempt to "make it feel more nervous," you might say, "Sasha is thinking that interrupting a passage with dashes here and there can create a feeling of nervousness, by making the reader feel like the words are stopping and starting. Would you agree that the pause created by a dash is less smooth than one you get from a comma? So sprinkling dashes throughout is sure to create a jerky, nervous feeling." To follow up, you might write on the chart, *Nervous feeling—interrupt with dashes more than once*, and copy down Sasha's passage as an example following the explanation. (It is often a good idea to jot down these notes on a pad or clipboard while the lesson is in progress and create the display chart later when you can concentrate on writing more legibly!)

Each shared passage should be read aloud with expression, by the writer or by you. Though you want to encourage students to have fun with their experiments (it would be difficult to do this lesson with absolutely no laughter), it is important as well to discuss seriously the effect their punctuation ideas have on the quality of their writing.

Possible Follow-Up Activities	Once the door has been opened, students may want to rewrite other entries from their writer's notebook. Variations on this activity could include:

- Rewriting the same entry more than once, trying out different internal punctuation each time. (Students might enjoy reading each aloud expressively to a friend and getting his or her opinions about which works best and why.)
- Rewriting another student's entry using different internal punctuation.
- Rewriting a favorite passage from a book.

Assessment	Certainly the most meaningful assessment of how students are internalizing this new expressive angle on internal punctuation is to look over their writer's notebooks and gauge the effect it has had on their independent writing. At first writers will probably overdo it, using way too much punctuation in an effort to add drama to their writing. This is a good sign, however, indicating a newfound passion for punctuation (!) and using punctuation as an expressive tool.

Punctuation Possibilities:
Collecting Ideas in Your Writer's Notebook

Rationale/Purpose At this point, children have had opportunities to:

1. Look at lots of examples of interesting internal punctuation.

2. Reflect on how punctuation affects a reader's understanding—rhythm, mood, emphasis, the sound or *cadence* of language, etc.

3. Mess around with punctuation themselves in their writer's notebook.

Now it's time for them to try out what they have learned in a piece of published writing. This lesson introduces a new writing/publishing cycle. Students may choose whatever genre of prose they like, as long as they try out as many new ways of using internal punctuation as possible.

They begin collecting ideas for topics that lend themselves to experimenting in this way by conducting a *punctuation notebook dig*—looking at old entries and letting the words generate ideas for new topics with interesting punctuation possibilities. Depending on time, they may or may not begin writing these entries but should end the lesson with a list of ideas for future work.

Materials/ Preparation Teacher:

- Two old entries from your own writer's notebook (one to rule out, the other to use in modeling—ideally ones children have seen before), copied onto chart paper, a transparency, or a SMART Board.

- Markers.

Students:

- Writer's notebooks and writing utensils.

Summary The notion of coming up with topics in connection with punctuation goals will be foreign to most students. Consequently, how you think aloud when you model the process is very important. Although you want to appear to be thinking in the moment, where and when you stop and jot down ideas should be carefully planned. Consider:

- Various punctuation possibilities (stretched-out phrases, fast-moving action, singsongy language, etc.).

- Various genres (personal narrative, essay, realistic fiction, etc.).

- Various types of words and phrases that trigger ideas (a piece of dialogue, poetic language, beginning or end of a sentence, etc.).

"Now that we've had so many conversations about internal punctuation and messed around with some old entries," you might begin, "it's time to go one step further and come up with new ideas for writing to try out all we've noticed. Today we'll generate ideas for punctuation pieces, so we can get some new entries in our notebooks. It doesn't matter what type of writing we end up deciding to publish—a story, an essay, an article— as long as we use lots of new internal punctuation and think about the *cadence,* or sound of the piece. To help us think of some topics, we will do a *punctuation notebook dig*—we'll look back at an old entry and let certain words give us ideas for new writing. The entry we choose might not be our favorite piece of writing, but it must have words that suggest new pieces in which we can concentrate on punctuation and cadence. Watch me demonstrate how to generate ideas for a punctuation piece with one of my own notebook entries."

Start by ruling out an entry, to discourage students from choosing the first one they come to. After reading a few lines out loud you might say, "I like the story in this one, but there aren't enough spicy words to give me ideas for new topics. I'll have to keep looking."

Display another entry and skim through it, thinking aloud about whether the words are inspiring. "In this one I tried to write in the voice of my best friend when I was little," you could reflect. "It probably has some interesting words, since he was always making up stories just to scare me. I see *German Shepherd* and *vampire* and *in disguise*—all good words to get ideas from. I think I'll use this entry for my punctuation notebook dig."

My Friend Dan Talks

You don't know this 'cause you're too little but you know the Schwartzes? That big dog? Stay away from that big dog. It's a German Shepherd, and German Shepherds are poisonous. They could kill you if they bite you.

You know Holder's Candy Store? Well, Mr. Holder is always in a bad mood, right? That's 'cause his daughter is a vampire. They're real, grownups just tell you they're made up. The metal door in the sidewalk that goes underground, it leads to a dungeon. His daughter's coffin is down there. She only comes out at night.

And Mrs. Whipple, in the green house, is a witch. There are bodies buried in her backyard. For real. All those cats she has have powers—they're witches too, in disguise. They can do that.

Read through your entry and think aloud about which words trigger ideas, circling or underlining particular words or phrases and drawing a line to the margin, where you'll write a few words explaining your idea, including the punctuation you want to try. "I like the phrase *stay away from that,*" you might say, "it makes me think of all the times my parents wouldn't let me do things! I could write about that, using punctuation to show how I'd start to do something and then suddenly be stopped by my mom or dad. So I'll circle those words and write, *Parents not letting me do things—punctuation to show stopping and starting.* Next, I see the word *poisonous.* I've always liked snakes, and think it's unfair that some people say bad things about them and call them poisonous even when they're not. Maybe I could write an essay called 'Unfair to Snakes!' and use punctuation to first make it seem scary—some ellipses to show a snake creeping up, perhaps—and then maybe some dashes to set off surprising, important information about the good things snakes do. So I'll circle *poisonous* and write, '*Unfair to Snakes!*' *essay—ellipses for scary parts, dashes for surprising info.*"

After coming up with three or four varied ideas, ask students to look in their notebook and first rule out an entry, then choose one to use for their punctuation notebook dig. "Once you've done this," you can instruct, "turn to a partner and explain why you ruled out the first one, and what made you choose the second." As writers briefly (a minute or two) discuss their decisions, circulate and listen in, noting interesting comments that could help them when they're working independently. "It was interesting to hear how Celine ruled out an entry about her dog, even though it had some interesting descriptions," you might mention, "since it didn't remind her of anything new and she didn't want to do another dog story. She ended up choosing another entry about feeling sad when her friend moved away, since some of the poetic language gave her ideas."

Then send students off to work independently, reminding them that once they finish hunting for ideas they may start writing. "You need to come up with at least five different ideas," you might conclude. "More would be better. Feel free to use a few different notebook entries for your dig if you like—the important thing is to think of lots of possibilities for punctuation pieces. If you finish, get started writing—but don't worry if you want to spend the entire period just gathering ideas. You'll want to have many to choose from over the next couple of days."

Independent Work   As students read through their writer's notebook and come up with ideas, your job is to be both cheerleader and coach. Some writers will take right away to the idea of thinking ahead about punctuation; others will have difficulty. Where children are able to come up with ideas but are confused about how to plan for punctuation, coach them by suggesting possibilities:

You: How do you want your reader to feel when reading this piece?

Student A: Nervous.

You: What about using dashes as interruptions, to break up short sections in sentences? That could leave the reader feeling unsettled and nervous.

Student B: Calm.

You: You may want to use long sentences, with sections broken up by commas, since we know that creates a smoother kind of pause.

Student C: Sad.

You: Using ellipses to have sentences drift off in the middle could make it feel sad. You may also want to use short sentences with very little punctuation so it feels kind of dry, with occasional long ones that list sad feelings, maybe separated by commas.

Student D: I want it to be funny.

You: Using lots of different internal punctuation could help with that—colons, commas, ellipses, parentheses, just to keep it surprising. Another idea is sometimes to unexpectedly put ending punctuation in the middle of sentences—like in the Lemony Snicket books when he uses sound effects with exclamation marks in the middle of sentences.

Throughout the independent work session, be a cheerleader as well, periodically sharing/ celebrating ideas children are coming up with. Besides building confidence and enthusiasm, this gives students ideas and allows you to connect children with classmates who have similar thoughts on punctuation possibilities ("Why not talk to Francisco about that? He is thinking about doing a cliff-hanger sports story too, and had some good ideas for using punctuation to make readers feel on the edge of their seats.")

While circulating, think ahead about which students should share, choosing a cross section of those writing in varied genres and using different kinds of punctuation.

Share Session

The main objective in this lesson is to come up with a variety of ideas for notebook entries and encourage children to approach their punctuation experiments with an intrepid spirit. Therefore, many students should share, each presenting one or two ideas. Preselecting writers to participate will ensure that students will encounter varied genres and many different ideas about how to use internal punctuation.

Possible Follow-Up Activities

The next couple of writing workshops (and writing homework assignments) should be devoted to trying out several of the ideas students have come up with in this lesson as notebook entries. (See the assessment section below for more on this important step in the writing cycle.)

Though you want to encourage children to use their own writing as a source for ideas, they may also try a punctuation dig with a page from a favorite author or magazine. Another possibility would be to trade notebooks with a partner and come up with ideas from his or her writing.

Assessment

As students begin to generate entries as homework and during the next couple of writing workshops, check their notebooks regularly, both to gauge understanding and gather student examples to use in your minilessons. You could take a couple home each night or look them over during your preparation periods, writing encouraging comments on sticky notes and duplicating excerpts to share with the class.

Punctuation Up Close: Mentor Sentences

When I sketch a great painting at the museum, I see things in it that aren't obvious at first glance. For example, I may notice how the edge of an object on one side creates an imaginary line to a shape on the other side. This alignment brings a sense of order I hadn't been conscious of just from looking, that creates harmony in the composition. I marvel at what's happening below the surface and realize I can do the same thing in my own work.
—Steve Ninteman, painter

But it is different to pay attention to how writers write at the sentence level. This means paying attention to the order and effect of words and punctuation, to the startling and evocative ways that some writers put these together. It means that we ask students to apprentice themselves in smaller, closer ways, so that they may generate only a sentence or two, but they consider carefully the placement of every word and mark.
—Mary Ehrenworth and Vicki Vinton

Rationale/Purpose

In their seminal book *The Power of Grammar* (2005), Mary Ehrenworth and Vicki Vinton propose that one powerful way for students to become better writers is to apprentice themselves to mentor passages in published books. In other words, students look closely at the way a particular sentence or passage is put together—its punctuation, its rhythm, how long or short, the meaning of each section of the sentence—and try writing something of their own that imitates this model. In literature classes this approach is called a *close reading*; but we seldom employ it at the word level, let alone in thinking about punctuation. Nevertheless, carefully considering one sentence can develop habits of mind that carry over to many sentences.

**Materials/
Preparation**

Teacher:
- Two mentor sentences, preferably drawn from a recent read-aloud or the sentence strips displayed in the classroom (see the examples on the next page).
- One of your own notebook entries, reproduced on chart paper or a transparency.
- Blank transparencies or chart paper.

Students:

- Writer's notebooks, with passages of interesting punctuation copied from earlier in the unit.

- Writing utensils and markers.

- *Optional:* Blank transparencies on which to copy work that will be shared.

Summary

In this lesson you model another strategy for experimenting with punctuation, building on earlier lessons. Earlier in the unit, students closely examined punctuation in passages from their reading and came up with theories about the author's intent. Here you take this idea one step further, imitating the structure of particular sentences. As always, first model and think aloud so students can see the process at work. Then have students try it on their own, either rewriting a passage from an old entry or starting with a new idea, perhaps one from the punctuation notebook dig.

Sample Language/ Sequence

"One way people learn to draw," you might begin, "is to copy the work of master artists, to see how they think and work. As writers learning about punctuation and cadence, it may help us to do the same thing with the work of great writers. Today we will pick sentences that inspire us and copy their structure; they will be our mentor sentences. In other words, we will write sentences just like them, substituting our own words and ideas. Watch as I demonstrate." Display the two mentor sentences you've chosen.

> **Mentor Sentences**
> Roger felt strangely secure, like an infant in a cradle. True, he was exhausted; true, his life hung by a thread.
>
> —Jules Feiffer, *A Barrel of Laughs, a Vale of Tears*
>
> Mig did not wave back; instead, she stood and watched, open-mouthed, as the perfect, beautiful family passed her by.
>
> —Kate DiCamillo, *The Tale of Despereaux*

"These are two passages I've collected in our study that inspire me," you'll think aloud. "They will be my mentor sentences. I love the way Jules Feiffer starts by telling how Roger felt, then pauses slightly with the comma and compares it to 'an infant in a cradle.' The pause of the comma makes the comparison more poetic and thoughtful. Then he divides the second sentence with a semicolon, which is a longer, more significant pause. The word *true* seems to announce each part, followed by a short breath—again indicated by the comma. The two parts of the sentence sound the same, and each has to do with Roger—but the first is about how he's feeling, and the second tells his situation. Feiffer is combining two ideas that go together but aren't quite the same. The drum language is different too; it goes on a little longer in the part after the semicolon. *Duh/duh-de-duh dut duh; duh/de-duh dut-de-duh-duh.* The shorter rhythm of the first half prepares you for the longer rhythm of the second."

The next step is to reflect on how to imitate the structure of the mentor sentence in your own writing. This can be done using a new idea or by rewriting a passage from an old piece of writing.

> **Notebook Example**
> Jeremy's four-year-old face is tear stained and flushed with rage. "GIVE IT BACK!" he yells. I dance around him, eight years old and tall enough to hold the stuffed animal just out of reach. At the same time I am thinking how cruel this is, why am I torturing him? But it's as if there are two people inside me—one who needs to tease his brother, and the other who is watching somebody else be so horribly mean. "MON-KEY MOE! Moooon-key!" I sing in a mocking voice.

"Looking back at my old notebook entries," you might say, "I see this one about teasing my little brother over his stuffed monkey. The funny thing was, at the same time I was doing it, I felt bad about it. These two things were both in my head, even though they were different feelings. It could be interesting to write a passage like Jules Feiffer's, using the semicolon to connect these seemingly opposite ideas. I'll need to decide where that would fit best. It wouldn't work right at the beginning, since the reader will need to understand a little about what is going on. I could put it in just after the sentence about 'watching somebody else be so horribly mean,' before the bit where I sing the Monkey Moe song." You may want to insert an asterisk at this spot, to make your intentions clear:

> But it's as if there are two people inside me—one who needs to tease his brother, and the other who is watching somebody else be so horribly mean.* "MON-KEY MOE! Moooon-key!" I sing in a mocking voice.

"In his passage," you continue, "Feiffer begins by telling how Roger feels and then comparing it to something. So I'll try the same with my feelings as I torture my brother Jeremy." On a blank transparency, chart paper, or a SMART Board write:

> I feel oddly unconscious, like a mummy sleepwalking.

"In Feiffer, that sentence prepares us for the one with the semicolons, where the two parts sound sort of the same. The first part tells how he is feeling, so I'll begin with that."

> Yes, I know it is wrong;

"The second part starts the same as the first, but in drum language it's a little longer. I think I will mess around with Feiffer's idea a little here—the second part will start with a one-syllable announcement, but it won't be exactly the same word."

> Yes, I know it is wrong; no, I cannot seem to stop myself.

"Now let's read the whole thing with my new sentence inserted, and see how it sounds."

> Jeremy's four-year-old face is tear stained and flushed with rage. "GIVE IT BACK!" he yells. I dance around him, eight years old and tall enough to hold the stuffed animal just out of reach. At the same time I am thinking how cruel this is, why am I torturing him? But it's as if there are two people inside me—one who needs to tease his brother, and the other who is watching somebody else be so horribly mean. *I feel oddly unconscious, like a mummy sleepwalking. Yes, I know it is wrong; no, I cannot seem to stop myself.* "MON-KEY MOE! Moooon-key!" I sing in a mocking voice.

Now that you have modeled the process, give students a chance to try it before going off to work independently. "Let's look at my other sentence, from *The Tale of Despereaux,*" you might say. "What is the first part about, and what does the semicolon do? What happens after the semicolon, and how do the commas divide that section? Turn to a partner and talk about what Kate DiCamillo did with this sentence."

As students briefly (a minute or two) discuss "the placement of every word or mark" in this sentence, eavesdrop and note their ideas. "Alex and Tess discussed how short the first section is and right to the point—*Mig did not wave back*—it tells you what she didn't do. Then Nathan and Ava pointed out that after the long pause of the semicolon, the commas do many different things. They create little pauses; they set off details, like how Mig stood and watched *open mouthed*; and they make lists, like *perfect, beautiful.* Put together, the second section gets across the rush of Mig's feelings by adding so many details at once, with just the slight pauses of the commas to connect them."

Conduct a brief shared writing activity in which you help the class construct a sentence modeled on this one. "Together, let's follow Kate DiCamillo's example and write a sentence describing the time we all went to the planetarium and couldn't take our eyes off the star show. How shall we begin? Remember, we want the first part to be short, and it should say what we *didn't* do."

After the class has composed a sentence together, remind them what they are expected to do independently. "First, you will need to choose at least two mentor sentences. These may be ones you gathered yourself, they may be ones classmates brought in that inspired you, or they may be from a book you read last night. The important thing is, they should use punctuation and cadence in a way you'd like to try in your own writing. Next, write sentences in your notebook modeled on the ones you have chosen. Your sentences can be added to an old entry, as you watched me do, or be about something completely new, as we did together. By copying the sentences of expert writers, we will begin to see details of how they put words and punctuation together—and learn from them so we can become better writers ourselves."

Independent Work   As students begin their independent work, monitor their choices of mentor sentences. Pick out a few examples ahead of time, preferably from familiar texts (read-alouds or books the class knows), that you can give to students who are struggling. The important element of this lesson is the writing; we don't want students to feel stressed because they cannot decide on a sentence.

Once writers are working on their own sentences, ask them to explain their thinking in your individual conferences, pushing them to go further with particularly good ideas. With stronger writers, you can speak broadly and ask them to make their own associations. With students having a harder time, you may need to be more specific in your suggestions. (For example: "This pair of commas in your mentor sentence is inserting information about the expression on the girl's face. How might you use a pair of commas in your sentence to add something about the look on your mom's face when she got home?") Questions/suggestions you might pose include:

- What is your mentor sentence about? When is a time you felt that way? Perhaps your sentence can be about a similar experience.

- Let's look at the different sections of your mentor sentence. Why do you think the punctuation separates them like that? Usually the parts of a sentence are about slightly different things that go together. How can you separate your ideas in the same way?

As you circulate and choose students to share, you may want to have them copy their sentences and mentor passages on overhead transparencies so others can see exactly what they have done.

Share Session   Depending on your students' level of comfort and understanding (which you can gauge during individual conferences), the share can be conducted in two slightly different ways:

- If students seem comfortable with the idea of imitating a model passage, the most valuable thing might be to expose them to as much variety as possible. In this case, you could opt for a simple round-robin share, with many students (selected ahead of time) sharing one after the other, presenting first the mentor sentence and then their own writing.

- If it seems that a significant percentage of students are having difficulty, you may choose two or three writers who "got it" to explain the thinking behind their writing in more detail. In this case, you will want to help them rehearse what to say, so it comes out clearly and no one succumbs to stage fright.

Say It with Feeling: Using Punctuation to Show Emotion

Rationale/Purpose Children who have been participating in writing workshops for any length of time know the importance of choosing topics they feel strongly about. One of the most concrete entry points for thinking about punctuation as a craft tool is the idea that it can very effectively express a range of emotions. This lesson, developed by fifth-grade teacher Alexandra Marron, asks students to connect their new thinking about internal punctuation to the familiar notion of writing from and about a strong feeling.

Materials/ Preparation Teacher:

- Blank chart paper and markers.

Students:

- Writer's notebooks and writing utensils.

Summary In this lesson:

- You model experimenting with punctuation to express strong feelings in your own writing, being sure to imagine the possibilities aloud.
- Students write a notebook entry doing the same.

Sample Language/ Sequence "Today," you might begin, "we will try another way to come up with ideas for punctuation pieces. One of the things we've noticed about internal punctuation is how authors use it to express a particular mood and make the reader feel a certain way. This has a lot to do with the way it makes the words *sound* in our heads—cadence again! In our personal narrative writing, we've seen how important it is to gather ideas by thinking back to moments when we felt strong emotions. It makes sense to put these two ideas together and write about those moments while paying close attention to how punctuation can help express feelings.

"To start, I'll need to search my memory for times I've felt strong emotions and imagine the possibilities for using punctuation to show those feelings. There are all sorts of emotions I've had in my life. I've felt incredibly scared at times. I've also felt so happy that I could barely stand still. I've felt excited—really looking forward to things. And nervousness—that's something I've felt a lot."

Model considering and ruling out different emotions, in order to encourage students not to choose the first idea that comes to them. "I remember a time I felt very sad," you might continue. "It was when I first found out my grandfather had died. I remember feeling more sad than I'd ever felt in my life. Maybe I could use punctuation to make the moment slow and dragged out, since that is how it felt in my head—like time was barely moving and the whole world had come to a stop." You could jot down on chart paper, *Grandfather dying—use punctuation to slow it down, show time standing still.*

"That's one possibility," you reflect out loud, "but it could be depressing to write about, and I'd have to use too many long sentences with commas to get that drawn-out feeling. It might be more interesting to try something that allows me to use different types of punctuation. Since I'd rather not write about a sad feeling right now, maybe I should think about an opposite mood. One memory is of a time I felt pure joy and peace. My family went on a vacation for a few days last summer, and that very first time on the beach felt so magical. When I first stepped onto that warm, soft sand and felt the bright sun, it was as if every pressure in the world had slipped away. I went to the beach alone first, to really escape and be by myself. This may be a moment I could write about—not only because it is interesting and powerful for me, but because there are so many opportunities to use punctuation to show my emotions to a reader." At this point, you might jot down, *First day at beach—calm and peaceful. Punctuation to show back-and-forth sound of waves, long sentences for feeling of beach stretching out.*

"Listen and watch as I write and think aloud about using punctuation to show that feeling of peace," you could instruct. "Afterward, I'll be asking what you noticed." As you model, write on chart paper for the class to see, stopping periodically to plan the next sentence or rethink something you have just written. For example:

> *Say:* "I remember standing at the edge of the water and feeling complete calm. The sand and dunes and water seemed to go on forever. So what does this sort of peaceful feeling sound like? Well, the ocean was lapping against a nearby boat. I want to recreate that sound for my reader . . . the rhythm, which seemed so calming."

> Write: *The ocean tide came in and out, splashing softly: on the boat, back to sea, on the boat.*

> *Say:* "I like the first part of the sentence—*the ocean tide/came in and out*—in drum language, that would sound like *duh dut-de duh/duh dut-de duh*, the same rhythm twice in a row. Then the colon stops the sentence to announce the motion of the waves, and the commas make it singsongy and back-and-forth, like the ocean—*on the boat, back to sea, on the boat*—they are all the same rhythm too, which helps it feel relaxing and calm."

> Write: *I could feel the sand beneath my toes. It was warm and soft.*

Say: "I'd like to draw the reader's attention to the warmth and softness of the sand, but the short sentence seems choppy—it takes away from the feeling of calm. Maybe it'd be better if I used a dash to set those two things apart rather than a period. It's a shorter pause, so they should seem more connected. First I'll cross out the old way, and then try it like that."

Write: *I could feel the sand between my toes—warm and soft.*

Say: "What else would show a reader how peaceful I felt at that moment? I remember the ocean and sand seemed to go on forever. Maybe I can re-create that by writing a long sentence, adding in a few breaths using commas. It will have to be long and smooth."

Write: *Far in the distance were the white shores, the green rolling dunes, the salty blue waters of the sea.*

Say: "My sentence is long and stretched out, like the horizon at the beach."

After this demonstration, ask students to turn and talk about the sorts of decisions you made while writing. Be sure to bring out that in order to express emotion in your writing you thought about:

- How the parts within a sentence sound together.
- Sentence lengths.
- Drum language (rhythm).
- Lengths of pauses created by internal punctuation.

"For today's notebook entry," you might conclude, "think first of a few different moments you felt strong emotions and jot down how you might use punctuation to describe them. These notes needn't be long—think of how I did it at the beginning of the lesson. Once you have an idea, try writing an entry using punctuation and rhythm to show your feelings to a reader."

Independent Work Some students will be able to make a connection between the small-moment narrative writing they are used to doing and the more recent punctuation work. You could direct those having difficulty to try:

- *Looking at early entries in their notebook for ideas.* There is no rule against writing about familiar topics, and it can be especially helpful when students are experimenting with a new technique.
- *Reading the charts and examples on display in the classroom.* Students may benefit from examining the examples from previous lessons and identifying ones that clearly express strong emotions.

- *Working with a partner.* Another strategy is to pair two students having similar difficulties and ask them to list strong emotions together; talking with a partner sometimes helps open up children's thinking. Once the list is completed, they may think of a time in their life when they felt each emotion, perhaps even making a T-chart in their notebook. They may then choose one that most lends itself to being expressed through punctuation.

Once students are past the idea-generating stage and producing entries, your conferences can help call students' attention to areas in their writing where punctuation will work to express feelings. These may include:

- *Descriptions of settings*—a creaky, scary porch at night; the peaceful feeling of a green meadow at sunset; the nervous bustle of a town at rush hour.

- *Descriptions of how a person or thing moves*—a tree blowing during a heavy storm; the peaceful lilt of the waves; the nervous, jerky movements of a person who is uncomfortable; the comforting strokes of a grandparent when we are upset.

- *Descriptions of how a character (or object) looks*—the soft look of a mother or father; the playful expression of a friend who makes us laugh; the sharp, annoying features of someone we don't like.

As always, be on the lookout for particularly interesting examples as you confer, and warn students ahead of time so they can copy their example on the board or a transparency. Listeners need to be able to both see and hear the passage being discussed.

Share Session

Today's share should include isolated passages or sentences written by several students, as well as verbal explanations of what they were trying to accomplish with their punctuation. It may be hard for some students, even those who have succeeded in using punctuation to express emotion well, to articulate exactly what they have done. You need to play an active role during the share by naming the strategy (for example, "Sydney has used a series of dashes to show how nervous she gets around her older cousin").

Possible Follow-Up Activities

It might be useful to create a chart entitled Ways Punctuation Can Express Emotion. Include examples from student writing as well as from read-alouds and independent reading, along with explanations of the way the punctuation is used to convey a particular feeling. Add to the chart as the unit continues and students begin to draft, revise, and publish their pieces.

Which Idea Works Best? Choosing an Entry to Develop

Rationale/Purpose
By now students have collected several different ideas and spent time experimenting with internal punctuation. They have looked at the way it can affect rhythm and mood, express emotion, break up related ideas, and call attention to certain words or phrases. They have discussed how the sound of language, or cadence, influences meaning. After all this preparation, it's time to choose a notebook entry to develop and publish. To do this, students need to reflect on the work they have done so far—what has been successful, and which punctuation possibilities they would still like to explore.

Materials/Preparation
Teacher:
- Overhead transparencies or charts displaying some of your own entries, preferably ones used earlier in the unit.
- Blank transparencies or chart paper, to use in modeling two-column reflections.

Students:
- Writer's notebooks and writing utensils.
- Sticky notes.

This is another lesson that does not follow the usual workshop structure. Though it occurs within one writing period, it is divided in two parts, each a brief minilesson followed by independent work. (There is a single share at the end of the period.)

Summary, Part 1
In the first half of the lesson, students reflect on their entries so far. You'll model how to reflect on punctuation moves they've already made and set goals for future work by attaching a small two-column chart (written on a sticky note) to each entry in the notebook.

Sample Language/Sequence, Part 1
"Before choosing which entry you'd like to develop into a published piece," you might begin, "it's important to spend time looking back at the work you've done so far and reflect on which punctuation and cadence experiments have gone well. You'll also want to think of goals you still have for using internal punctuation, and which entries would be the best ones to develop to try them out. So for at least three entries, jot your ideas down on sticky notes in the form of a two-column chart, one side noting what you've done well, the other stating what you'd like to try. Listen and watch as I demonstrate with my own writing."

Show the class a notebook entry you've used in a previous lesson, and draw a two-column chart on transparency or chart paper, labeling the left-hand side Punctuation/Cadence Moves That Worked and the right-hand side Punctuation/Cadence Goals. The entry and chart need to be side by side, so you can model moving back and forth between reading and reflecting, and filling in the columns. (Be sure students understand that they will be creating the chart on sticky notes.)

Unfair to Snakes!

Slithering . . . hissing . . . twisting . . . what's that crawling across the floor? A snake! Will it bite me?! Sisters scream, mothers yell: everyone is ready for the attack of the monster.

But is it really fair?

The truth is, very few snakes in North America are poisonous; the myth of the deadly serpent is closer to a horror movie than to real life. Even more important, pet shops—those that sell snakes at all—will not let you buy an animal that could hurt you in any way.

"I think the first few lines of this entry use punctuation in interesting ways," you might begin. "The ellipses help express the way some people feel about snakes, like they are scary creatures that creep up on you. The short sentences gradually get longer, which builds the tension—*A snake!* goes to *Will it bite me?!* to *Sisters scream, mothers yell.* Then the colon brings it to a sudden stop, and announces the reason everyone is panicking. So I'm going to record that on the left-hand side of my chart, under Punctuation/Cadence Moves That Worked.

Punctuation/Cadence Moves That Worked	Punctuation/Cadence Goals
• Ellipses to show a scary, creepy feeling • Short sentences getting longer, to build tension • Colon makes sudden stop, announces reason	

"Going further with this entry, I might try listing facts I know about snakes mixed in with reasons people should think differently about them. Since semicolons can be used to show connections between ideas that seem separate, I might want to try using them to put facts together with opinions. I'll put that in the right-hand column."

Punctuation/Cadence Moves That Worked	Punctuation/Cadence Goals
• Ellipses to show a scary, creepy feeling • Short sentences getting longer, to build tension • Colon makes sudden stop, announces reason	• Use semicolons to put facts about snakes together with reasons people should think differently

To wrap up the first of your two minilessons, instruct students to reflect on their own entries and make two-column sticky notes for as many of them as possible. It may be helpful to give a minimum number: "as many entries as possible, but at least three" or whatever number you decide.

Independent Work, Part 1	Some students will be more adept than others at naming what they have tried to do with punctuation and varied sentence lengths than others. In addition to taking an active role with those having difficulty, you could pair writers strategically, asking a student who has the hang of it to work with one who doesn't.

Questions you might ask during these reflection-type conferences include:

- Would this entry be different if you mixed up the lengths of sentences (long, medium, short; one section, two, three; etc.)?

- Which internal punctuation have you not yet tried? Which entries would work best to try them?

- Are there things you've done in one entry that you may want to try in another? Which?

- Which passages displayed in our classroom give you ideas for things to try? What entries would you try them in?

After ten or fifteen minutes, once the majority of students have completed two or three sticky notes, call the class back to the meeting area.

Summary, Part 2	For your second minilesson, you will model choosing one entry to develop into a published piece, thinking aloud about:

- What topic will sustain your interest.

- Reasons to rule out one or more entries (not enough punctuation opportunities, for example).

- Punctuation moves you have applied to your entries successfully, and which new ones you'd like to try.

- The effect you'd like to have on a reader (e.g., convince them of something, make them feel sad, put them at the edge of their seats), and how punctuation can help you achieve it.

Depending on how much time you have, you may want to model ruling one entry out before deciding. In that case, you'll need to prepare two entries and sticky notes (on transparencies or chart paper) ahead of time.

Sample Language/ Sequence, Part 2	"Now that you've looked over the different entries in your notebook," you might think aloud, "it's time to make an important decision. Which one will be the most interesting to spend time on, planning, drafting, and revising? And since you will be accountable for trying out punctuation ideas we've been exploring, which will be the best for that purpose?

"I've narrowed down my choices to two: the 'Unfair to Snakes' essay, and an entry about a lucky catch I made once in a softball game. Watch as I compare them and decide which makes more sense to develop and publish."

Very first hitter, very first pitch—crack! A sharply hit line drive seemed to be moving a hundred miles an hour right toward my head. Terrified, I lifted my mitt to keep the ball from permanently injuring me. I closed my eyes.

Pop! It was the sound of the ball landing squarely in my mitt. "Nice catch!" a female voice called out. Opening my eyes, I saw the girls' gym class walking past at just that moment. My teammates cheered and gave me high fives. The gym teacher made a point of complimenting me in front of everyone. That night I got phone calls from friends in other classes who had heard about the incredible play.

Of course there was a problem with all this attention. My catch, as impressive as it was, could not be chalked up to skill. The fact was—I could not tell a lie—it was luck. When the ball was hit to me, I had two choices: (1) catch it; (2) die.

Now what? The girls all thought I was a good fielder . . . the boys were picking me first for teams . . . my gym teacher was considering changing the grade on my report card . . . but it was all a lie. I was going to be found out. The next time a ball came my way I would miss it and everyone would know the truth.

Punctuation/Cadence Moves That Worked	Punctuation/Cadence Goals
• Good mix of long and short sentences to keep action moving at a steady pace • Dash to set off sound effect in an exciting way (*crack!*) • Ellipses to show how thoughts went slowly from one idea to the next • Colons to list my two choices in a funny way • Two dashes to insert thinking in an interesting way (*I could not tell a lie*)	• Use a mix of slow and fast punctuation, like dashes and ellipses, to show my thoughts going out to the field and then the quick action when the ball is hit • Semicolons to connect two ideas: liking the attention and worrying about being found out

"My entry about the lucky catch has a good variety of punctuation," you might reflect, "and a mix of different sentence lengths, which keeps the action going steadily. The essay entry on people being unfair to snakes is a good one too, for different reasons. In that one I did a good job of building tension by having the sentences start short and get longer. One thing I'd like to try is to go back and forth between long and short sentences, so it never settles into one thing. That might be a good way to show an uncomfortable feeling, like the one I had walking onto the field before the softball game. I'd also like to try putting two ideas together with semicolons. That could work with either piece. In the snakes essay, I might connect false beliefs people have about snakes with the true facts; in the lucky-catch story, I could link what people thought about my catch with the truth about me being a bad fielder.

"In the essay I would mostly be showing one feeling—anger at the people who are unfair to snakes. In the softball piece there are a lot of changing emotions: fear when the ball comes at me, happiness when everyone thinks I am a great fielder, and doubt when I worry I will get found out, just to name a few. The more different feelings, the more chances to use different punctuation and cadence ideas. I think I'll go for the soft-ball story."

Before sending students off to choose which entry to develop, remind them to be sure to think about (a) whether the idea will keep them (and a reader) interested and (b) what punctuation goals they will work on in the piece. "During today's share session," you may explain, "you will need to tell a partner which entry you chose, and why."

Independent Work Part 2

The challenge here is making sure students carefully consider which entry is the best one to develop and publish rather than select their most recent work or pick randomly. In your conferences, you could ask students to articulate their reasons and suggest things to try in their writing (particular punctuation, different sentence lengths, etc.) as they plan and draft. Possible questions/suggestions include:

- What punctuation goals have you set for yourself in this piece? Why is this entry the best one to develop to meet those goals?

- How will you use internal punctuation and different-length sentences to affect mood? Pace (fast and slow)? Rhythm?

- How do you want readers to feel as they read your piece? How will you use internal punctuation to make them feel that way?

Share Session

After students have had time to choose the entry they want to develop into a published piece, have them share with a partner what they picked and why.

Assessment

As students share, circulate and listen in, taking notes and gauging their understanding. Start thinking about how to match children for small-group instruction over the next lessons, and which students could potentially serve as mentors for those having difficulty.

Planning for Punctuation and Cadence

Usually we plan by making timelines and stuff. This is different. You can hear your writing better.
—Fifth grader Julia Cohen

Rationale/Purpose

Once students have chosen which idea to develop and publish, they will need to plan a draft. Since the unit's objective is to expand the way students think of cadence and punctuation, plan with these goals in mind. Most children are used to plotting out a piece using outlines, lists, or timelines. In this lesson they use a graphic organizer to imagine where in their piece punctuation and cadence can affect meaning. Thinking through this lens will add a dimension to their planning today and in future writing.

Materials/ Preparation

Teacher:

- Notebook entries and punctuation goals (from last lesson).

- A punctuation/cadence planning sheet for each student (on page 154; see the example on page 155).

- A transparency of the punctuation/cadence planning sheet (it may be filled out in advance; a filled-out example is provided in the lesson sequence).

To facilitate the demonstration, your chosen entry, your punctuation goals, and the punctuation/cadence planning sheet (blank or filled out in advance) must all be visible.

Students:

- Writer's notebooks and punctuation goals.

- Writing utensils.

Summary

After briefly discussing the importance of planning before drafting, you'll think aloud about how to use punctuation and cadence in your piece. This is best done with an entry familiar from previous lessons, to reinforce the notion that such planning is a natural next step. As you think aloud about specific punctuation and cadence ideas, stress that they are a means to an end. Writers pay attention to these things because of the way they affect mood, rhythm, pacing, and how ideas may be separated or combined.

Sample Language/ Sequence

"Before beginning any first draft," you might begin, "it is a good idea to make a plan. Normally we do this by thinking ahead about *what* to say. For stories, that could mean deciding what we want to happen; for an essay, it could mean plotting out our ideas and evidence. Since we have already thought about punctuation and cadence in our piece, it makes sense to plan not only *what* to say but also *how* to say it. For example, where will I use semicolons to connect ideas—in the beginning or in the middle? To help plan, I will use a graphic organizer to map out my punctuation and cadence moves. Watch as I demonstrate, and notice the sorts of things I think about."

Next, refer to transparencies of the blank or filled-in punctuation/cadence planning sheet (there are copies at the end of this lesson) and your chosen entry. "I'll begin by planning what to say in each section of my lucky-catch story," you might continue. "Next to each part, I'll think about how internal punctuation and cadence can help get my message across to the reader."

Whether you decide to think aloud and fill out the planning sheet in front of students or show one you have prepared in advance, you need to talk through your choices and explain the thinking behind them. "The first scene in my story," you may begin, "will be me walking out onto the field, feeling worried about what might happen and thinking what a bad fielder I am. The whole thing makes me uncomfortable, unsettled—so I want the reader to feel that way too. This is a place I can try out one of my goals from last lesson—mixing very long and very short sentences so it never settles down. I'll also use dashes and ellipses to change speed a lot, which will make it very annoying.

"Next comes the part where the ball gets hit hard right at me and I make my accidental lucky catch. I'll want to start with long sentences that use lots of commas to show things happening quickly, one after the other. Then I'll change over to short, sharp sentences, peppered with dashes and exclamation points, to show fast and exciting action.

"After that I'll skip to later, when I'm home thinking about my new popularity—but at the same time worrying it will all come to an end when people discover I'm a terrible fielder. This will be my chance to use semicolons to show the conflict in my head—how I was feeling both these things, even though they seem like opposites."

Now ask students to open their notebook to the entry they have chosen to develop and talk to a partner for a minute or two about their plans for punctuation and cadence in the first section of the piece. Listen in to these conversations and note ideas to share with the group before sending them off to work independently. Mention two contrasting ideas to show students varied possibilities for the planning they are about to do.

You could sum up the minilesson something like this: "Caitlin and Pedro were talking about using commas to show the back-and-forth, repetitive movements of a boring Ping-Pong game. Eliza is thinking of starting with long sentences, then making them shorter and shorter, to describe how her dog falls asleep on the bed. During your independent work you will record your ideas on a punctuation/cadence planning sheet to map out what you want to try with punctuation and cadence in the different sections of your piece."

Independent Work   As students plan their pieces, remind them to look over the goals for using punctuation and cadence they decided on last lesson. At the same time be open to—and celebrate—new ideas that come up as writers fill out their planning sheets. At this stage they will probably want to overuse certain punctuation (ellipses are a notorious offender). Though this is certainly a concern moving forward, for now it is better to downplay it; better to overdo than feel stuck about what to do, especially in the initial stages of writing. When students move on to the revision and editing stages, they may realize on their own the need to use ideas in moderation. If they don't, you can point it out then, when there are examples to look at.

Questions/suggestions to encourage students to plan for a variety of ideas include:

- Do you want the pace or rhythm of the piece to change as a reader moves from one section to another? Why or why not? What will you do to show those changes?

- It is especially important to set a strong mood at the beginning. How do you want to grab the reader's attention? What punctuation will help you do that? How long will the sentences be, and how will that affect the feeling of the piece?

- At what point will the feeling or mood of the piece change? What will you do differently to show that?

While circulating, be on the lookout for students whose plans show an understanding of shifting mood, rhythm, and pacing from one section to the next. Ask individuals ahead of time to present at the share and spend a moment or two helping them prepare what to say.

Share Session   You could start the share by inviting students to "steal" ideas from one another. "As a community of writers," you might explain, "it is important to share our thinking. If someone likes your idea so much that she or he wants to try it too, that is a high compliment—remember, they are not copying your exact words but your plan about *how* to write the piece."

As students share their plans, point out similarities and differences in their ideas. "Nora and Thurston are both trying to create a sad feeling in their middle section," you might say, "but they are approaching it in different ways. One of them is doing it with drum language, making the sentences feel monotonous with the same rhythm, while the other is drawing out the sad feelings with ellipses. Would either of these ideas work for your piece? What are some other ways to get the same effect?"

Possible Follow-Up Activities   For students having difficulty planning in this new way, you could:

- *Conduct a small-group shared writing activity.* Using one of their ideas or an entry familiar from an earlier lesson, gather four or five students in a separate area and fill in a punctuation/cadence planning sheet together.

- *Limit the planning.* Ask writers to think in terms of just one section of the piece at a time. Alternatively, asking a child who feels intimidated by having to decide on the number of sections to plan a beginning, middle, and ending may prove liberating!

Assessment

To gauge how much individual students have internalized, you could set up a checklist of particular punctuation and cadence ideas discussed in class. Collect their planning sheets and use these checklists to determine how many different things they've tried. If you find that one child has not thought to vary sentence lengths or another never uses dashes to insert information, you can encourage these writing strategies in future conferences, once they have started drafting.

Punctuation/Cadence Planning Sheet

Content		Punctuation/Cadence Goals
	⇨	
	⇨	
	⇨	

Sample Punctuation/Cadence Planning Sheet

Content		Punctuation/Cadence Goals
Walking out to the shortstop position, worrying what will happen	⇨	Make the punctuation annoying—change speeds a lot—ellipses to slow down, dashes to speed up; mix short sentences with very long ones (ellipses)
Ball gets hit hard straight at me—lucky catch, everyone sees	⇨	One long sentence to describe the pitch and the hit, with commas to show things happening one after the other—then short sentences, dashes, exclamation points, to show the catch
Later on I feel happy to suddenly be popular; at the same time filled with doubt, worried I will be found out	⇨	Connect two opposite feelings with semicolons, to show the conflict in my mind

-Dash-

A dash is when you pause to think about what you're going to do and how you're going to do it. Also when you use a dash your voice changes too. Calm level and it sounds like you sure of what you're going to do.

Sammy Keyes and the Hollywood Mummy

And after Grams came back from visiting Lady Lana — after I'd heard about the things she'd done — I knew someone had to do something and the only someone I could think of was me.

Fifth-Grade Dash Example and Theory

Celine's Punctuation Planning and Final Piece

Punctuation Planning Sheet

CONTENT	PUNCTUATION WORK
I start to get really nervous starting out, + then the coach blows the whistle. I start off well	I'll show I'm nervous by putting in dashes. And then I'll make the sentences really choppy when the coach goes "5-4-3-2-1". Then elipses to hold the reader. Next I'll make the sentences smooth to show I was doing well.
Then I get a cramp I start to feel pain, horribly tired.	I'll make uneven sentences to show my breathing. And long lasting sentence to show my pain was really there to stay. I'll do, elipses to show I'm tired.

800 meters
by Celine

"Oh no-oh no-oh no-oh no" I thought beginning to panic. I started to hop in anxiety. Up-down-up-down was the rhythm of my foot. Sweat began to trickle down the back of my neck even though the race hadn't begun, "drip, drip drip" "Oh no" I think Last time, "oh-no". The coach was starting to count down. This was bad, really bad! 5-5-5-5-5-4-4-4-4-3-3-3 2-2, There we go again... "Hey" I thought, "this isn't half bad... I jogged around the track passing all my friends.

And then, could it be - a small knot in my stomach - a miniscule pain started to grow. It was like watching your best friend slowly swallowed up by quicksand, larger and larger it became swallowing you up... It hurt like thunder.

Fifth-Grade Guided Share

We've Noticed Internal Punctuation Can:

1. Affect how loudly or softly you say words

Keeta Logan: "Here we are, surrounded and under attack." —The Cello of Mr. O - Cutler
→ commas make the words before and after stronger + louder

Julia: "I tried to hold my breath and counting to 30 — I only got to 10 before I hiccuped again." - The Princess Diaries - Cabot
→ dash makes you say "I only got to 10" with more emphasis

2. Make your voice deeper or higher

Tamara: "Yes, like a maze." —The Tale of Despereaux - DiCamillo
→ Your voice gets deeper after the comma

Max Z: "Lana's eyes — heavily circled in Bobbi Brown — widened." —Princess in the Spotlight - Cabot
→ The words inside the dashes are deeper than the words outside

Rachel Sophie: "Some, like Mama's friend Marya, stay because they have no place else to go." —The Cello of Mr. O - Cutler
→ The words inside the commas are said higher, like details you forget

Max Levi Alex: "A good night kiss from my mother meant a great big hug as well; I learned that this was a great way to extend the experience." —The Last Kiss - Fletcher
→ The words before the semi-colon have a higher pitch than the ones after

3. Change the speed of the sentence

Max Z: "My father and most of the other fathers, the older brothers — and even some of the grandfathers — have gone to fight." -The Cello of Mr. O - Cutler
→ You say the part inside the dashes faster, like an add-on

Leo Sam: "Loch wanted to cry out to Zaidee, to warn her — but he didn't dare." —Firebirds Rising - Aleen
→ The dash makes you say "but he didn't dare" stronger, slower, and more articulately

Glennon Peter: "Nonetheless, he was able to return to the sport, sailing, in which he could handle his handicap." —Amazing but True Sport Stories - Hollander
→ The commas make the sentence slower by forcing you to pause

4. Affect the Mood of a Sentence

Sydney: "Worse yet, Shelly was probably afraid of her too." —Franny K. Stein - Benton
→ The commas make you pause and think, which gives the sentence a sad tone

Ikey Noah: "Hey, what's going —" Frank started to yell but was interrupted. —Hardy Boys Case Files #54
→ The dash raises tension by cutting off the sentence

Cynthia Shilen: "Thank you," said the girl happily. "It's just like Christmas." —Olfie Undercover - Tavlarios
→ The comma gives it a happy tone, almost like a poem

Max Z: "Many people have left." —The Cello of Mr. O - Cutler
→ The lack of internal punctuation gives it a blank and empty tone

Marisa Radini: "Our story unfolds unfortunately, on a very unfortunate day." —The Jester has Lost His Jingle - Saltzman
→ The commas make it smooth and sing-songy — kind of playful

5. Instruct a reader about what is coming next

Vida Zina: "Just this: his male scent, the faintest remnants of morning aftershave lotion, and the whisker stubby contour of his proffered cheek." —The Last Kiss - Fletcher
→ The colon tells you details are coming

Max Levi Alex: "He looked at glitter creek, home to the fish he found so appetizing, the tar rode, across which tasty rabbits were known to hop, Jayse wood, where meaty chipmunks sometimes shittered before dawn." → The semicolon adds more information, like a "P.S." in a letter

by Lizzy   January 2

    Looking out-over the treetops, under the skyscrapers. The sky, was smudged with an array of colors. The Sun sinking... sinking... Sinking... Sinking under the sea of buildings.
    I pulled my sweater tight around me. It's getting cold, I thought — then looked down at Central park: magnificent greens, a range of blues, and pink skies. Maybe a couple more minutes... or hours, I thought. All so pretty... and calm... and beautiful... and so per—
Swash, somebody flushed a toilet. What? Oh Yeah, there's a bathroom up here, but who'd want to come up just to use the bathroom — Oh NO! I must be someone from the buildings. I'm not supposed to be up here, I thought. My mind was going through the roof rules: no food, no drinks, no pets, can't play with equipment (jump rope, balls, tennis rackets, etc.) a whole bunch of other things, and, last of all, kids must be accompanied by an adult — wich I was not. Most of these rules I broke daily, but if I got caught up here alone one more time...
    I hid behind a plant. The cold air around me froze. I tried to stifle a yawn - no use. Horrible thoughts danced in my head. What if I get caught? Or freeze to death, or get stuck up here? or... or...

Lizzie's Piece, Fifth Grade

! ~ ... ; - ? , : ' ! ~ ... ; - ? , : ' !

Reflection

How am I thinking about punctuation differently?

I think now that planning punctuation is like painting a picture, because you have to know what you're painting, before you do it. Also, I used to think that punctuation was just something you did to make the sentence correct, but I now I realize that punctuation supports what you write, and the more you do it, the more that section of your piece gets emphasized. Suddenly, punctuation seems so important to me.

An example of something I tried in my piece:

Something I tried in my piece was, like I said before, to emphasize my writing. For example, if I was unaware of what was happening, I used lots of question marks and punctuation that I would use in short sentences, like commas. I used semi-colons to make an inference or philosophy where it says in my narrative, "Time passed quickly; as in life, your worst moments are your chapted." these "tests" were very helpful to me.

What do I still want to try with punctuation?

Something I still want to try with my punctuation is to learn more from other writers. This makes reading an advantage for me, like an opportunity to learn from other writers. If I learn to do this, then my writing might sound more meaningful than me writing myself. Also, I might try more of a selection of punctuation marks, rather than commas & periods.

! ~ ... ; - ? , : ' ! ~ ... ; - ? , : ' !

Morris' Reflection Sheet, Fifth Grade

Other Fifth-Grade Reflection Sheet

! ~ ... ; - ? , : ' ! ~ ... ; - ? , : ' !

Reflection

How am I thinking about punctuation differently?

I used to think of puncuation as just periods and comas - not knowing that there was a whole other world out there using semi-colins, dashes, and ellipses. Now I'm in that other world using more and more puncuation to make my writing much more interesting.

An example of something I tried in my piece:

For the first time in any of my writing pieces, I used 1 word sentences. I used to never use 1 word sentences unti now. I'm happy I started because it really fits my writing when neccesary.

What do I still want to try with punctuation?

What I would still love to use is semi-colins. The reason I haven't used it yet is because, I don't feel comfortable using them because I don't really know when to use them. YET!

! ~ ... ; - ? , : ' ! ~ ... ; - ? , : ' !

Punctuation Cupcakes, Fifth-Grade Cadence Celebration—baked by Ms. Levenherz and Ms. Marron!

Drafting: Where to Start?

Rationale/Purpose   The hardest part of drafting is often getting started. Adding to this difficulty, focusing on rhythm and sound in language can be particularly intimidating. The work students have done in their notebook can serve as a good entry point however, especially if they begin to draft where the mood is strongest and there are interesting possibilities for punctuation—whether or not that point is at the beginning. Many young writers see writing as a linear process, and never consider starting at the middle or the end and working on the beginning later. This lesson suggests the possibility that writing at the "hot spot" first can sometimes help a writer move into a piece more easily.

**Materials/
Preparation**   Teacher:

- Transparencies of your filled-in planning sheet and notebook entry from the last lesson.

- Blank transparencies or chart paper.

Students:

- Writer's notebooks and planning sheets.

- Sticky notes.

Summary   It is important to allow students to make their own decisions and not *require* them to begin drafting at a fixed point; the objective of this lesson is to raise the possibility that the best place to start may not be the beginning. First think aloud about the difficulty of getting started, and then use your planning sheet and notebook entry to identify a place where writing comes more easily.

**Sample Language/
Sequence**   "Now that we've planned out how to use punctuation and cadence to help express our ideas," you could say, "it's time to begin drafting. For many authors, this is the hardest part of writing. Sometimes it makes it easier if we start somewhere in the middle, where we have things we are bursting to say. Watch as I think aloud about how to begin my baseball story. When I finish, I'll ask what you noticed about how I made my decision. Those are the sorts of things you'll want to think about as you figure out where to start your own draft.

"As I look at my planning sheet," we might continue, "the first thing I see is the opening section, about walking out to the shortstop position before the game. My idea for that section was to make the punctuation annoying by changing speeds a lot. Doing this is important to set up the shock of everything that happens later, but it is not the heart of the piece. My entry starts a bit further in, right when the ball is hit. I'd say that is one of the two most important parts, along with the conflict in my mind afterward about admitting I was really a bad fielder. The way I wrote in my notebook about the ball being hit feels rushed. This is an action-filled moment, and the whole rest of the story hinges on what happened—so it makes sense to stretch it out. More important, I know just what I'd like to try here with punctuation and cadence in those first long sentences about the pitch and the crack of the bat. I'm going to try that out now to see if this is a comfortable place to begin writing."

On a blank transparency or chart paper, demonstrate writing one specific idea from your think-aloud.

> The pitcher's arm wound in a circular motion, gathering force, releasing the ball toward home plate. I froze in fear—the pitch approached the hitter fast, too fast, his bat snapped forward, CRACK!

"This is not the start of the story," you might say, "but it feels like a good place to begin writing. It's a critical part of the story and it makes sense to write it when I'm fresh. Also, I know from here the next part will be short, sharp sentences to show how scared I was and how quickly it all happened—so I won't be stuck for how to continue. The first section can be written later."

At this point have students spend a moment reflecting on where they might begin their own writing and briefly share this idea with a partner. "Take a minute to look over your planning sheet and entry," you might explain, "and decide where the hot spot of your piece is. It should be the place that is easiest for you to get started and where the reader is most drawn into the piece. Once you've found that spot, tell a partner what it is and why you've chosen it."

As students talk for a minute or two, listen and take notes on their ideas, deciding which to share with the group before sending them off to work independently. "Erin has decided to start writing her essay on cruelty to animals at the end, where she wants to use a series of short sentences and colons to sum up her argument, like one punch after another. Christian wants to start at the beginning of his story about the birth of his baby sister, where he plans to use long sentences with commas and ellipses to show how slowly the time went and how impatient he was. The important thing is to choose a place that is one of the crucial spots in the story, and start right in without worrying whether it is the first section or not. This is something writers do both to help themselves get started and to give their first burst of energy over to one of the most important parts. When you go off to start your draft, jump right in to that part and don't worry about filling in what came before. You can get to that later, once you are already into the piece."

Independent Work Since one of the purposes of today's lesson is to find a place to begin drafting where they will not feel stuck, many students will dive right in. However, after this initial burst of energy and ideas, some will run out of steam and need coaching. Others will do just fine with their hot section but may need help later in figuring out how to backtrack and write the parts leading up to where they started.

Questions/ideas for individual conferences include:

- The part you have chosen to write first is a hot spot in the piece, one of the most important for getting your meaning across. What do you want the reader to think about/feel after reading this part? How do you get *that* message across?

- Can punctuation help in getting this meaning across? Different sentence lengths? How?

- I see you are having a hard time deciding which section would be best to use as a starting point. You may want to see how it would feel to start in different ways before making a decision. Try drawing three large boxes on a page in your writer's notebook. Then write the first sentence or two of the beginning section in one box, a couple lines of the middle part in the second box, and the first sentences of the final section in the third one. Which feels like the best starting point for drafting, and why?

- Now that you've written the middle section, what information will the reader need to know in order to understand it? You will want to be sure that the first section leading up to it includes the important information.

- What questions do you want to put in the reader's mind that will be answered by the middle section? How will you raise those questions in the first section?

Be on the lookout for children to share who represent a range of possibilities. Ideally this means choosing a student who has started in the middle, one who began drafting the final section, and another who opted to begin at the beginning.

Share Session Since the objective of this lesson is to open students to the idea that they need not draft strictly from beginning to end, this share should be as much about decision making as about content. Identify in advance the children you would like to share and coach them on how to articulate the reasons behind their choices, i.e., what made them decide to begin at one section rather than another. At the end of the session, take a tally of how many students have started at beginning, middle, or ending sections and make a chart of their reasons to display in the classroom.

A Menu of Drafting Lessons

Rationale/Purpose   As students get deeper into drafting their pieces, the support lessons they need may be quite different. At this point it may not make sense to present the same minilesson to everyone. Rather, you can draw on your knowledge of individual children's strengths and struggles to differentiate accordingly. Remember too that not every writing workshop needs a minilesson; sometimes a quick check-in at the meeting area is enough to get started. Once the class is engaged in ongoing work, you can call together students with similar needs for small-group lessons.

Although you will of course want to address the needs of your particular students, this menu presents suggestions for small-group instruction in three areas where it is typically needed:

1. **Revisiting the use of mentor sentences** to express particular moods or ideas. *This lesson may be appropriate for students ready for an extra challenge.*

2. **Working back to the beginning**—writing earlier sections when drafting began in the middle or at the end, filling in necessary information and using punctuation and cadence to create contrast. *This lesson may be a good fit for writers having difficulty with sequence. It could also be adapted for students whose sections are too similar in punctuation and cadence.*

3. **Revisiting the plan.** *This lesson might work well with students who become stuck on their first idea, or who have trouble rethinking their writing when they run into trouble.*

These lessons are ideally done with groups of three to five students. You can present several in a single workshop for different groups, or stretch them out over a number of sessions. They may be used as whole-class minilessons as well, if appropriate for most of your students.

**Materials/
Preparation**   Teacher:

- Some of your own notebook entries, on transparencies or chart paper.

- Blank transparencies or chart paper.

Students:

- Writer's notebooks and writing utensils.

- Sticky notes.

Revisiting Mentor Sentences

Summary

Lesson 8 asked students to try modeling their own punctuation and cadence on mentor sentences from familiar texts and authors. At that stage of the unit they were working in notebooks, not necessarily thinking of how to fit their experiments into larger pieces of writing. In this lesson students try incorporating sentence structures from favorite authors into their drafts, perhaps finding examples with mood or meaning similar to their own (a sentence about a character being angry, a before-and-after sentence, etc.).

Sample Language/ Sequence

"Now that you are drafting," you might explain, "you are probably coming to parts where it's tricky figuring how to use punctuation and cadence to get across a certain feeling. For example, you may want to show sadness or boredom or make the reader feel excited and not know how to do it. One thing that writers sometimes do when they can't figure out a way to say something is look at how other authors express the same type of feeling—they will find specific sentences to imitate. That doesn't mean they use the exact words of that other author, but they will copy the structure of the sentence, how the punctuation is used, and how the sentence is broken up into parts. We tried this when we first began experimenting with punctuation, but this time our goal is to create sentences to use in our actual drafts. Watch as I try this in my own writing, to see how it might look.

"In looking over the examples of interesting punctuation I've collected, a sentence that stands out is the one from *The Tale of Despereaux* that we looked at before."

> Mig did not wave back; instead, she stood and watched, open-mouthed, as the perfect, beautiful family passed her by.
>
> —Kate DiCamillo, *The Tale of Despereaux*

"One place I am having trouble is at the part right after I make my lucky catch, just before all the people start to congratulate me. The reader should know that I was stunned, in a daze, couldn't believe the ball had landed in my mitt. That is the way Mig feels when she sees the princess; she is stunned and can't even react. I'm going to try modeling my own sentence after Kate DiCamillo's and see if it helps me solve my problem.

"The sentence begins with a short phrase, right before the semicolon, telling what Mig *didn't* do. One thing *I* didn't do after catching the ball was look up—my eyes were glued to the mitt. I'll try writing that like Kate DiCamillo's sentence."

> I could not look up;

"Next, she explains what Mig did *instead*, how she stood there frozen, and that she did it with her mouth open. I stared at my mitt with my eyes wide open."

> I could not look up; instead, I stared, eyes wide,

"Already there are three commas—but Kate DiCamillo uses one more before she's through. The last part of the sentence tells what *caused* Mig to freeze—the family passing by—and uses two adjectives to describe that family. The comma between *perfect* and *beautiful* gives a sense that these thoughts are coming into Mig's mind in that moment. What caused *me* to freeze was the realization I'd actually caught the ball, and my thoughts were about how impossible that seemed and how hard the ball was. Let's see if I can express that in the same way."

> I could not look up; instead, I stared, eyes wide, at the rock-hard, impossible ball in my mitt.

"Though my sentence is about something completely different from Kate DiCamillo's," you can conclude, "it is structured the same way and expresses a similar feeling. Look over the examples of interesting punctuation you collected earlier in the unit or in the book you are reading now to see if there are any sentences that could work for your piece. If so, imitate the structure of that sentence as you've watched me do and see how it works for you."

Working Back to the Beginning

Summary

Students who started drafting their piece at a middle or ending point rather than the beginning may find working backward challenging. This lesson addresses backtracking with punctuation and cadence in mind, considering not just information that must be filled in but also which types of sentences and pauses build most effectively to the heart of the story. Though the lesson focuses on writers who have begun drafting somewhere other than the beginning, the notion of using one type of punctuation or pattern of sentences to build to another is useful for any student.

Sample Language/ Sequence

"Those of us who began drafting in the middle or end," you might begin, "now have the challenge of going back to fill in the beginning. To do this well means figuring out what information was left out that the reader needs to know. It also means thinking about what punctuation to use and what sorts of sentences will best lead up to what you've already written. Notice what I work on as I do this with my own draft. Afterward, you will go back to your own writing and think in a similar way."

> The pitcher's arm wound in a circular motion, gathering force, releasing the ball toward home plate. I froze in fear—the pitch approached the hitter fast, too fast, his bat snapped forward, CRACK!

"My middle section starts with the climactic action," you reflect, "but it leaves out the important buildup of how I felt walking onto the field. I was scared and nervous; when you know that, you really feel the shock of my lucky catch. The part I've already written is also fast moving, with long sentences that use lots of commas to create a feeling of rushing ahead. To build to that, my beginning should move slowly, with mostly short sentences. That way when I get to the action it'll seem different and surprising."

Think aloud while composing an opening section on chart paper or a blank transparency. "Since I want the reader to know my discouraged feeling," you might say, "I'll start with some short, sad sentences."

Softball again. Gym class can be torture.

"Now that I've set the mood, I'd better give readers the information they need to know to understand the story. For example, it's important to know I was playing shortstop and was worried about being a terrible fielder. I'll need a longer sentence to get that all out, but then can go back to shorter ones to show my sad thoughts."

Softball again. Gym class can be torture. I walk to the shortstop position, dreading the start of the game. Somehow they'd find out. A ball would be hit at me. I'd botch the play. Some would groan. Others would laugh.

It was a slow walk.

"Before you go back to your own writing to try this kind of work," you conclude, "take a minute to look over what you've already written. What information does the reader need to know? How can you use punctuation and plan long and short sentences so they lead up to what you've already written? Tell a partner about your plans, and then jot them down so you'll remember."

Revisiting the Plan

Summary

Many upper elementary and middle school writers are inflexible when it comes to planning a draft. Once they have committed ideas to paper, they become tied to them and are reluctant to change, even if the way the writing is going calls for a shift. In this lesson you model rethinking and revising your original plan as you look over a draft-in-progress.

Sample Language/ Sequence

"One of the hardest jobs of a writer," you might explain, "is going back over your plans and admitting the way you thought to do it at first isn't the best way. This doesn't mean you were wrong, just that once the piece got underway things changed and you had better ideas. The truth is, writers almost always change parts of their plan—if you don't, that probably means you are not rereading to check whether it is coming out the way you want. Watch as I look over my writing to see whether there are things in my plan that need to be changed, now that I am into a draft. Then I'll ask what you think needs to be changed in your own plan. Here's the draft of my middle section."

> The pitcher's arm wound in a circular motion, gathering force, releasing the ball toward home plate. I froze in fear—the pitch approached the hitter fast, too fast, his bat snapped forward, CRACK!

"And here's my planning sheet."

Content		Punctuation/Cadence Goals
Walking out to the shortstop position, worrying what will happen	⇒	Make the punctuation annoying—change speeds a lot—ellipses to slow down, dashes to speed up; mix short sentences with very long ones (ellipses)

Content		Punctuation/Cadence Goals
Ball gets hit hard straight at me—lucky catch, everyone sees	⇒	One long sentence to describe the pitch and the hit, with commas to show things happening one after the other—then short sentences, dashes, exclamation points, to show the catch

Begin your demonstration by reflecting on what you've written so far. "I began my draft with the middle section," you could explain, "and used long sentences as planned. The commas separate the different things that happened, but they don't slow down the action. I think the punctuation here did what I wanted, creating a sense of things moving quickly one after the other, and making it exciting."

Next, look over other parts of your plan and think aloud about what will have to change. "Now that I've written the middle part," you observe, "my original plan for the beginning section doesn't make sense. I had thought that mixing long and short sentences to change the speed would give it an unsettled feeling, and let the reader know how worried I was. Looking it over now, I see that my beginning should move slowly, with mostly short sentences. That will show how sad and worried I was feeling, and when I get to the action it'll seem different and surprising. I guess I'll have to change my plan."

At this point, you can rewrite the plan for students to see.

Content		Punctuation/Cadence Goals
Later on I feel happy to suddenly be popular; at the same time filled with doubt, worried I will be found out	⇨	Connect two opposite feelings with semicolons, to show the conflict in my mind

Then, if you like, you can demonstrate realizing the new plan by rewriting the opening passage, as you did in the Working Back to the Beginning lesson (see page 163).

"Take a minute to look over your plan," you can conclude, "and think about which parts will have to change. Once you have decided, jot yourself a note with your new ideas and share them with a partner." As always, eavesdrop on student conversations and share interesting thinking with the group before sending everyone off to work independently.

Independent Work Look for work that will influence others in the class. You could call attention to what they are doing then and there. ("Writers, I want you all to see what Rodrigo is doing with mentor sentences. Listen to how he used this passage about sadness from *Charlotte's Web* as a model for the part in his story where his grandmother passed away."). Another option is to choose two or three students to share at the end of the period. If you've taught minilessons to different small groups, think about which writers will most effectively communicate the new strategy to classmates who were not part of the lesson.

As you confer with students working with mentor sentences, you could ask:

- Of the sentences we have studied, which do you especially like? Where could you use a sentence like that in your piece?

- In the mentor sentence, the part *after* the comma tells more about the first part, which helps the reader understand it better. What new information do you plan to add after your comma, and how will it help the reader understand?

You could ask students working back to the beginning:

- What information will the reader need to know that was not included in the section you've already written?

- How will you use punctuation in the first section so that it contrasts with what you've already written?

- How will you vary the lengths of sentences so the beginning contrasts with what you've already written?

Questions for writers revisiting their plan include:

- Which part(s) need to change from the original plan, and why?

- What is it about the way you have written your draft so far that makes this change a better idea?

Share Session   Though the idea is to teach each lesson to the students who will most benefit from the strategy, it's best to let each student in the room know what others are working on. If you've taught the minilessons separately to different groups, students can share by explaining the teaching points to others in the class who did not participate in the lesson. This may be done with the whole class in the meeting area; one small group can present their ideas to another small group; or pairs of students may share their ideas with each other. Hearing these ideas may open up possibilities that writers hadn't thought of. At the very least, it's a good way to encourage the notion that the class is a community of writers who are all working on individual things together.

Drum Language, Revisited

Rationale/Purpose
In many workshops, revision and editing are treated as separate stages of the writing cycle; revision is defined as the process of "making it better," editing as "fixing the mistakes." In truth, the line between the two is unclear, especially when punctuation is treated as a craft tool rather than a set of rules. While for teaching purposes it sometimes makes sense to think of them as distinct steps, revision strategies can often be seen as editing, and vice versa. This lesson revisits the notion of drum language (see Lesson 5) as a way to look over writing for rhythm and flow (*prosody*). Is this revision or is it editing? One could make convincing arguments either way.

Materials/Preparation
Teacher:

- Overhead transparencies or charts of passages from your current draft (one where the drum language works, another where it needs to be revised).

- Blank transparencies or chart paper.

Students:

- Completed first drafts.

Summary
Though students have been thinking all along about the rhythm and "sound" of their writing, they now step back and look over the draft as a whole through this lens. Specifically, they find places where the rhythm works well and identify parts that need to be revised. Demonstrate this process by:

- Sounding out and acknowledging a place in your draft where the drum language works well.

- Revising another passage so it has a more effective rhythm.

Sample Language/Sequence
"While drafting," you might begin, "one of the things we thought about was the sound and rhythm of particular sentences. A while back in reading workshop, we talked about how authors break up sentences with punctuation to make the words rise and fall a certain way, and how using different-length sentences—some short, some long—accomplishes the same thing. To hear this more clearly, we sounded out the rhythm without the actual words—and called it *drum language*. Now it may be useful to do this with our own drafts, to figure out places where the sound and rhythm should flow better. Watch as I demonstrate with this passage from the second half of my shortstop story."

> It was no good. Sooner or later they'd know. I was a phony, a fake. I'd never make another catch like that, and never had before.

"I think this passage works pretty well," you might reflect. "The drum language builds nicely, with the second sentence just a little longer than the first—*dut-de-dut-duh/dut-de-duh-dut-de-dut-duh.* This gives the feeling of slowly realizing that I can't continue pretending to be a good fielder. The next two sentences also work well. Both of them are divided in the middle by commas, so there are short pauses, and the drum language builds from a shorter one to a longer one as well—*dut-de-de-duh-de, dut-duh/duh-dut-de-dut-de-dut-de-duh-de-duh-dut-duh, duh-dut-de-duh-dut-duh.* In fact, the whole passage builds gradually, with each of the four sentences getting longer as you go. So let's move on."

> But how could I let people know without embarrassing myself? You can't just put up a sign at your school advertising that you made a lucky catch—and besides, I was enjoying my new popularity.

"The drum language in this passage doesn't feel right. The second sentence especially has problems. That *you can't just put up a sign* part is way too long, and the section after the dash is a totally different rhythm that doesn't go with the first part of the sentence. Put them together and the whole thing seems clunky and awkward, not smooth. What I wanted to express is the conflict I felt between wanting all that attention and worrying about being found out. Looking back at my original goals, I thought about connecting these two ideas with a semicolon. If I do this, it will give me a nice long breath in the middle to break up the parts. That should allow the reader time to take in the first idea, pause, and consider the second."

Begin to compose a revised version on chart paper or a projected transparency. "It makes sense to start with a shorter question, to get the reader ready for the main conflict."

> How to let people know?

"In drum language that would be six beats—*dah-de-dut-duh-de-duh.* Now I'll try the next sentence. Since it's going to be divided by a semicolon, I'll make each part kind of short, with a similar rhythm."

> How to let people know? I loved the attention; I feared the next game.

"In drum language, *I loved the attention* is *de-duh-dut-de-duh-duh*—six beats again. It's followed by *I feared the next game,* which is five beats—*de-dut-duh-de-duh.* That works well, like it's answering the rhythm of the first part—*de-duh-dut-de-duh-duh/de-dut-duh-de-duh.* Now that I've set that up, I can write a longer sentence to fill in more information. This one should probably be broken up too, but with a shorter pause—I'll try a comma."

How to let people know? I loved the attention; I feared the next game. As soon as a ball came my way, they were bound to find out.

"Look over your draft now as you've watched me do," you'll continue, "and choose one part where the drum language works well. Put a star next to it. Then find a passage that you think should be rewritten for smoother drum language. Put an X there. Last, share what you've marked with a partner and see if she or he agrees with your choices."

As students turn and talk for a minute or two, listen in and gauge their understanding. Rather than taking time to share what writers have said at this moment, call attention to interesting efforts during the independent work session.

"Once you get back to your seats," you can conclude, "rewrite the section you have identified in a few different ways, trying out the drum language yourself or with a friend. After you are satisfied, read through the rest of your draft carefully to see what other passages may need smoothing out."

Independent Work As students begin this complicated work, you may need to take a more active coaching role than usual, modeling how to read aloud in drum language until they get the hang of it. In order to provide support to as many students as possible, you might partner writers having an easier time verbalizing the drum language with those having a harder time. (Being more or less conversant with this idea may not break down strictly along the lines of who are the most sophisticated writers.)

Questions/suggestions you may want to pose as you confer today include:

- Which sentences in particular need to be rewritten?

- For the longer ones, what length pauses do you want, and which internal punctuation would create those pauses?

- For shorter ones, what is the drum language like in the sentences that come just before? Do they lead in well to the one you are revising?

- How many beats do you want in this part? If the sentence is divided in two parts, how many beats do you want in each?

While conferring, note students' successful attempts to rewrite passages. It is particularly important to preselect writers for the share session who are able to articulate their thinking on how punctuation, sentence length, and pauses impact the rhythm of their work. Helping them decide how to explain their thinking ahead of time may be useful.

Share Session

As in Lesson 5, you will more than likely need to help verbalize the drum language in students' writing as they share. The trick is to acknowledge that this work is a little unusual and amusing but does bring us to a greater awareness of how to make our writing better. You'll need to strike a balance between having fun and keeping the conversation productive.

A good sequence is to have two students share, one who revised a longer sentence or passage and another who worked in shorter chunks—this will provide a point of entry for as many writers as possible. Each student should read the passage and its drum language before and after revision (with or without your assistance), and explain the thinking behind the change.

Possible Follow-Up Activities

Now that they have had the experience of trying out the drum language idea as a writer, students may return to their independent reading and further investigate the rhythm of particular passages in their books. A possible homework assignment is to identify sentences or sections where the rhythm does or doesn't work and bring them in for group discussion. Students might even want to rewrite sentences from their books and compare them to the original versions.

Assessment

The best way to assess whether students have begun to think more consciously about the rhythm in their writing is to give them opportunities to read it aloud expressively. You may want to have them—with a partner, in small groups, or as a whole class—practice explaining what they were trying to achieve with their drum language in a particular passage and then read aloud to illustrate.

Don't Overdo It!

Rationale/Purpose   In her seminal first book *Lessons from a Child* (1983), Lucy Calkins discusses how student writers at a certain developmental level can "do anything except do something in moderation." As examples she cites third graders who have just learned about exclamation marks using "hundreds of them," children newly introduced to dialogue filling up their stories with "chitchat," and others beginning each story with sound effects. Once children have become conscious of internal punctuation and how it affects meaning, they will undoubtedly develop favorite tricks and use them over and over—a plethora of semicolons perhaps, or parenthetical commas in every other sentence. Like anything done in excess, a perfectly good punctuation idea can lose its effectiveness when overused. Though this tendency may be developmentally appropriate, it also points the way to future teaching moves. You need to train student writers to be critical about their own work, and make decisions about where an idea works best and places it should be cut.

**Materials/
Preparation**   Teacher:

- A section of your draft, displayed on chart paper or a transparency, in which one type of punctuation is overused.

- Blank transparencies or chart paper.

Students:

- First drafts.

- Writing utensils.

Summary   Simply telling students to go over their writing and eliminate overused punctuation is likely to confuse them. If they understood that repeating the idea over and over would kill its effect, they wouldn't do it in the first place. In this lesson you first model how to decide when too much repetition is monotonous, and then make decisions about what to keep and what to change.

**Sample Language/
Sequence**   You'll first display an example of your own draft in which a particular type of punctuation is overused, and then begin your think-aloud. "One of the most important things a writer needs to be able to do when a draft is finished," you may begin, "is to read it over and see what needs to change. Since we have been working on using internal punctuation and different sentence lengths, one thing to look out for is whether we have overdone anything—too many short sentences, or too many semicolons, for example. Even a really good idea can lose its power if we overdo it. Watch as I look over my own

draft, and notice the kinds of things I think about. When I'm done I'll ask you to do the same with your own writing."

> I had made up my mind—the first person I would tell was Mr. Spraker, the gym teacher. I'd wait at the end of class—he usually stood at the door as we filed out—and ask if I could speak to him privately. The truth—however embarrassing—would be better than continuing to pretend.

Read your excerpt aloud, emphasizing the overuse of dashes, even exaggerating the repetition for effect. Then model rewriting the passage, anticipating problems and thinking aloud through possible solutions.

"In reading this over, I see there are five dashes—in only three sentences! More important, that quality of interrupting a thought you get from using a dash is lost. It happens so often the reader gets used to it, and there's no surprise—it just feels jerky. The place I most want that effect of interrupting is in the last sentence: *The truth—however embarrassing—would be better than continuing to pretend.* I'll have to rewrite the first two sentences. Come to think of it, they are both pretty long. Rewriting them will give me the opportunity to make them shorter as well. The first one is pretty straightforward. I'll just divide it in two, and take out the word *I* in the second part, so I'm not using the same word too often."

> I had made up my mind. The first person to tell was Mr. Spraker, the gym teacher.

"The second sentence is a bit trickier. To make this work, I'll need to change the order of things in the sentence and rewrite some of it."

> I had made up my mind. The first person to tell was Mr. Spraker, the gym teacher. He usually stood at the door as the class dismissed. I'd lag behind and speak to him after the others had gone.

"The last part can stay as it was. I like how the dashes show I'd finally reached a very difficult decision, even knowing how embarrassing it would be to let people know the truth. Let's hear how the whole passage sounds rewritten."

> I had made up my mind. The first person to tell was Mr. Spraker, the gym teacher. He usually stood at the door as the class dismissed. I'd lag behind and speak to him after the others had gone. The truth—however embarrassing—would be better than continuing to pretend.

At this point give students a couple of minutes to look over their drafts for internal punctuation they may have overused and begin thinking what to take out and what to leave in. Another option is to have students look over their partners' draft and tell what punctuation seems to be overused from a reader's perspective. If you choose this road, first spend some time discussing how to give feedback without being overly negative.

As always, listen in on students' conversations to gauge their understanding and briefly report back to the group before sending them off to work independently. "I want to compliment you on being so honest in looking over your writing," you might say. "It's difficult to go over something you've worked so hard on and find places that need to change, but that is the job of a writer. Rhonda realized she had overused semicolons, but already has some thoughts on which ones to change. Jorge saw that he had put in too many dashes, like me, and is planning to divide some of the sentences in two. Remember, everyone should be able to find at least one or two places where you overdid a particular type of punctuation, and rewrite them. You may do these revisions in your writer's notebook before copying the final, published draft. In today's conferences I'll be asking you which parts you are planning to rewrite."

Independent Work

By now you should know what sorts of punctuation individual writers have tried—and what they may be overusing. With a little advance planning your conferences can be brief and numerous; the objective today should be lots of short, check-in conversations. You may want to convene small groups or partners with similar issues and coach them on how to break up long sentences, combine short ones, or mix up internal punctuation to vary the lengths of pauses. Questions or suggestions you might raise include:

- Which place does that punctuation work best? Where is it most important? Why?

- Once you take away this punctuation, how might you rewrite it? Try three different ways in your writer's notebook and then read them to a partner to see what they think works best.

- Are there places you use too many long sentences in a row? Too many short? How might you mix them up?

Look for students whose work can teach something to the class. A rule of thumb is to think about issues that have come up for a number of students, and look for writers who have found solutions to these problems. As in earlier lessons, you may ask these children to copy before-and-after sections of their revisions onto transparencies so that classmates can see how punctuation has been reworked.

Share Session

Most writers favor particular punctuation to express shades of meaning; it is in part what constitutes their voice, or style. The hope is that this unit of study will open students to the idea that the way they treat the rhythm of language—where they put the pauses and how they vary their sentence lengths—is as important as their choice of words. As that awareness develops, they will need to be conscious of overusing favorite punctuation.

One purpose for this share could be to begin developing a repertoire of alternatives for punctuation they may use too often. In facilitating the conversation it is important to make generalizations students can tuck away for future use. "Notice," you might say, "how Cara realized she was overusing dashes and changed one to a colon. When a dash is being used to announce or call attention to something, a colon may work just as well. Aaron had a great idea here how to cut down on places he used a pair of commas to insert information. In this place, where the extra information was especially important, he used a pair of dashes instead."

Possible Follow-Up Activities

To continue building this repertoire of strategies once the unit has ended, you may want to create a chart that remains on display in the classroom (see the example below). Begin by including things that came up in the share, and add to it as ideas come up in future conferences, shares, or whole-class conversations. Giving credit to the student who initially used the idea provides an incentive for others to find more strategies.

Writers need to think of ways to keep from overusing favorite punctuation. For example:

. . . *when Cara realized she was using too many dashes, she changed some to colons.* When your dash is calling attention to something important, sometimes a colon can be used instead.

. . . *when Aaron saw he was using pairs of commas to insert information too often, he tried a pair of dashes in some places.* A pair of dashes can sub for a pair of commas when you really want the information to stand out.

Reflecting on What's Been Learned

Rationale/Purpose   Metacognition is a necessary step in solidifying understanding. As Ellin Keene and Susan Zimmermann (2007) have written, "thoughtful, active, proficient readers . . . think about their own thinking during reading"—and the same is true of writers. Throughout these lessons students have stepped back and taken the point of view of the reader, imagining how the use of punctuation and cadence will affect the way their writing is understood. To end the unit, you'll encourage students to continue this metacognition and reflect on how they have changed as writers and readers after having looked at punctuation and cadence differently.

Materials/
Preparation

Teacher:

- Excerpt(s) (copied onto chart paper or a transparency) from your published piece and/or notebook illustrating something you have done with punctuation that you have never done before.

- Blank reflection sheets to distribute to students (the example at the end of this lesson is adapted from a sheet created by fifth-grade teacher Jackie Levenherz).

- A transparency or SMART Board image of the reflection sheet.

Students:

- Published pieces.

- *Optional*: Writer's notebooks.

- Writing utensils.

Summary   So far you've modeled strategies for students before asking them to practice independently. This session is a bit different. Rather than model writing a reflection sheet, first think aloud about a specific thing you have done differently with punctuation, then have students discuss their own examples with a partner before filling in a sheet on their own.

Sample Language/
Sequence

Once students have gathered in the meeting area with their published pieces, discuss the importance of reflecting on all they've learned. "You've done a lot of hard work on this piece," you might begin, "and soon we'll celebrate. But what's even more important than the work you've completed today is how you've improved as a writer by thinking differently about punctuation and cadence. During our celebration, we'll do more than just look at one another's pieces. We'll also share our new thoughts about punctuation and what we will do differently in future writing. To do this well, it is important to look for specific things you have done in your piece or in your notebook that you will probably do again."

Call attention to the excerpt(s) from your own writing.

> Yes, I know it is wrong; no, I cannot seem to stop myself.

> I loved the attention; I feared the next game.

Now think aloud about what you have done. "Looking over the work I have done these last several lessons, one thing I never did before was use a semicolon to separate two opposite ideas, and then have the two halves follow the same structure. For instance, in my first example, the first part starts with the word *yes* and a comma; the second part starts with the word *no* and a comma. In the second example, the first part starts with *I loved*, and the second part begins with *I feared*—opposite ideas, similar structure. That is definitely something I will try again in future writing.

"Take a moment to look over your published pieces and find something you tried with punctuation or cadence you hadn't tried before—and that you will probably do again in future writing. Then share it with a partner."

As students briefly (no more than two or three minutes) read through their pieces and talk to partners, listen in and note the strategies students identify as useful. After calling them back to attention and sharing one or two examples, introduce the reflection sheet and give students instructions on how to fill it out.

"In preparation for our celebration," you might explain, "each of you will need to fill out a reflection sheet, which you will share along with your final piece. You'll see that the first question asks how you look at punctuation differently now, both as a writer and as a reader. The second question asks what you will do differently as a writer now that you've spent so much time thinking about punctuation and cadence. Next, you're to give an example of something you tried that you think you will probably try again, as we've just discussed. Last, list something you'd still like to try with punctuation or cadence. These sheets are very important; they are a way for you to remember and for me to know what you've learned and where you want to go next as a writer and punctuator. For the first part of independent work today, talk with a partner about what you want to say on the reflection sheet. Then, when I signal to end the discussion, fill it out."

Independent Work Students may not immediately be able to think of things they have tried and goals they have set for themselves throughout the unit. Your job is to refer to conference and assessment notes and remind them. In addition, partners may read each other's pieces and comment on interesting things their classmates have done with punctuation and cadence.

Once conversations have ended and students are filling in reflection sheets, confer with individuals, pushing them to be specific in their answers, give examples, etc. Possible questions/suggestions include:

- What are you noticing in your reading about how authors use punctuation, now that you have thought about it so deeply yourself?

- What are some things you will think about now as you use punctuation and cadence in your writing?

- Look over your piece for examples of things you have tried, but also look through your notebook entries. Are there things you've done more than once, that you can make part of your writing style? Are there things you did in your notebook that you'd like to continue experimenting with?

| Share Session | As each preselected student shares his or her answer to one of the four questions, comment on how he or she "thinks about thinking." "It's so interesting," you might point out, "how Nora noticed that paying so much attention to punctuation in her writing has affected her reading. Evan was very smart in the way he looked at the thing he did well in his piece, mixing long and short sentences, and decided a future goal would be to try many short sentences in a row, with an occasional long one to break them up."

Before ending the share, mention that hearing one another's reflections may have given students new ideas for what to include in their own. "If hearing from your fellow writers made you think of new things to put in your reflection sheet, feel free to add them."

! ~ ... ; - ? , : ' ! ~ ... ; - ?

Reflection Sheet
(adapted from the classroom of fifth-grade teacher Jackie Levenherz)

How am I thinking about punctuation differently?

_____
_____
_____
_____
_____

One thing I will do differently as a writer as a result of this study:

_____
_____
_____
_____
_____

Something I tried in my piece that worked, which I will do again in future writing:

_____
_____
_____
_____
_____

What do I still want to try with punctuation?

_____
_____
_____
_____
_____

Punctuation Celebration

Rationale/Purpose   When writers in the world complete significant projects, they typically mark the accomplishment in some way—going out to dinner, having a party, or putting together a public reading. Student writers are no exception; in addition to needing to celebrate, it is important they take stock in some way and reflect on what they have learned.

Materials/ Preparation

Teacher:

- Refreshments!

Students:

- Published pieces.
- Filled-in reflection sheets.

Possible Approaches   You'll want to invite parents and/or students from other classes to attend, and combine sharing the work with some sort of party (refreshments, music, etc.). Two types of celebrations that work well are:

- A *museum share*, in which each student's work is displayed on tables, and everyone moves around the room reading and writing brief comments.

- A *reading*, in which each writer reads aloud one or more excerpts (full pieces take too long!) that show their most successful punctuation experiments.

Though there are many ways to organize celebrations of student writing, a few considerations are particularly important in a study of punctuation and cadence:

- *Explaining the study*: Because the study is unusual, you may want to begin with a brief description of how it differed from a traditional string of punctuation lessons. (You may deliver this introduction, or students may prepare and present it.) "Welcome parents and friends," you might begin, "and thank you for coming to our celebration. In this study we looked closely at the sound of our writing, and how this affects the way a reader understands it. For example, a group of short, choppy sentences might create a fast-moving, action-packed feeling. A long sentence with lots of commas may be a good way to show something rolling out slowly, like waves lapping up on the shore. A dash in the middle of a sentence might make our voices rise up a little, calling attention to the thing that comes after. To work on this, we thought about how to use internal punctuation to make different connections and pauses, and put together longer and shorter sentences to give it some variety. The way our voices go when we speak or read aloud, pausing in certain places, slowing down or speeding up, going lower or higher, makes a rhythm and a sound, which we call *cadence*. As you listen to/read our work, pay careful attention to these things—and perhaps think about the way you use punctuation and cadence in your own writing."

- *Sharing reflections*: Though finished pieces are of course important, equally significant in this study are student reflections on how their thinking about punctuation has changed. Part of the celebration, preferably at the beginning, should be devoted to sharing these reflections. You might:

  - Have one or two students prepare a reflection to read out loud at the start, before pieces are shared. These individuals may be chosen by the class or selected by you.

  - Have students display their reflection sheet along with their piece, for readers to look over as they move about the room.

- *Seeing the punctuation*: A critical element in sharing students' experiments with internal punctuation is that readers see the work, so they understand exactly what the author has done to create pauses, particular intonations, etc.

  - In a museum share, readers will of course look at the pieces as they go.

  - If you are having a reading, you may want to have students copy the excerpts they will read aloud onto chart paper or a transparency, which they can then display as they share.

- Optional: *Providing special "punctuation refreshments"*! Just for the fun of it, some classes may want to prepare "theme" refreshments. Jackie Levenherz and Ali Marron, fifth-grade teachers in Manhattan, decorated cupcakes with punctuation marks on top. Veggies cut up to resemble particular punctuation are another option. Be inventive!

An Internal Punctuation and Cadence Glossary

One of the most interesting things about looking at punctuation guides is noticing the differences from one to the next. Sometimes there are flat-out contradictions, such as whether there should be a comma before the word *and* when we use commas to divide items in a list (see the Comma Comma Comma Comma Comma Chameleon section at the end of Chapter 3).

In other instances the differences are more subtle; this is particularly apparent in the widely varying attitudes toward the controversial semicolon. In her wonderful (and quite amusing) book *Woe Is I* (1996), Patricia O'Conner advises: "For whatever reason, many of us avoid it. Maybe it intimidates us; it shouldn't. (See, wasn't that easy?)" In her somewhat more formal (but no less useful) guide *Grammatically Correct* (1997), Anne Stilman warns: "Even if you can justify each individual use, having semicolons show up in sentence after sentence becomes tedious. Don't make the mistake of trying to make your content look more important by peppering it with fancy punctuation." Though the two passages don't exactly contradict each other, the bias of each author comes through—and these are the sorts of conversations that make a punctuation study such a rich experience.

So as you refer to the following selective glossary of definitions and suggestions, don't think of it as the final word. Instead, consider it a place to go for a general idea and, perhaps, a beginning point for further research.

Colon

Colons are unattractive for several reasons: firstly, they give you the feeling of being rather ordered around, or at least having your nose pointed in a direction you might not be inclined to take if left to yourself, and, secondly, you suspect you're in for one of those sentences that will be labeling the points to be made: firstly, secondly and so forth, with the implication that you haven't sense enough to keep track of a sequence of notions without having them numbered.
—Lewis Thomas (1979)

The colon seems at first to be one of the more straightforward forms of internal punctuation, but is more complicated than it appears. Though its most common usage is to introduce or announce, at times it makes less obvious connections. Children will need to see lots of examples of these more subtle functions and practice them in their writing repeatedly in order to use them correctly.

> *Think of the colon as a traffic cop, or punctuation's master of ceremonies. Use it to present something: a statement, a series, a quotation, or instructions. But remember that a colon is an abrupt stop, almost like a period. Use one only if you want your sentence to brake completely.*
> —Patricia O'Conner (1996)

> *A colon tells the reader that what follows is closely related to the preceding clause. The colon has more effect than the comma, less power to separate than the semicolon, and more formality than the dash. . . . Join two independent clauses with a colon if the second interprets or amplifies the first.*
> —Strunk and White (2000)

> *The colon is next to the period in the strength of the stop. It often introduces quoted matter, a list, or a clause that amplifies the preceding statement.*
> —Lederer and Dowis (1999)

> *A colon serves to cue readers that a sentence consists, in a sense, of a question and an answer.*
>   The situation was becoming desperate: supplies were running low, and winter would soon be setting in.
> —Anne Stilman (1997)

We should remind students that the words before a colon must be a complete independent clause; colons should not be used before a sentence fragment.

We might explain the colon to students like this: *A colon is like an announcer. It stops the sentence for a moment, to let the reader know important information is coming up.*

Dash

Once a class gets the hang of it, the dash tends to become contagious. Don't be overly concerned, however; student writers tend to first overuse a writing technique before learning to use it in moderation. The best approach may be to celebrate initial attempts, even if they seem excessive. Once it seems children have a true understanding of how to use dashes correctly, gently suggest alternatives (e.g., commas, parentheses) when appropriate.

> *The dash is used to interrupt a sentence and insert parenthetical material. Expressed in words, a dash would be something like "Oh, by the way . . . ."*
> —Lederer and Dowis (1999)

A pair of dashes can be employed in two ways: to draw particular attention to elements you wish to emphasize, and . . . [to] veer off in a different direction temporarily and then get back on the original track.
—Stilman (1997)

The dash is like a detour; it interrupts the sentence and inserts another thought. A single dash can be used in place of a colon to emphatically present some piece of information: It was what Tina dreaded most—fallen arches. *Or dashes can be used in pairs instead of parentheses to enclose an aside or an explanation:* Her shoes had loads of style—they were Ferragamos—but not much arch support.

Dashes thrive in weak writing, because when thoughts are confused, it's easier to stick in a lot of dashes than to organize a smoother sentence.
—O'Conner (1996)

Use a dash to set off an abrupt break or interruption and to announce a long appositive or summary. A dash is a mark of separation stronger than a comma, less formal than a colon, and more relaxed than a parenthesis.

His first thought on getting out of bed—if he had any thought at all—was to get back in again.
—Strunk and White (2000)

Use a dash to separate a final clause summarizing an idea, or series of ideas, from that which precedes it.

Money, fame, power—these were his goals in life.

Use a dash to indicate an interruption in thought.

When I was in college—but I have already talked about that.

Do we—can we—dare we ask for more money?

Use a dash to introduce a word or group of words to which you wish to give emphasis.

What he needed most he never got—love.

Use a pair of dashes to enclose words or ideas which you wish to emphasize sharply or emphatically.

I think—no, I am positive—that you should go.

My mother can bandage that—she's a trained nurse, you know—so that it won't hurt at all.
—Shaw (1993)

We may sum this up for students as follows: *A dash is a way of interrupting a sentence. It creates a more sudden stop than a comma, and authors use it to put in extra information. When you add a second dash after the extra information, it takes you back to the interrupted sentence.*

Ellipses

In many writing workshop classrooms, ellipses have become cliché. Student writers take to them with enthusiasm, exploring the melodramatic potential of these three dots in building suspense or expressing longing—a sort of slow drum roll or corny string section. As much as children love to use this punctuation within a phrase or sentence to create drama, few reference books even mention that particular usage. Overwhelmingly, they discuss the function of the ellipsis in showing text has been omitted (*Fourscore and twenty years ago, our forefathers brought . . . . a new nation*) or signifying a trailing off of thought. More often it is described as a form of ending punctuation, to show something has been left out or unresolved (see the ending punctuation glossary in Chapter 2). The few guides that do discuss the way ellipses bring out emphasis within a sentence do so in a rather condescending way, as though it were a thing to be avoided. Nonetheless, it can be an effective, if somewhat cartoonish, form of punctuation that students may use to not-so-subtly evoke tension or emotion.

> Ellipses may be used:
> - *To indicate the passage of time.*
>   The day wore on from sunrise to midmorning . . . steaming noon . . . blistering afternoon . . . cooling sunset.
> - *To separate short groups of words for emphasis.* Such use of ellipsis periods is a favorite device of advertising writers. Here, ellipsis periods are used not so much to indicate omission as to set off, to emphasize, the selling message itself:
>   Do it soon . . . do it today . . . do it today. See . . . your local dealer. (Shaw 1993)

We might explain ellipses to students as follows: *Ellipses are three dots that make a slow pause in a sentence. They are usually used to create suspense, and make readers sit on the edge of their seat waiting to find out what comes next. When they are used at the end of a sentence the author usually wants readers to finish it in their head.*

Parentheses

> *You can't hear me talk now. I'm in parentheses.*
> —Steven Wright

Parentheses are often discussed more in terms of their function than how they make a passage *sound*. (Stilman's explanation below does a good job in teasing out the difference between inserting information with parentheses versus a pair of dashes or commas.) Nonetheless, they do create a pause when we read them aloud, and contribute to the mood and flow of a sentence.

> *The function of parentheses is to set off an element that "inter-*
> *rupts" a flow of thought. . . . [Such] elements may be set off with*
> *either commas, dashes, or parentheses. Thus, how do you decide*
> *when it's appropriate to use each? In general, commas serve to*
> *integrate a digressive element unobtrusively; dashes serve to*
> *draw particular attention to it; and parentheses serve to deem-*
> *phasize it, signaling to the reader that the text is temporarily*
> *getting off the track.*
> —Stilman (1997)

> *There's not much debate about the use of parentheses, but they are*
> *often used when commas or dashes would serve as well and be less*
> *distracting. Some manuals say that material in parentheses carries*
> *less emphasis than material set off by commas or dashes. But that*
> *distinction is a fine one at best.*
> —Lederer and Dowis (1999)

We might explain parentheses to students as follows: *Parentheses are used to put extra information in the middle of a sentence that makes it more interesting but isn't necessary to understand the sentence. They make a shorter pause than dashes, and don't feel as much like an interruption.*

Semicolon

> *[W]ith a semicolon . . . you get a pleasant little feeling of*
> *expectancy; there is more to come; read on; it will get clearer.*
> —Thomas (1979)

> *Alright, semicolon. Comma or colon? Pick a side; we're at war.*
> —Steven Colbert

The semicolon is probably the least commonly understood of all internal punctuation and frequently the place where children (and adults!) have the most trouble. Its perhaps unde-served reputation as a "fancy" or snobbish form of punctuation seems to intimidate many student writers. Best used in moderation, it nevertheless works well to unite related thoughts and create a beat between ideas. Students should be encouraged to experiment with this controversial connector; with enough practice, they may be the generation to conquer the fear of semicolons once and for all!

> *The semicolon is one of the most useful but least used punctuation*
> *marks. For whatever reason, many of us avoid it. Maybe it intim-*
> *idates us; it shouldn't. (See, wasn't that easy?) If a comma is a*
> *yellow light and a period is a red light, the semicolon is a flashing*

red—one of those lights you drive through after a brief pause. It's for times when you want something stronger than a comma but not quite so final as a period.
—O'Conner (1996)

[A semicolon] indicates that two or more statements are not suffi-ciently related to require commas but are too closely related to justify being put in separate sentences.
—Shaw (1993)

Consider using the semicolon in place of a conjunction:
    His offer sounded too good to be true, so I didn't believe it.
    His offer sounded too good to be true; I didn't believe it.

Consider using the semicolon to unite two separate sentences:
    His old apartment had been dark, cramped and dirty; his
new one was worse.
—Stilman (1997)

We may explain semicolons to students as follows: *Semicolons are a good way to connect two ideas that could be in separate sentences. Authors use them when they want to make the reader think about how the ideas go together. They make us pause and wait for the second idea. They are less sus-penseful than ellipses, and interrupt less than dashes.*

Writing Mechanics Grade by Grade

Deciding on End-of-Year Expectations

Once a school has begun to think deeply about the way it approaches the teaching of mechanics in general and punctuation in particular, the next step is to come to an agreement about what is expected from one year to the next. One way to set up such conversations is through forming what Carmen Fariña and Laura Kotch (2008) call an Articulation Team. In this structure, one teacher representing each grade comes together with other relevant staff (e.g., literacy coaches, administration) around a particular subject area or instructional issue to come up with ideas.

The document below is not intended to be the final word on what elementary grades should be working on year to year in writing mechanics or punctuation. Rather it is an example of what one group of educators working in a Mechanics Articulation Team came up with for their particular population, and should be used as a starting point for similar conversations in other schools. It is worth noting how certain strategies are introduced in one grade, with mastery not expected until the following year. Meaningful learning takes time!

Thanks goes to the PS 6 Language Systems Committee and Writing Articulation Team, which includes Barbara Rosenblum, Barbara Pinto, Jackie Levenherz, Marissa Vassari, Nicole Silva, Patty Tabacchi, Emily Schottland, and Tammy Rimoin.

Kindergarten

1. Lowercase Letters
   - Recognizes lowercase letters
   - Begins to use lowercase letters more than capital letters
2. Letters and Words
   - Understands that letters make up a word
   - Understands the difference between a letter and a word
3. Spacing Between Words
   - Begins to use spaces between words
4. Capitalization
   - Uses proper capitalization and lowercase letters in their first name
   - Uses proper capitalization for *I*

5. Ending Punctuation
   - Recognizes ending punctuation marks in shared reading
6. Sentence Structure
   - Begins to use full, simple sentences in their writing

First Grade

1. Lowercase Letters
   - Uses lowercase letters appropriately
2. Spacing Between Words
   - Uses spaces between words appropriately
3. Capitalization
   - Uses proper capitalization at the beginning of sentences
   - Uses proper capitalization for the days of the week
   - Uses proper capitalization for the months of the year
   - Uses proper capitalization for the names of specific people
4. Ending Punctuation
   - Uses periods at the end of a sentence correctly
   - Begins to use exclamation points
   - Begins to use question marks
5. Commas
   - Attempts to use commas in the date
6. Apostrophes
   - Reads contractions containing apostrophes
7. Punctuating Dialogue
   - Recognizes quotation marks as indicating dialogue
8. Sentence Structure
   - Writes full, simple sentences consistently
   - Varies sentence openers
   - Varies sentence structure
   - Begins to embed literary language

Second Grade

1. Lowercase Letters
   - Uses lowercase letters appropriately

2. Capitalization
   - Meets all of K and 1 end-of-the-year expectations
   - Uses proper capitalization for names of people and holidays consistently; also begins to use capitals for titles of books and movies

3. Ending Punctuation
   - Uses periods consistently
   - Attempts to use other ending punctuation where appropriate: exclamation points and question marks

4. Commas
   - Begins to use commas in a series
   - Uses commas in the date
   - Uses commas in the greeting and closing of a letter

5. Apostrophes
   - Uses apostrophes in contractions

6. Other Uses of the Period
   - Uses the period in abbreviations: Mr., Mrs., Ms., Dr.

7. Sentence Structure
   - Begins to understand that there are varying types of sentences, including questions, statements, and exclamations
   - Begins to use complex sentences—the connection of two simple sentences with a connecting word (e.g., *and, but, because*)
   - Uses sentences with transitional words (e.g., *first, then, next*)

8. Parts of Speech
   - Knows what nouns are
   - Recognizes the difference between singular and plural nouns
   - Demonstrates noun/action-verb agreement
   - Uses article/noun agreement (e.g., an apple, a boy, a gray elephant)
   - Knows what verbs are
   - Uses proper words for past, present, and future verb tenses
   - Knows what adjectives are
   - Attempts to use adjectives in writing

9. Punctuating Dialogue
   - Begins to place quotation marks around spoken words in own writing

Third Grade

1. Capitalization
   - Uses proper capitalization for all proper nouns

2. Ending Punctuation
   - Uses all ending punctuation (periods, exclamation points, question marks) consistently
   - Uses ellipses to indicate omission and statement left unfinished

3. Commas
   - Uses commas between city and state
   - Consistently uses commas in a series correctly
   - Uses commas after introductory phrases consistently
   - Begins to use commas to combine sentences
   - Begins to tuck in information (i.e., with appositives: Barbara, a third-grade teacher, loved teaching punctuation)

4. Apostrophes
   - Begins to use singular possessive apostrophes
   - Has mastered and consistently uses apostrophes in contractions correctly

5. Internal Punctuation
   - Recognizes a variety of internal punctuation in reading

6. Other Uses of the Period
   - Uses the period in abbreviations of a.m., p.m., ft., in., lb., yd. (American standard units of measure)

7. Sentence Structure
   - Uses complete sentences (noun/pronoun, verb) consistently
   - Uses a variety of types of sentences in a published piece of writing consistently
   - Uses more complex sentences

8. Parts of Speech
   - Can name parts of speech (nouns, pronouns, adjectives)
   - Differentiates between common and proper nouns and attempts to use them in their writing
   - Know what pronouns are and tries to use them in writing
   - Uses adjectives appropriately to craft their writing

9. Punctuating Dialogue
   - Begins to place quotation marks around spoken words in their writing
   - Begins to capitalize first letter inside quotation marks
   - Begins to understand that punctuation is placed before end quotation mark: *"I think we'd better finish this right away!"*
   - Begins to understands the comma replaces a period when the tag is at the end: *"I had a great time at our meeting,"Kate said.*

10. Paragraphing
    - Understands a paragraph is a group of connected sentences
    - Writes an idea-based paragraph connected to their reading
    - Begins to change paragraphs when a new person is talking

- Begins to change paragraphs when there is a change in scene
- Begins to change paragraphs to show time passing

11. Use of Tense

- Uses the past tense correctly

Fourth Grade

1. Capitalization
   - Meets all K–3 end-of-the-year expectations
   - Has mastered and consistently uses capitals for specific places and people

2. Ending Punctuation
   - Consistently uses periods with complex sentences

3. Commas
   - Uses commas before a conjunction (e.g., *I went to the store, but I forgot my money.*)
   - Uses commas with appositives

4. Apostrophes
   - Uses the singular possessive apostrophe
   - Begins to use the plural possessive apostrophe

5. Internal Punctuation
   - Knows that parentheses enclose explanations inserted in the text [e.g., *Giraffes are herbivores (eat plants).*]

6. Sentence Structure
   - Uses a variety of sentence structures in their independent writing
   - Continues to understand and use compound sentences (two or more simple sentences joined by a coordinating conjunction)

7. Parts of Speech
   - Balances the use of proper nouns and pronouns
   - Knows what conjunctions are and how to use them properly
   - Knows what adverbs are and attempts to use them in their writing

8. Punctuating Dialogue
   - Identifies speaker at the beginning (e.g., *Stacey's mother shouted, "You need to finish your homework!"*)

9. Paragraphing
   - Has mastered and consistently uses third-grade paragraphing strategies
   - Begins to use paragraphing when new chunks of meaning are introduced

10. Use of Tense
   - Uses past tense correctly

Fifth Grade

1. Ending Punctuation
   - Varies ending punctuation to improve writing

2. Internal Punctuation
   - Uses commas to set off words in apposition (e.g., *Barbara, a third-grade teacher, works in room 221.*)
   - Consistently uses commas after an introductory word or phrase correctly (e.g., *however, yes, for example, therefore,* etc.)
   - Is exposed to and experiments with all types of internal punctuation
   - Is held accountable for the correct usage of ellipses, parentheses, and the comma usage above

3. Apostrophes
   - Has mastered and consistently uses apostrophes in contractions correctly, both singular and plural
   - Has mastered and consistently uses possessive apostrophe correctly, both singular and plural

4. Sentence Structure
   - Uses compound sentences in their independent writing
   - Uses commas to punctuate compound sentence (see section on commas)
   - Uses compound sentences (two or more simple sentences joined by coordinating conjunction)
   - Combines two simple sentences with a coordinating conjunction
   - Incorporates quotes and citations

5. Parts of Speech
   - Knows what adverbs are and uses them properly
   - Uses prepositions properly

6. Punctuating Dialogue
   - Has mastered and consistently uses appropriate ending punctuation inside quotation marks
   - Introduces quotation marks when speaker is identified mid-quote (e.g., *"Hello," Tim said, "how are you?"*)

7. Paragraphing
   - Meets the paragraphing expectations from third and fourth grade

8. Use of Tense
   - Consistently uses correct tense within a text

Punctuation Interviews

In studying any craft, we want to learn from the masters. Hearing what accomplished writers have to say about punctuation can inform and expand our ideas on the subject and provide ideas for our own teaching and writing.

To explore this notion, I was fortunate to be able to interview Frank McCourt, a memoirist; Jimmy Breslin, a journalist; Natalie Babbitt, a children's book author and illustrator; and Colum McCann, a novelist. The similarities and differences in their approaches to punctuation are fascinating. One thing they all seem to agree on is that the way a writer uses punctuation is about choice and craft first and that the rules and conventions are less important than clarity and rhythm.

Quoting the experts to student writers can be quite powerful as well. Aside from being fascinating reading, these conversations are filled with pithy lines we may use—forgive the pun—to punctuate our instruction.

Interview with Frank McCourt, January 17, 2007

Frank McCourt is perhaps our greatest living memoirist. He won the Pulitzer Prize and National Book Critics Circle Award for Angela's Ashes *and is also the author of* 'Tis *and* Teacher Man. *McCourt is a former New York City high school teacher.*

FM: So what are you doing about punctuation that's new?

DF: The idea of the book is that punctuation should be taught as a craft tool rather than as a set of rules.

FM: What fascinated my students was going back into the history of the English language. They were fascinated to think that at one point in time there was no regard for punctuation whatsoever. We went from sentence to sentence and you had to figure it out for yourself. They didn't know this. It was not easy to read—I used to photostat manuscript stuff from various English literature books to show them what English was like, and they couldn't believe that Anglo-Saxon was English, that Middle English was English, and that punctuation was the new kid on the block as far as the language was concerned. They just couldn't understand it; they were able to grasp the period and the comma, but beyond that, the semicolon and the colon were—and for me still are—areas of mysticism. They didn't care about them. So what I used to do, to overcome my own ignorance, and maybe this is a cheap trick—you were required by the Board of Education to write the aim of your lesson on the board, *Aim, A-I-M*—so I'd write AIM—colon—"to study why Hamlet was mean to Ophelia," or something like that. But then I would say this is a very important lesson, so we are going to use a super colon. And I would put three dots up instead of two. The number of dots will indicate the importance or the intensity of the sentence.

DF: Sounds like rating a movie.

FM: Right. Then I used to do fatigued explanation points. I'd put the exclamation point under the sentence to show it wasn't that important, or have it tilted one way.

DF: To sound like it's just a little exciting.

FM: It wasn't much, but it made it more interesting. I did all kinds of things to amuse them and lure them in. That was my way of seducing them into punctuation.

DF: Did they start punctuating more after that?

FM: Oh, yeah. I think they did. I got around all the hostility. That is one of the missions of a teacher, to overcome hostility to lessons on technical English, punctuation, and so on.

DF: So why do you think students and grownups are so hostile to the idea of punctuation? Mention punctuation to nine out of ten people and they groan.

FM: There is hostility toward the teaching of grammar, punctuation, and technical English in general. You have to tell, seduce them in another way. You just play around with language to show it's a living thing. If you look at a page of Hemingway—minimum punctuation. Period.

DF: Frank McCourt, another wonderful writer, does not use much punctuation at all. I have not analyzed every page of every book, but generally you seem to avoid it except when absolutely necessary. In terms of internal punctuation, I didn't notice much more than a comma and occasional dashes.

FM: That's correct. I began with *Angela's Ashes*, and that's told from the perspective of a child, from four to nineteen, really, and then I continue that in *'Tis*. I tried to be a little more sophisticated in *Teacher Man*. I started using standard punctuation, quotation marks and so on. My editor would say, "Why are you doing that? The barenaked sentence worked before, leave it alone." I just started thinking to show off a little, I could use punctuation marks, quotes—but she was right, why not leave it alone? Joyce never used quotation marks, he used a dash. A lot of Irish writers, for some reason, and a lot of English writers use dashes—but I don't even use a dash.

DF: Why not?

FM: You are leaping in the dark. If I can't write a sentence or a speech that you can't recognize by itself—if you don't know that line belongs to the teacher in the classroom, rather than the kid or the mother, then there's something wrong with the sentence. Each person speaks, has a distinct way of speaking. In a sense I was challenging myself—and I think it worked. Nobody's complained that any of the lines were murky. If you look at a page of Hemingway, sometimes you do get lost. If you look at a page of *The Sun Also Rises* where there's dialogue, sometimes you have to go back yourself. When Jack, the hero of *The Sun Also Rises*, speaks and then another guy and then another guy, sometimes you have to go back because you get lost, unless you are paying close attention, and you shouldn't be required to pay that close attention.

DF: Do you make a conscious effort when you're writing—forget about teaching, but writing—to achieve some sort of rhythm or musical feeling, pay attention to the sound of it?

FM: Well, you know, if you are going to reproduce the dialogue and speech of New York kids, it has a certain rhythm. Irish kids will have a different way of talking completely. When *Angela's Ashes* came out a lot of the critics were talking about the lyricism in there. Well, all right, the structure of the sentences are a little different. For instance, when my brother Mike came over to the States, and I met him and brought him to my apartment up in Washington Heights, and I had to go to work at four that afternoon. And Mike said, "Is it the way now that you have to go to work?" Americans say, "Are you going to work? Do you have to go work?" *Is it the way*, that comes directly over from Gaelic—is it the way you have to eat, is it the way you have to walk. A lot of that stuff stuck, because I spent years thinking about *Angela's Ashes*, I retained a lot of that structure—and excuse me, *lyricism*.

DF: *How much of that is about punctuation and how much about varied sentence length?*

FM: I think the English and the Irish tend to speak in longer, more complicated sentences. They're not in such a hurry. There's a kind of an enjoyment of language that you'll find. And they seem to speak spontaneously, off the cuff, very easily. Everything depends on the individual, what you're learning, what your feeling about language is, your enjoyment of language. Some people can barely talk, they might be intelligent people, and they may write like angels, but when it comes to talking, it's another story.

DF: *What is the main purpose of punctuation?*

FM: That is a good question! You're very conscious if you are writing a sentence that the next one is going to have something to do with the first—after the topic sentence, the rest has to be of that paragraph, so to speak. Punctuation is effective in helping with that.

DF: *The first person I interviewed, a poet, said: "I have only one thing to say about punctuation— good fences make good neighbors."*

FM: Oh, yeah, yeah, but it divides and connects at the same time. The fence is there and it shows what's what. You don't go over, but that's a very poor parallel for me. A period is not a fence. A period is a pause—take a breath and then you go on to the next place, but it should go with the last one. And then it is a series of instructions, and maybe the punctuation is the plaster that holds all of them together.

DF: *What's a comma?*

FM: A gasp.

DF: *A dash?*

FM: It is a mild pause—a period is more serious. Remember Joseph McCarthy? He said "The State Department is loaded with communists, period!" He ruined that punctuation for everybody—period. Let's not have the period be so very somber. It puts an end to a particular thought. But you should have hope then, because you are going into the next sentence, where the previous thought can be expanded. I think it's not to be taken too seriously. That's why we have editors in the publishing business, to worry about this sort of thing. They have a man in my publishing house, a world-famous expert, I think, on punctuation. He's Irish. He called me up and we spent all kinds of time on the phone and I had to justify my periods.

DF: *How did that go?*

FM: Don't ask. You know, you could learn a lot from him. I did, I suppose, but I don't care in the long run. It goes back to total rhythm. Sometimes you have an instinct. I don't know if it would be very interesting, if you could look into the history of the colon and semicolon. I don't remember colons and semicolons in Shakespeare or Swift. I think they were period and comma men. I don't even know if they used quotation marks.

DF: Do you edit as you go, wait until the end and read over the whole thing, or stop every few lines and go back?

FM: I write first in longhand, and then put it into the computer, and with the computer you can revise as you go along. I would spend so much time as a high school teacher going over thousands, millions of high school kids' words. I suppose I developed a sense of clarity, a sense of simplicity and lucidity, if you want to call it that. Always compelled to make things clear. When I was teaching at the community college, the people there were foreigners. They were from all over. They were Chinese, they were Cambodian, Cubans. I arrived in America with English—the only gift I had. I was aware they were frustrated, so I wanted to make myself clear. I had to speak slowly and be clear and maybe all of that was building up in my mind when I was writing *Angela's Ashes*, that desperate desire to be clear.

DF: What part does punctuation play in that desire?

FM: Oh, a lot—you can't go rushing on, so it stops you. This is the one thing I learned from the years of teaching—simplify, simplify, simplify.

DF: How does punctuation help you do that?

FM: It makes you pause and look at the reader. You see sometimes that what you are saying is not getting through to them. So there's a pause, maybe a comma up here or a period or not. So it is rhythm, that's about all it is. We each have our own rhythm. You look at a page of Faulkner, completely different kind of rhythm. Look at a page of Jane Austen and a page of Joyce, different rhythms all together. I suppose it all depends on the individual. Journalists have a different kind of rhythm. A sharp, snappy, where why. It depends on the individual and the message, what are the circumstances, what do you want to get across. Everything depends.

DF: Part of it too seems to be where you separate the ideas, put in breaths or pauses.

FM: Yeah, the paragraph itself is a form of pause. You arrive at the end of a thought you have developed. Take the key and go down a space and you follow that to a new adventure.

DF: Would you say punctuation is better defined as a set of rules or as a craft tool?

FM: It is a craft tool. You use it whatever way you want to use it, as long as you have a courtesy for the reader. Punctuation is in your subconscious. I don't know what the absolute truth is, no one does. Every person has their own set of rules, a set of urgencies which have nothing to do with what we teach about punctuation, and maybe you can bring that up into the conscious level when you write. There should be thousands of different rule books of punctuation, since everyone divides their thoughts differently.

DF: What do you think of the idea of having kids think about punctuation as they plan their work, rather than just using timelines or plotting out what is going to happen?

FM: I like that. I keep linking it to music. Music is what they love, most of them. Can you read music?

DF: Yes.

FM: So there you are. You have the advantage over the rest of us, if you can read music. You know when you have the words set to the music of a song, why this is here, why that is there, why you pause.

DF: Actually, the length of the rest, unlike a comma, dash, or whatever internal punctuation, is prescribed. It's not a guessing game in music—the time is defined, you know how long to wait.

FM: Well, yeah. I'm very conscious of the music of language. That's why I like to listen to New Yorkers having arguments. Offering platitudes, you don't hear it so much. But the arguments, this stuff has music and I think it's wonderful. I listen to people when I sit on the park benches. Listen to all the people talking about their illnesses or a fender bender down the street, and two of them screaming at each other, and there's going to be a fight, but the light turns green—gone again. It's all music.

DF: So anger is where you find the music of language?

FM: Oh, yeah. The passion, the grief, anger. That is when people let down their guard mostly. Otherwise people are always saying I could never speak in public, but somebody pushes them on the subway and they are sounding like Abraham Lincoln.

DF: So you think in terms of the music of language. What I am pushing in this book is that you don't teach kids to be an artist by studying anatomy first—you'd turn them off. You let them finger paint. You let them mess around, go nuts, you know. Perhaps they should be allowed to start off that same way as they learn about punctuation.

FM: The Suzuki method. You know, just let them play.

DF: Right, exactly. Then you kind of slowly make them aware. That's what I have been trying to have kids do with punctuation—think about it, mess around with it, and like with anything else, once they are sold and conscious of it, they have reason to learn the rules, or conventions.

FM: Then you need to have them write stories about punctuation. The poor lonely period looking for a sentence. Or the comma wanted to be used, and the writer wouldn't use him. So how does a comma get into the writer's subconscious? *Please, I'm here, use me! You are using nothing but periods. What about me? What about me?* That kind of thing. Exclamation point! The exclamation mark would make a very long sound. You're getting me all excited. I may want to renew my teacher's license. Go back to punctuation.

Interview with Jimmy Breslin, January 15, 2008

Jimmy Breslin is a true American hero. A Pulitzer Prize–winning journalist, he worked for many years as a columnist for the Daily News *and* New York Newsday, *where his distinctive style and expert investigative reporting often worked to uncover scandal and injustice. He is also the author of several novels.*

DF: What's the purpose of punctuation?

JB: To make it easier to read, purportedly.

DF: Why purportedly?

JB: Because they use so many commas in sentences now that you don't know where you are sometimes. I dunno. Under the rules, you're supposed to have the commas, but if you look at it with your eye, it's nuts. Too many of them.

DF: So punctuation guides where your eye goes on the page?

JB: I think so. You read with your ear. When you write it comes from the ear, I think.

DF: So is punctuation like dynamic markings in music, to tell your voice when to rise and fall and pause and all that?

JB: No, you get going and then you do things. I mean, Wolfie does it, Tom Wolfe does a ton of those things and they're very effective for him. God bless him.

DF: So if you watch someone's eyes following a piece of text, would that be following what they're hearing in their head?

JB: I don't know . . . individual cases, I guess. I hear it in my ear, not in my head.

DF: Well, your writing sings.

JB: Well, that's where it comes from. It's an emotion, a sound. Wolfe plays the sound almost like he's got an instrument when he gets going good.

DF: Your stuff is very lyrical to me.

JB: Yeah. . . . Well, I took the trumpet when I was a kid. I always thought that was the most valuable thing for me.

DF: How so?

JB: 'Cause you get tunes in your ear, sounds in your ear, and the sound of a trumpet can become words on a page with the same impact on your ear. You can hear them. That's why.

DF: So, on any conscious level do you actually think of being lyrical like a trumpet solo as you're writing, or is it just intuitive?

JB: It better just come, 'cause I can't freaking think that good.

DF (Laughs): How does punctuation help?

JB: When you try something, there are times you have to use commas. As much as I'm not in love with them, I know how to use them. And a lot of times I just freaking refuse and I won't do it. Like in apposition to something, *too bad* if they don't know! You know, I just keep going.

DF: It becomes a macho thing.

JB: It's my own personal beef. Or you'll get the thing, you know, *It is*, comma, *being*, comma, *something*—one word after the comma! They got me crazy, all that stuff . . . the ignorance is deep. And what's another one? *That* and *who*. When you're dealing with a person it should be *who*, not *that*—it's a person. They don't know that one. And then *it's* is a beauty, with an apostrophe, *it's* . . . I mean I've seen big people who don't know that.

And then the other thing in the *New York Times*—I don't read it that much, but this I've watched. It's supposed to be the smartest because they get all Harvard graduates or something. It's supposed to be the smartest, and they know everything, and they put out the best newspaper, and they start a sentence with *it*. And you do a computer search on how often they do and it's voluminous. They all use *it* to start a sentence somewhere in the game. I'll show you, now if you're so smart, you're helping the readers along, you get to the next sentence: *it*. What's *it*? What are you talking about? I don't know what you're freaking talking about. I mean that's the pet peeve I've got.

DF: So it's the lack of clarity?

JB: Yeah, simple declarative English sentences: subject, verb, and object, one after the other, forming a rhythm. What else is there?

DF: So you think they're trying to be too fancy and not making it clear?

JB: Just look at their opening sentences and count the number of words. I tried it once—fifty-one words! Look at Norman Mailer—fifteen words. Hemingway, maybe five. I don't know who these *New York Times* guys are writing for, maybe the universities. I mean sometimes you go off on a flight in the middle, sure, that's part of it. But start with the short sentences, give the thing some motion. Have some consideration for the reader.

DF: This is the stuff you become aware of when punctuation is taught differently. The idea is for kids to think of writing rhythmically, to think of written language as rhythm.

JB: You mean *think* of it? You better freaking do it. Don't think. Jeez, don't think!

DF: Let's talk for a minute about the role punctuation plays in journalism as opposed to other types of writing. Does it vary depending on the type of article you're writing?

JB: Well, with journalism you've got to be so particular, though, and tell the people who *he* is, you know. *Feigelson, comma, the principal of PS 6, comma*—I'm sorry, you know, that you got to do. Or you could put the title in *front* of the guy's name—*the principal of PS 6, comma, Feigelson, comma.*

DF: So there are times when you're using it just for clarity?

JB: Always. Clarity should be your whole goal in everything you're doing unless you've got a reason to sound mystical.

DF: We've talked before about rhythm and lyricism and now you're talking about straight-ahead clarity. Is that a more important consideration in journalism?

JB: No, with anything . . . business writing, anything. It's got to be very clear, whoever you're dealing with. Don't get too carried away with your ideas of rhythm. Do what you want but make sure it's clear.

DF: Let's look at one of your sentences. This is from one of your pieces, about a funeral in Mexico: "Sway forward on the left leg, sway back on the right foot, sway forward, sway back, sway, sway, sway, dance the young man to his grave." The way you use the commas here is interesting.

JB: It's good.

DF: It comes off like a seesaw.

JB: Yeah, there's motion. You're trying to capture it—you can hear it almost. It's there.

DF: How do the commas help achieve that?

JB: Well, it keeps it from getting cluttered. It separates the motions out just enough to give the sentence its own legs, its sway, its movement. If you didn't have commas, what would you have?

DF: So to push this point a little further, there's another passage from one of your books that was intriguing: "An instant, a shrug of concrete and metal, and the floor under Eduardo went. Down Ed-

uardo went, so quickly that he made no sound. The third floor fell into the second floor and the second fell into the first and everything fell into the basement."

JB: The key to it there is *went* instead of *horrible crash* or something. That comes from sports writing. Oh, yeah, that's old.

DF: What do you mean? How does that come from sports writing?

JB: Well, at the key part of the thing, at the height of the action, you use the freaking flattest word you can come up with. That's very important. Everybody that ever did it good, like Red Smith . . . that would be his game. He would use the word *fled* instead of *racing, running, flying around the bases*—*fled*. Just one word, you know? Understatement.

DF: That's an amazing tip. Pressing on, I want to ask you about the sequence of sentences. You follow that first line with: "Down Eduardo went," and you have one comma, then: ". . . so quickly that he made no sound."

JB: Period.

DF: Then in the next sentence you have no commas at all. It just goes straight through: "The third floor fell into the second floor and the second fell into the first and everything fell into the basement." You don't pause at all. I mean you could have said, "The third floor to the second floor, comma, the second floor to the first, comma. . . ."

JB: I wouldn't have done that, no.

DF: So it was a building of rhythm?

JB: Yeah, that's deliberate. Works better than doing it the correct way.

DF: It's like a snowball . . . several pauses, then fewer pauses, then no pauses.

JB: Yeah, that's right. That worked. It just suggested a rhythm. And you just type it out, like it told you what to do. As you look at it, you write it and then you can see it moves forward— third floor went into the second, second went into the first. I love that.

DF: With something like that, are you listening in your head to hear if it sounds right, or are you looking at the page and seeing it?

JB: I don't see it on the page, no. I hear it.

DF: To me that's a masterful use of punctuation.

JB: Yeah, but it's natural. It's not rule-book punctuation. If you did it rule book, after the second floor you'd have a comma—and the second fell into the first—and you wouldn't have a comma before *and* at the end. You'd be tempted—*and everything fell into the basement*—but a comma in there would have screwed it all up, I think. Nothing belonged in the way of this thing—third second first—you don't put a pause in there. It's the motion that produces the rhythm, doesn't it? But you've got to be able to spot it, the motion in your notes . . . and maybe as you start typing it you notice there's a rhythm.

DF: What about the semicolon?

JB: That's the least used key on the typewriter, isn't it? It's a way to move the sentence without having to use a period, and when a comma obviously wouldn't do it. Sometimes it actually works. It replaces a period in order to keep it going. That's the idea behind using it. You use a semicolon when you want to be able to get in that last thing, without too many stops and starts.

DF: You don't use exclamation points very much.

JB: If the words don't produce the exclamation, what's the point? Why put *horse* under the picture?

DF: So it's overkill?

JB: *Here, I mean this! You do it!* This is just a tomfoolery on people, but if you were writing something important enough, you don't need an exclamation point.

DF: How is punctuation connected to oral traditions? How much does it have to do with replicating the sound of speech?

JB: Breath.

DF: What do you mean?

JB: Well, you figure the end of a paragraph would be a breath, huh? There would be breathing involved. Punctuation is about where you breathe. That's how you could link those two, I would say. And then, the oral thing—we go back to a musical instrument. I would tell every writer to take a musical instrument. Or hang out in bars and talk incessantly, like the Irish do.

DF: Thank you for doing this.

JB: I'm sorry I couldn't give you more.

DF: You gave me a lot.

JB: I had nothing original.

DF: I wouldn't say that. We've been talking for an hour and eight minutes.

JB: Wow. I don't have that much on my mind.

Interview with Natalie Babbitt, March 3, 2008

Natalie Babbitt is a much loved children's author and illustrator. Her many books are staples of children's literature. Among them, Knee-Knock Rise *was a Newbery Honor selection and* The Eyes of Amaryllis *was made into a film. She is probably best known for her classic novel* Tuck Everlasting, *also adapted (twice!) for the screen.*

DF: Could you describe what goes on in your head as you make decisions about punctuation?

NB: I've been thinking about that all day and wondering how to describe it. The thing is that I am fundamentally a visual person. I can't get used to the idea that people like what I write, because I never thought about being a writer. I wanted to be an illustrator. But creating a page of writing does have a certain visual quality to it. I am not an actor or theatre person at all, but everybody around me is—and punctuation is kind of like stage directions. I think if the punctuation and the layout are right, they give you a clue on how to read it.

DF: The novelist Colum McCann described how he sometimes steps back from a page and squints, to see how the words fall visually.

NB: I don't know if I've ever done that deliberately. I think I do it instinctively.

DF: *When you step back to look at the page, what do you notice?*

NB: I notice breaks in the text. I notice the length of sentences and paragraphs that don't go on for four pages, which tires you out just looking at it. I can read that kind of thing now, but there were times in school when I had a very hard time sticking with certain texts because they were so awful to look at. That's not a good reason, I know that perfectly well, but it's there just the same or at least it was for me. Dialogue helps to break it up, and punctuation helps. I like dashes, and I use them a lot. I am not allowed to use a lot of exclamation points, nor do I wish to. Italics help, a couple here and there—it makes a difference, the page looks interesting.

DF: *I was looking at your use of dashes in* Tuck Everlasting *and noticed a lot of examples where you used them like parentheses, to simulate an interruption in a thought.*

NB: Yes, it is a stage direction. It's just a way to read it. You know, pause and then go on, then pause again and go on. It gives you time to think about what you're reading. I've never talked about this with kids. I think it would bore them to death. But I think it works.

DF: *I'd like to ask you to comment on one sentence from* Tuck *that I think is very interesting to look at in terms of punctuation:* "She made her way to her seat in the stern, and Miles handed her two old cane poles—'Watch out for the hooks!' he warned—and a jar of bait: pork fat cut into little pieces."

NB: I'm not too good with colons. I think I may have had a dash there, and my editor suggested the colon would go better. I'm not sure, but I don't think it would have occurred to me to do that. Colons and semicolons are funny. I don't really understand them.

DF: *Since you bring it up, I didn't see a single semicolon in the book. I didn't comb the entire book—*

NB: Well, it seems to me, Dan, the least you could have done was go over the entire book. (*Laughs*) I always get them mixed up—the semicolon is the one with the comma and the dot, or is that the colon? I guess I do use those occasionally, but I don't like them.

DF: *The opening of* Tuck *is very interesting. There are a series of long sentences with lots of commas, and the effect on the reader is that you ease into the story. It feels like you are going down a windy path.*

NB: Well, I am delighted to hear you put it that way, because the book really has three first chapters, and children are aware of that. They sometimes have trouble with it, and I get a lot of letters that say, "Well, I didn't like the way it started, but then I got into it."

DF: *What is the purpose of punctuation, and what role does it play in fiction as opposed to other genres?*

NB: I think when we can get far enough away from what we are writing to see what we are directing the reader to do, it's a good thing. Punctuation is a sort of road sign.

DF: *What about the rhythmic aspect of punctuation? Your writing, again, is very lyrical, and this seems to imply some attention to rhythm.*

NB: When I started writing, my husband wrote the story for the very first book. I had always written verse. When he decided he didn't want to do it anymore, I had to start writing my own and the first two were in verse. I feel very comfortable with verse, the way it looks and sounds. I think that if you have grown up with that feeling of rhythm it comes out in prose as well. Let me give you a good example. Children ask me, "In *Tuck*, why does the man in the yellow suit wear a yellow suit?" I can tell them exactly why. It's because I needed a two-syllable color, and nobody wears purple. So because it's a phrase that's used many times, it has to have its own internal rhythm. It had to be two syllables—try it in your own head once with brown or black. It ruins it.

DF: Sorry to be so focused on one book, but I have another question about Tuck Everlasting. *For the first several pages all the sentences end in periods. Then the first ending punctuation other than a period is a question mark—and there you have three questions in a row, sort of a one-two-three punch (Reads): "How deep, after all, can it go? If a person owns a piece of land, does he own it all the way down, in ever narrowing dimensions, till it meets all other pieces at the center of the earth? Or does ownership consist only of a thin crust under which the friendly worms have never heard of trespassing?"*

NB: The voice is different too. I mean it talks about something that really isn't part of the story, and this was the purest form of self-indulgence.

DF: How?

NB: Because it is something I've always thought about, and I don't know who you ask for the answer to that question. My books are pretty full of unanswerable questions, actually. People want to know, "Why are you writing for children?" but I think most of the questions that really matter to us are questions that arose when we were quite young.

DF: So it was self-indulgence in the sense that you were asking a question you actually wondered about—but I'm also interested in how it worked rhythmically and in terms of cadence, the rising and falling of the voice. It does shake things up a bit to suddenly have these three questions.

NB: It is like being on stage, Dan—and you're doing your lines and then you come to one that you never understood, and you turn and face the audience and say in effect, *Hey, wait a minute!*

DF: So these questions are in effect an interruption of the story. Earlier you talked about using parenthetical dashes too, which are another kind of interruption—for example, when Winnie is thinking about the jail cell and you write, "But she had not dared to sleep, for fear she would kick off the blanket and give herself away—give the Tucks away—unwittingly." Can you talk about the difference?

NB: I use the questions as an interruption to the narration, to talk directly to the reader. Dashes are to interrupt the thinking of the character, inside the story.

DF: Getting back to thinking rhythmically, my background in music influences the way I write. Sometimes if a passage feels awkward or clunky I'll actually say it to myself without the words, just the syllables, to hear how it sounds—so Hello, Natalie *would be* dut-duh duh-duh-duh.

NB: Oh, absolutely, I do the same thing. I have a background in music too. I think before we start, wouldn't you agree we know what it is we want to say? And there are a hundred different ways to say it. So I don't necessarily read it out loud, but I read it over and over and over and the changes that I make have to do with how it sounds. Just as a piece of music, if you want to call it that. I think this is a very big part of it. It's important, and it also makes it a lot more fun. Kids understand it without even being told. They have a lot of rhythm in their nature. Even if they can't carry a tune, it's there.

DF: Is it more important to think of rhythm in phrases that repeat, like the man in the yellow suit?

NB: I think with titles it shows up more sharply than anything else. Some of my books have titles that really don't sell the book very well, but they sound nice. Like *Eyes of the Amaryllis*.

That's a hard word, *amaryllis*, and I don't think it's done the book any good. But anyway I'm bound by it—and it looks pretty good. All of those things matter, they really do, and as I said it's one of the things that gives me pleasure. It's a challenge to find exactly the right way to say it, and when you do find it, it's certainly a matter of preference, not correctness. It's what pleases your own ear, and you just have to hope the people agree.

DF: So to what extent is punctuation a craft tool and to what extent is it a set of rules?

NB: I think you need to observe the fundamental use of periods and commas and question marks, the basic stuff. Quotation marks, certainly. These things are pretty fundamental—but where you use them and when and how to a large extent is up to you.

Interview with Colum McCann, February 2007

Colum McCann is a contemporary Irish novelist. Named Esquire *magazine's Writer of the Year in 2003, he has won the Pushcart Prize and was inducted into the Hennessy Writers Hall of Fame. He is the author of several titles, including* Dancer *and* Zoli.

DF: OK, let's start right in. What is the purpose of punctuation?

CM: That's a good question. I think it's to time the reader in. It's that little guiding hand at the back of the reader's mind that sort of says, OK, halt, or OK, stumble here a little bit or allow yourself a breath or don't allow yourself a breath. Or the marvelous semicolon, you know, it suggests a pause, but also can be as a comma. So I think punctuation sort of modulates our rhythm. It says this is the music and here is the music sheet. In fact, in a funny way, punctuation marks do look like musical notations, don't they sometimes? So I think ultimately it's a service for the reader, and the writer decides where that service comes in and where it doesn't.

DF: So what you're describing has to do with pauses and breaths, like the rests in music.

CM: Yes, or sometimes no rests at all. I really don't know the rules, but I've read enough to sort of intuit them, and I know what's wrong and I know what's right. And punctuation can sometimes stutter a text so much that it puts the wrong emphasis in places and stops you. I once wrote a sentence, in my novel *Dancer*, which is about thirty-five pages long. But you see, that was a scene that was about the 1970s. It was charged with flashing disco lights. It was movement, movement, and it was about a time before excess became tragic, right? So I had to make a decision as a writer. How am I going to capture the texture of those times? Well, I can use punctuation. I use commas, I use semicolons, and I use certain breaks in the text, too, because it was just too much on the eye of the reader to keep going—

DF: Too claustrophobic.

CM: Yeah, and I wanted to bring the eye to certain places. The thing that a lot of people forget is the way the text looks on the page is so important. Roddy Doyle's a great example of a master writer when it comes to knowing how to use punctuation—dashes as opposed to quotation marks and all that stuff. But for me, that was a big scene in that it's the one time in my life I absolutely hammered all the rules of grammar, hammered them to pieces, and I felt like it was successful, because it just sort of plowed the reader through. Like a big river of text.

DF: But you do use commas and semicolons to break it up.

CM: The seminal text for this is the last chapter of *Ulysses*, the Penelope chapter with Molly Bloom. It's one of the great chapters in literature, but he uses no punctuation whatsoever. None. And it is, again, about forty pages. And only the very best actors can read it. And I want my readers to be actors in certain ways and be involved in the text. I don't want to throw them out of the book. But every now and then you've got to stop and help them listen to the music of the text. So there are italics there, which are important 'cause they draw attention in a big block of paragraph. Your eye will automatically go to it. I think a lot of writers forget about what the eye of the reader does. Ultimately, we're here as writers to be servants of the reader, right?

DF: So it's not just about the sound of it or the music of it. It's about the appearance of it, what it looks like in the reader's eye.

CM: I would say it's primarily about the sound, the cadence, the rhythm, and how that's going to bring the reader along on the journey. But it's also about what the eye does on the page. And I think that's enormously important. All artists know that. I mean, if you talk about the way Picasso draws your attention to the left-hand corner of the painting, why shouldn't writers feel the same way about a page of text? I'm always interested in how my text is going to look on the page. What is the typeface? Is it sans serif? Is it loud? Is it quiet? How long should the page be?

DF: But it also gets into the design of the paragraph, how long the sentences are.

CM: Sometimes when I'm writing, depending on the piece, I will write certain parts in italics on my computer. It won't end up in italics in the final thing. If I'm looking for a different character's voice, I nearly always give them a different typeface because I don't want it to be the same voice as came before. And these are sort of the little tricks . . . and it's so funny, because I've never talked about these before.

DF: You do this for yourself?

CM: I do this for myself, to achieve a different voice, to achieve a different texture, to achieve a different rhythm. But it annoys me sometimes when I get into deep arguments about grammar with my editors. For example, in *This Side of Brightness*, the phrase for the second part, really the opening salvo of the book was, "They arrive at dawn in their geography of hats." Right? Now, I had a long, long, long talk with my editor, you know, a fantastic woman, an editor I really trust and admire. But we argued for two weeks 'cause she said, "You can't arrive in a hat. That's wrong." It's prescriptively wrong, I said, but it's descriptively right, because people say, "He's arriving in a hat." She said, "Well, they should arrive at dawn *wearing a geography of hats*." But you see, it didn't have the same rhythm to me. They don't arrive at dawn *wearing* a geography of hats. They arrive at dawn *in* a geography of hats, because the hats are talking about all the places that they come from, and a nice short word like *in* works much better than a longer, stretched-out word that draws attention to itself like *wearing*.

DF: In Zoli *you have different sections told by different characters. How do punctuation and cadence figure in achieving those voices or establishing differences in voice?*

CM: Different punctuation can get at different characters. Dialogue marks are very interesting, drawing attention to the dialogue using dialogue marks, or using a dash, which is the European way, or not using any dash whatsoever. Cormac McCarthy does it in a really interesting way sometimes. You don't know what's dialogue and what's not. And you come to the end of a sentence and you realize, oh, that's description. There'll be two characters talking and it'll be rapid-fire—boom, boom, boom, boom, boom—and then suddenly, "And then they went over the fields in the dusty sunlight." And then, all right, OK, it gives me pause and makes me think about what's just gone before and think about the dialogue again. So it's for the purpose of arresting people's attention and, like I said at the start, guiding them through the text. And some of the great ones about this were the new journalists of the early 1970s who were using this wild, wild, wild punctuation, like huge amounts of dots, like forty dots in a row and thirty dashes all over the page. They were looking at a page and saying, OK, what does that mean and what can you do? Because basically we have how many symbols? Twenty-six? But we have a lot more when you take all of the grammatical symbols and exclamation marks and—that's another thing. The writer's fear . . . how would you put it? The anxiety over the exclamation mark. (*Laughs*) Like, shoot, should I put it in there or should I not?

DF: Frank McCourt talked about how every writer has an individual set of rules when it comes to punctuation.

CM: I'd say almost every *story* has its different rules. The writer doesn't always have his coherent logical patterns that he's going to follow for his or her whole life. There's not this deep DNA of grammar inside you, you know, the story finds its own grammar. It's like the way, you know, stories find their own form? Sometimes stories find their own grammar. This is far more interesting to me than I thought it would be—I haven't ever talked about this. Are you finding people are saying that?

DF: How is punctuation connected to oral storytelling?

CM: Every writer knows, even from readings, that the exact same text one night goes down like a lead balloon and sort of sparks the roofs in another place. You don't know why that is, so it seems to me that you have to find some sort of framework to have your pauses, to have the atmosphere of the room right, to have it match to the fluorescent light or to the candlelight. And so, if you can capture in the grammar some sort of oral tradition of how to tell the story or how to listen to the story, and if you get the right one you get all the readers on board with you. It's as if you're whispering intimately into their ears, but they're all getting the same story told to them at the same time. Punctuation and grammar put the whisper into things and put the loud shout into things. It brings across the exact way you want the story to be listened to.

DF: What about using punctuation and cadence to angle your writing, to draw importance to certain things?

CM: Well, you do it all the time. That long sentence would be sort of taken over and drawn attention to with two short sentences that follow it. Rhythm . . . I mean it all comes back to song and to music, the way you can use dashes in the middle of a sentence to say, you know, *Look at this*. I think most good writers will read their stuff aloud and they will know then what's happening to the reader on the page, because I think in a certain way we all read aloud anyway. I think that readers, in their head, are involved in the rhythm. And if the words are too messy, and if they're not bumping up against each other right or they're calling too much attention to each other, we sort of give up on it.

DF: The notion of rhythm and the music of it, the sound of the language and how you convey that on the page, is often ignored, isn't it?

CM: I will tell you that it troubles me my kids will have too many manners put on their writing. You put these kids in little boxes that they don't necessarily fit in and what will it do? Take away all their wildness, all their inspiration? I mean, I think that for a writer to be good he has to know or at least intuit the rules in order to break them, but constantly demanding that we should write in perfect ways sort of denies all the ways that we live our lives.

Works Cited

Alborough, Jez. 1994. *Where's My Teddy?* London: Walker.

Anderson, Carl. 2000. *How's It Going?* Portsmouth, NH: Heinemann.

Angelillo, Janet. 2002. *A Fresh Approach to Teaching Punctuation.* New York: Scholastic.

Babbitt, Natalie. 2008. Interview with author. March 3.

Bomer, Randy. 2006. "Reading with the Mind's Ear: Listening to Text as a Mental Action." Newark, DE: International Reading Association.

Boynton, Sandra, and Sara Boynton. 1982. *Moo Ba La La La.* New York: Simon & Schuster.

Breslin, Jimmy. 2008. Interview with author. January 15.

Brinckloe, Julie. 1986. *Fireflies.* New York: Simon & Schuster.

Calkins, Lucy. 1983. *Lessons from a Child.* Portsmouth, NH: Heinemann.

———. 1994. *The Art of Teaching Writing.* Portsmouth, NH: Heinemann.

Chase, Naomi. 2006. Conversation with author, May 23.

Chicago Manual of Style. 2003. *Chicago Manual of Style,* 15th ed. Chicago: University of Chicago Press.

Cronin, Doreen. 2000. *Click, Clack, Moo—Cows That Type.* New York: Simon & Schuster.

Cutler, Jane. 1999. *The Cello of Mr. O.* New York: Dutton.

Danzinger, Paula. 1997. *Amber Brown Sees Red.* New York: Putnam.

DePaola, Tomie. 1975. *Strega Nona.* New York: Simon & Schuster.

DiCamillo, Kate. 2003. *The Tale of Despereaux.* Cambridge, MA: Candlewick.

Durrell, Lawrence. 1962. *The Alexandria Quartet.* New York: Dutton.

Ehrenworth, Mary, and Vicki Vinton. 2005. *The Power of Grammar.* Portsmouth, NH: Heinemann.

Fariña, Carmen, and Laura Kotch. 2008. *A School Leader's Guide to Excellence: Collaborating Our Way to Better Schools.* Portsmouth, NH: Heinemann.

Feiffer, Jules. 1998. *A Barrel of Laughs, a Vale of Tears.* New York: HarperCollins.

Fletcher, Ralph. 1993. *What a Writer Needs.* Portsmouth, NH: Heinemann.

———. 1995. *Fig Pudding.* New York: Dell Yearling.

Heard, Georgia. 1989. *For the Good of the Earth and Sun.* Portsmouth, NH: Heinemann.

Hest, Amy. 2003. Conversation with author, April 12.

Keene, Ellin Oliver, and Susan Zimmermann. 2007. *Mosaic of Thought,* 2d ed. Portsmouth, NH: Heinemann.

Konigsberg, David. 2007. Conversation with author, October 12.

Lamott, Anne. 2002. *Blue Shoe*. New York: Riverhead.

Lederer, Richard, and Richard Dowis. 1999. *Sleeping Dogs Don't Lay (and That's No Lie)*. New York: St. Martin's Press.

Lowry, Lois. 1979. *Anastasia Krupnik*. New York: Bantam Doubleday.

———. 1989. *Number the Stars*. New York: Bantam Doubleday.

MacLachlan, Patricia. 1985. *Sarah, Plain and Tall*. New York: HarperTrophy.

Marron, Alexandra. 2007. Conversation with author, April 15.

McCann, Colum. 2007. Interview with author, February 19.

McCourt, Frank. 2007. Interview with author, January 17.

McDonald, Megan. 2000. *Judy Moody Was in a Mood*. Cambridge, MA: Candlewick.

Ninteman, Steve. 2006. Conversation with author, March 12.

O'Conner, Patricia T. 1996. *Woe Is I*. New York: Riverhead.

Rylant, Cynthia. 1999. *The Cookie-Store Cat*. New York: Blue Sky.

Schuster, Ed. 2003. *Breaking the Rules*. Portsmouth, NH: Heinemann.

Shaw, Harry. 1993. *Punctuate It Right!* New York: HarperPaperbacks.

Stilman, Anne. 1997. *Grammatically Correct*. Cincinnati, OH: Writers' Digest Books.

Strunk, William, and E. B. White. 2000. *The Elements of Style*, 4th ed. New York: Allyn and Bacon.

Thomas, Lewis. 1979. "Notes on Punctuation." *The Medusa and the Snail: More Notes of a Biology Watcher*. New York: Penguin.

Truss, Lynne. 2003. *Eats Shoots and Leaves*. London: Profile.

Waber, Bernard. 1962. *The House on East 88th Street*. New York: Houghton Mifflin.

Wood, Don, and Audrey Wood. 1984. *The Little Mouse, the Red Ripe Strawberry, and the Big Hungry Bear*. Swindon, UK: Child's Play Library.